P9-AQR-736

Women Memoirists

volume two

WOMEN WRITERS OF ENGLISH AND THEIR WORKS

Women Memoirists
volume two

Edited and with an Introduction by

Harold Bloom

CHELSEA HOUSE PUBLISHERS

Philadelphia

ON THE COVER: Kay Sage, American, 1898–1963. *I Saw Three Cities*, 1944. Oil on canvas, 91.5 x 71.0 cm. The Art Museum, Princeton University. Gift of the Estate of Kay Sage Tanguy. Photo by Clem Fiori.

CHELSEA HOUSE PUBLISHERS

EDITOR-IN-CHIEF   Stephen Reginald
MANAGING EDITOR   James D. Gallagher
PRODUCTION MANAGER   Pamela Loos
PICTURE EDITOR   Judy Hasday
ART DIRECTOR   Sara Davis
SENIOR PRODUCTION EDITOR   Lisa Chippendale

WOMEN WRITERS OF ENGLISH AND THEIR WORKS:
  Women Memoirists: Volume Two

PROJECT EDITOR   Pamela Loos
CONTRIBUTING EDITOR   Kara Donaldson
SENIOR EDITOR   Therese De Angelis
INTERIOR AND COVER DESIGNER   Alison Burnside
EDITORIAL ASSISTANT   Anne Hill

First Printing
1 3 5 7 9 8 6 4 2

Library of Congress Cataloging-in-Publication Data

Women memoirists / edited and with an introduction by Harold Bloom.
    p.   cm. — (Women writers of English and their works)
  Includes bibliographical references.
  ISBN 0-7910-4654-0 (v. 2 : hc). — ISBN 0-7910-4655-9 (v. 2 : pbk.)
  1. American prose literature—Women authors—History and criticism. 2. English prose literature—Women authors—History and criticism. 3. Women authors, American—Biography—History and criticism. 4. Women authors, English—Biography—History and criticism. 5. Autobiography—Women authors. I. Bloom, Harold. II. Series.
PS366.A88W64   1998   97-35879
810.9'9287—dc21   CIP

CONTENTS

Women Memoirists

volume two

HAROLD BLOOM

I APPROACH THIS SERIES with a certain wariness, since so much of classical feminist literary criticism has founded itself upon arguments with that phase of my own work that began with *The Anxiety of Influence* (first published in January 1973). Someone who has been raised to that bad eminence—*The Patriarchal Critic*—is well advised that he trespasses upon sacred ground when he ventures to inquire whether indeed there are indisputable differences, imaginative and cognitive, between the literary works of women and those of men. If these differences are so substantial as pragmatically to make an authentic difference, does that in turn make necessary different aesthetic standards for judging the achievements of men and of women writers? Is Emily Dickinson to be read as though she has more in common with Elizabeth Barrett Browning than with Ralph Waldo Emerson?

Is Elizabeth Bishop a great poet because she triumphantly meets the same aesthetic criteria satisfied by Wallace Stevens, or should we evaluate her by criteria she shares with Marianne Moore, but not with Stevens? Are there crucial gender-based differences in the representations of Esther Summerson by Charles Dickens in *Bleak House*, and of Dorothea Brooke by George Eliot in *Middlemarch*? Does Samuel Richardson's Clarissa Harlowe convince us that her author was a male when we contrast her with Jane Austen's Elizabeth Bennet? Do women poets have a less agonistic relationship to female precursors than male poets have to their forerunners? Two eminent pioneers of feminist criticism, Sandra Gilbert and Susan Gubar, have suggested that women writers suffer more from an anxiety of authorship than they do from influence anxieties, while another important feminist critic, Elaine Showalter, has suggested that women writers, early and late, work together in a kind of quiltmaking, each doing her share while avoiding any contamination of creative envy in regard to other writers, provided that they be women. Can it be true that, in the aesthetic sphere, women do not beware women and do not suffer from the competitiveness and jealousy that alas do exist in the professional and sexual domains? Is there something in the area of literature, when practiced by women, that changes and purifies mere human nature?

I cannot answer any of these questions, yet I do think it is vital and clarifying to raise them. There is a current fashion, in many of our institutions of higher education, to insist that English Romantic poetry cannot be studied in the old way, with an exclusive emphasis upon the works of William Blake, William Wordsworth, Samuel Taylor Coleridge, Lord Byron, Percy Bysshe Shelley, John Keats, and John Clare. Instead, the Romantic poets are taken to include Felicia Hemans, Laetitia Landon, Charlotte Smith, and Mary Tighe, among others. It would be heartening if we could believe that these are unjustly neglected poets, but their current revival will be brief. Similarly, anthologies of 17th-century English literature now tend to include the Duchess of Newcastle as well as Aphra Behn, Lady Mary Chudleigh, Anne Killigrew, Anne Finch, Countess of Winchilsea, and others. Some of these— Anne Finch in particular—wrote well, but a situation in which they are more read and studied than John Milton is not one that is likely to endure forever. The consequences of making gender a criterion for aesthetic choice must finally destroy all serious study of imaginative literature as such.

In their *Norton Anthology of Literature by Women*, Sandra Gilbert and Susan Gubar conclude their introduction to Elizabeth Barrett Browning by saying that "she constantly tested herself against the highest standards of male-defined poetic genres," a true if ambiguous observation. They then print her famous "The Cry of the Children," an admirably passionate ode that protests the cruel employment of little children in British Victorian mines and factories. Unfortunately, this well-meant prophetic affirmation ends with this, doubtless its finest stanza:

XIII

They look up with their pale and sunken faces,
    And their look is dread to see,
For they mind you of their angels in high places,
    With eyes turned on Deity.
"How long," they say, "how long, O cruel nation,
    Will you stand, to move the world, on a child's heart,—
Stifle down with a mailèd heel its palpitation,
    And tread onward to your throne amid the mart?
Our blood splashes upward, O goldheaper,
    And your purple shows your path!
But the child's sob in the silence curses deeper
    Than the strong man in his wrath."

If you read this aloud, then you may find yourself uncomfortable, on a strictly aesthetic basis, which would not vary if you were told that this had been composed by a male Victorian poet. In their selections from Elizabeth Bishop, Gilbert and Gubar courageously reprint Bishop's superb statement explaining her refusal to permit her poems to be included in anthologies of women's writing:

> Undoubtedly gender does play an important part in the making of any art, but art is art and to separate writings, paintings, musical compositions, etc., into sexes is to emphasize values in them that are *not* art.

That credo of Elizabeth Bishop's is to me the Alpha and Omega of critical wisdom in regard to all feminist literary criticism. Gender studies are precisely that: they study gender, and not aesthetic value. If your priorities are historical, social, political, and ideological, then gender studies clearly are more than justified. Perhaps they are a way to justice, or at least to more justice than women have received throughout thousands of years of male domination and aggression. Yet that is a very different matter from the now vexed issue of aesthetic value. Biographical criticism, like the different modes of historicist and psychological criticism, always has relied upon a kind of implicit gender studies and doubtless will benefit, as other modes will, by a making explicit of such considerations, particularly in regard to women writers.

Each volume in this series contains copious refutations of, and replies to, the traditionally aesthetic stance that I have advocated here. These introductory remarks aspire only to a questioning, and not a challenging, of feminist literary criticism. There are no longer any Patriarchal Critics; they are all dinosaurs, fabulous beasts fit for revival only in horror films. Sometimes I sadly think of myself as Bloom Brontosaurus, amiably left behind by the fire and the flood. But more often I go on reading the great women writers, searching for the aesthetic difference that yet may prove to be there, but which has not yet been found.

GERTRUDE STEIN AND EUDORA WELTY are among the most eminent writers in this volume, but Virginia Woolf necessarily occupies a central place in any consideration of women memoirists. Her vast *Diary* and the reflections gathered in *Moments of Being* are crucial parts of her subtle autobiographical venture, and yet her novels and critical essays, though displacements of her meditations, are equally involved in her lifetime of self-representation. Here I will center upon a single essay, "How Should One Read a Book?" which concludes *The Second Common Reader* (1932). In just 12 pages Woolf reveals her inmost self, as reader both common (in Dr. Johnson's grand sense) and uncommon.

The sheer love of reading has no more eloquent celebrant than Virginia Woolf, who was no kind of an ideologue, unlike so many of her professed academic disciples. As great a solitary reader as Dr. Johnson, William Hazlitt, and Charles Lamb, Woolf read for aesthetic pleasure and for no other cause whatsoever. When we think of her as a memoirist, we should consider first what she most passionately reread, and only then refect upon what she herself wrote, and whom she did (or did not) love.

Woolf's literary culture was large, comprehensive, and centered particularly upon Shakespeare, Jane Austen, Laurence Sterne, Emily Brontë, and three great critics: Thomas DeQuincey, William Hazlitt, and most importantly, Walter Pater. Pater indeed was the prophet of Woolf's particular aesthetic sensibility, the theorist of what he called "privileged moments," her "moments of being." Tutored by one of Pater's sisters, Woolf absorbed so much from Pater that he constituted her authentic anxiety of influence, rarely to be mentioned. Her key metaphors for the reading process—impression, perception, sensation—are Pater's; he was, in the world of literature, what Perry Meisel called "the absent father."

Woolf might have preferred Dr. Johnson or Hazlitt, but as a reader she remained always Walter Pater's daughter, a critical impressionist of rare genius. From Pater she learned the Epicurean lesson that the reality of reading inhered in accurately apprehending a concourse of perceptions, a flux of sensations, a cognitive music of impressions. For a Paterian-Woolfian aesthete, love for an actual woman or man is frequently only a disguise for the love of reading. Personality, to such an aesthete, is the highest value, but this means personality in the high Shakespearean sense: Falstaff, Hamlet, Cleopatra. Woolf reads to encounter great personalities, be they Hamlet or Jane Austen, and thus to reveal her own remarkable personality to herself.

Writing about DeQuincey's autobiography, Woolf made a distinction that is also relevant to her own role as a memoirist—an artist of the self and the truths of personality:

> To tell the whole story of a life the autobiographer must devise some means by which the two levels of existence can be recorded—the rapid passage of events and actions; the slow opening up of single and solemn moments of concentrated emotion.

The world outside the self is a whirl of sensations and perceptions, but the "single and solemn" moments of being imply a concentrator, the reader's solitary self. Borges, the modern writer whose love of reading rivals Woolf's, tends to fuse that self into a larger self that somehow performs all reading and writing, a kind of universal Shakespearean being. Woolf refreshes, particularly now, in a bad time for disinterested reading, because she will not yield her individuality to even the most literary of abstractions. "How Should One Read a Book?" insists passionately upon the self's needs and wishes, its program of enrichment through the words of otherness:

> Indeed, it is precisely because we hate and we love that our relation with the poets and novelists is so intimate that we find the presence of another person intolerable. And even if the results are abhorrent and our judgments are wrong, still our taste, the nerve of sensation that sends shocks through us, is our chief illuminant, we learn through feeling; we cannot suppress our own idiosyncrasy without impoverishing it.

The salient words here are "sensation" and "idiosyncrasy," indications again of how distant the high aesthete Woolf is from her Feminist following among academic Resenters. My own credo as a reader, since first I encountered it more than a half century ago, is the wonderful final paragraph of "How Should One Read a Book?":

> Yet who reads to bring about an end however desirable? Are there not some pursuits that we practise because they are good in themselves, and some pleasures that are final? And is not this among them? I have sometimes dreamt, at least, that when the Day of Judgment dawns and the great conquerors and lawyers and statesmen come to receive their rewards—their crowns, their laurels, their names carved indelibly upon imperishable marble—the Almighty will turn to Peter and will say, not without a certain envy when He sees us coming with our books under our arms, "Look, these need no reward. We have nothing to give them here. They have loved reading."

ANNE MORROW LINDBERGH
b. 1906

ANNE SPENCER MORROW was born in Englewood, New Jersey, on June 22, 1906. Her mother, Elizabeth Cutter Morrow, was a strong and energetic woman who stressed the importance of education. Elizabeth attended Smith College from 1895 to 1899 and then traveled and studied in Europe for two years. In 1903 she married Dwight Whitney Morrow. A graduate of Columbia Law School, Morrow began working for the banking firm of J. P. Morgan and Company in 1914 and was made a partner within the year. After World War I, both Elizabeth and Dwight Morrow were active supporters of the League of Nations. A college classmate of Calvin Coolidge, Morrow was made ambassador to Mexico in 1927. It was there that Anne Morrow met Charles Lindbergh in 1928, soon after he had completed his historic cross-Atlantic flight.

Bring Me a Unicorn (1971), the first volume of Anne Morrow's diaries and letters, covers her years at Smith College and the beginning of her relationship with Charles Lindbergh. She entered Smith in 1924 and began to receive recognition for her writing abilities. She won two awards for essays and contributed to college publications. Her first story was published in the April 1927 edition of *Smith College Monthly*, and her first poem, "Height," was published in *Scribner's* magazine in 1928.

After graduating from Smith, Anne Morrow married Charles Lindbergh, on May 27, 1929. She was suddenly thrust out of a quiet and contemplative life into one of action and celebrity. She learned to read flight maps and flight equipment, earned her pilot's license, and became navigator on long flights with her husband. In 1930, soon after completing a cross-country flight that set a speed record, Anne gave birth to Charles Lindbergh Jr. on her birthday, June 22. Within a year she joined Charles Sr. on a trip across Canada and Alaska to Japan and China. While on this trip, in 1931, Anne learned of the death of her father. Accounts of this trip and the effect of her father's death are described in both her diary and her first book, *North to the Orient* (1935).

Further tragedy occurred on March 31, 1932, when Charles Lindbergh Jr. was abducted from the family's home in rural New Jersey. For two long months, the family hoped he would be returned alive. When his body was found at last, it was determined that he had probably been accidently killed the night of the abduction. Anne turned to her writing for the first time in three-and-a-half years and began her draft of *North to the Orient*. She also writes about this time in the second volume of her diaries and letters, *Hour of Gold, Hour of Lead* (1973). The "hour of lead" began to come to a close with the birth of the Lindbergh's second son on August 16th of that year. The pain was rekindled, however, when the suspected kidnapper, Bruno Hauptmann, was arrested in the fall of 1934 and tried in 1935. In response to the media furor caused by the trial and the persistent invasion of privacy, the Lindberghs left the country—not returning until the approach of war in 1939.

In 1934 Morrow Lindbergh's article "Flying around the North Atlantic" was published in *National Geographic* magazine. Harold Nicolson, who was writing a biography of her father, gave favorable feedback on her writing. And when the Lindberghs moved to England, they rented a house from Nicolson and his wife Vita Sackville-West. During the next couple of years, Morrow Lindbergh continued to fly on long surveying trips with her husband, worked on her second travel book, *Listen! the Wind*, and gave birth to her third son. She eventually had three more children, a son and two daughters.

With the outbreak of World War II, the Lindberghs once again gained celebrity. With Anne's publication of *The Wave of the Future* (1940) and Charles's outspoken activities for the America First Movement, they became known as antiwar and anti-interventionist. When the U.S. entered the war, they became notorious. Charles was not accepted for active duty, but worked as a test pilot for Ford. Morrow Lindbergh wrote her first novel, *The Steep Ascent* (1944), during this time.

After the war, the Lindberghs retired to private life and turned their energies to the preservation of wildlife and the environment. In 1955 Morrow Lindbergh published her best-known work, *Gift from the Sea*, in which she uses the circular pattern of sea shells as a metaphor for women's lives. Morrow Lindbergh's reputation as a writer increased further when she began publishing her journals in the 1970s. Her first two volumes are described above. Her third volume, *Locked Rooms and Open Doors: 1933–35* (1974), recounts her recovery from grief after the loss of her child and her continuing explorations in flights with Charles. *The Flower and the Nettle: 1936–39* (1976) describes their years in Europe before the war. *War Within and Without: 1939–44* (1980) describes her anxieties about and during World War II.

CRITICAL EXTRACTS

HELEN BEVINGTON

"Let her speak for herself," says Anne Morrow Lindbergh in her modest introduction to a remarkable gathering together of her early diaries and letters
⟨Bring Me a Unicorn⟩. Covering six years from 1922 to 1928, this is the first volume of a personal record, to be continued through 1947, of one of the great
stories of the 20th century. The account in Anne Morrow's own words begins
when she was 16 with a letter to tell Grandma Cutter that "we children" are
having a fine time traveling with Mother and Daddy in Scotland, and ends in
1928 with a letter to Corliss Lamont: "Apparently I am going to marry Charles
Lindbergh."

The decision not to shape this extraordinary material into an autobiography took courage and, I think, perfect wisdom of choice. At first it seemed too
bad: young Anne Morrow, who wanted intensely to be a writer ("I want to
write—I want to write—I want to write and I never never never will"), is left
struggling to compose, full of transport and exclamation marks, rapture and
despair. In her diary at Smith College, she is given to calling clouds "great
archangel wings"; she has an understanding with some lavender sweet peas, is
recklessly lost in a daisy; she is smothered with joy when praised for her
English theme and permanently hounded by final exams. It seemed ironic that,
having become the successful writer she yearned to be, Mrs. Lindbergh should
not use that professional skill to rescue Anne Morrow from her youth.

But I was wrong. The picture that emerges is neither girlish nor partial. In
a charming self-portrait that might be labeled "before and after meeting
Colonel Lindbergh," she reveals herself as the complex person she was—
strong-willed yet meek, firm yet apologetic, timid yet independent, terribly
vulnerable, a poet fond of unicorns, a girl falling in love.

Mrs. Lindbergh confesses in the introduction that when she sat down to
read over these diaries and letters, wondering how to dispose of them, she was
struck not only by what a young, shy, selfconscious adolescent she had been
but by "what an extraordinary life this quite ordinary person led." ⟨. . .⟩

How could Mrs. Lindbergh from this distance retell that love story now?
She had no need to try. Anne Morrow gives her own testimony, pouring out
the tale, bringing to intense life every moment as she lived it. The first flight
she ever took in an airplane was with Colonel L. as pilot, and she felt exalted.
("God, let me be *conscious* of it! Let me be *conscious* of *what* is happening, *while*
it is happening.") He had swept out of sight all the other men she had known.
"All my life, in fact, my world—my little embroidery beribboned world is

smashed." But he didn't hear her as she thanked him. He hadn't really noticed her. She expected never to see him again.

Most of the year 1928 she spent thinking of him and his remote world in the sky, watching birds because they too mounted on wings. When she went to the dentist, the drill roared in her ear like a plane overhead. "Wouldn't it be nice," she asked herself, "if I were wrong about Colonel L.—if he liked me?" Yet, "Fool, fool, fool. You are completely and irretrievably opposed to him. You have nothing in common. You don't even sincerely care a damn for his world."

By July, after graduation from college, feeling fat and old with her teeth all cavities and the lilacs fading in the vase ("It's no good—they *always* fade!"), she knew she wanted to be married and never would be asked. Colonel L. was going to see Elisabeth in New York, "Elisabeth of course again." Anne speculated with her younger sister Constance about the wedding they thought inevitable now. Her dream of heroes was dead. Then on a Wednesday morning he telephoned Anne at her home in Englewood, arranged to come out for an interview, offered to take her flying. She set it down in her diary like a young Fanny Burney, pages and pages of dialogue between them, remembering every word. After that there were the secret meetings. He taught her to fly. When a Mexican paper reported: "Lone Eagle no longer lonely—courts Elisabeth Morrow," she wept with rage.

Once the thought crossed her mind, "How absurd this will sound in fifty years," but it doesn't sound absurd, not at all, endearing rather, moving and delightful. She is so honest a witness. Her feelings are so contradictory—as comical as they are touching—the dilemma of a sheltered, introspective girl in love with a Lindbergh. She writes Con: "Lord, that man is cold, always on guard, with a one-track mind, and his coat doesn't fit"; and in the next breath: "Colonel L. is the kindest man alive *and* approachable. . . . He *really does* like us!"

She analyzes him in her diary: Why is he a great man? She lists his shortcomings: He never opens a book (a hideous chasm between them); he plays practical jokes; he clings to facts, facts, facts. "I don't want to marry him—God forbid. I don't even want to go up in the plane!" Yet he is "the biggest, most absorbing person I've ever met." He has no sense of humor; he has a sense of humor, vision besides. He is amazing, overwhelming, extremely forceful, and "we are utterly opposed."

Only one letter in the book is written to Dear C[harles], and that a demurely noncommittal one. A few months before her marriage, there is the final letter, addressed to Corliss Lamont. Anne Morrow, no longer tentative or unsure, knows only too well the life she is entering with its "horrible, fantastic, absurd publicity." She knows also that where he goes she has to go: "Don't

wish me happiness—I don't expect to be happy, but it's gotten beyond that somehow. Wish me courage and strength and a sense of humor—I will need them all."
　　—Helen Bevington, "Bring Me a Unicorn," *The New York Times* (27 February 1972): 3

CATHARINE R. STIMPSON

Sincerity is the sinew of Anne Morrow Lindbergh's third volume of diaries and letters 〈*Locked Rooms and Open Doors*〉. She is, she says in her introduction, now over 60 years old. She claims a "last chance" to bear accurate witness to her past.

Part of a later generation, I must work to grasp a sense of the charisma that Anne Morrow Lindbergh and her husband Charles radiated in that past. To their honor, they refused to massage their wild celebrity. The diary mentions neither press agents nor business managers. The pictures of the Lindberghs are appealing: a handsome, brave, ardent, self-sufficient couple, free spirits too devoted to each other to be lonely. Yet if the diary, prose and photographs, shows how attractive the Lindberghs were, it fails to tell why they provoked such frantic awe.

Such an omission is deliberate. Anne Morrow Lindbergh's purpose is not to explore our mass compulsion to create and then to touch that special category of being—the famous—but to record the strains of being one of its members. She notes the tensions, and pleasures, of public and domestic events. 〈. . .〉

Unifying the happenings of Anne Morrow Lindbergh's life is the effort to create a stable sense of self, a serene "I." Her confessions are more reticent and less gamey than those of, say, Vita Sackville-West, but they document an unexpected anguish and anxiety. "Locked Rooms and Open Doors" is an autobiography of being imprisoned in bad dreams, great demands, self-doubt, and painful fatigue. From 1933 to 1935 "The Terror" often enveloped her. Sometimes, she physically feared death, as she flew with Lindbergh as radio operator, navigator and co-pilot. At other times the terror was psychic. Often an insomniac, she would remember, as if it were a garish mental tic, the death of her first child, or, as if she were regressing to a state of adolescent panic, she would believe herself to be a duckling as useless as it was ugly.

Her love for Lindbergh steadied her. A muffled conflict of the diary is that of her love and desire for Lindbergh's happiness, of her sense of children as the nurturing core of life, of her wish to write and of her feminism, which she calls proving to the world that a woman can do anything a man can. Lindbergh tends to dominate the conflict. 〈. . .〉

⟨. . .⟩ Despite the evocations of joy, ⟨Charles⟩ Lindbergh remains opaque, a heroic mask.

Other parts of the diary also call for amplitude. Many entries are terse: the brevity of a hard-working aviator or of a shy woman who fears that self-revelation may be a dangerous self-indulgence. Among the scenes that suffer from abbreviation is the account of a visit by the Charles Lindberghs to the George Putnams. The two wives—Anne Morrow Lindbergh and the great flyer Amelia Earhart—ask each other if they have read Virginia Woolf's essays about the condition of women, "A Room of One's Own." The answers? Unrecorded. An incidental interest of the diary is its evidence of the influence of the literature of Virginia Woolf. For Anne Morrow Lindbergh and some of the favored, intelligent, earnest, often perplexed people whom she knew, Woolf crystallized their sense of the tenuous structures of being.

The sensibility that most vividly animates "Locked Rooms and Open Doors" is moral, psychological and esthetic. Anne Morrow Lindbergh looks to art for a consoling sense of form; to writing for proof of consciousness.

—Catharine R. Stimpson, "Locked Rooms and Open Doors," *The New York Times Book Review* 11, no. 28 (24 March 1974): 8

ANNE FREMANTLE

Anne Morrow Lindbergh prefaces her introduction to this third volume of her autobiography ⟨*Locked Rooms and Open Doors*⟩ with a quotation from Thoreau: "A traveller is to be reverenced . . . going from—toward; it is the history of everyone of us." It is supereminently hers. In this volume, she goes from the golden glory of her marriage and the tragedy of her eldest son's murder to almost a half year's exploratory air travel round the Atlantic with her husband and second son, Jon, to the death of her beloved elder sister Elizabeth, to her flight to England with husband and son to escape the almost ceaseless publicity, the constant threats and the fearful lack of privacy that almost eroded her sanity and threatened her marriage—all in two years.

Anne Lindbergh was fortunate in having a wonderfully warm family life, a happy childhood, a brilliant and devoted husband and the deeply felt conviction that she was a writer. But she has paid dearly for these assets. Here is such an agonizing sensitivity that she seems, at times, flayed alive, every nerve of body and soul raw. Hers, too is a constant awareness of danger, whether physical or spiritual—she is "frightened to death in a back cockpit in stormy weather," in fog, in sandstorms, in accidents; she is searingly wounded by casual remarks about their tragedy, even when made by strangers in darkest Africa; she is fiercely protective of her private life under circumstances that were necessarily public, for the Atlantic survey flight the Lindberghs undertook was not only physically grueling, but also had to be undertaken with enormous publicity. Everywhere, she and Colonel Lindbergh were received with royal honors, greeted by governors, prime ministers, heads of state, feted at embassies. Also the flight took her away from her small Jon for months, with news of him scarce and no contact possible with those left in charge of him.

She is pitilessly, luminously clear about the cost—the suppression of her natural feelings, she admits, created "terrible inner tensions, distorted fears," and her nights were full of suppressed rebellious feelings, "ballooning like monstrous toadstools." Since she was "well, though sleepless," it never occurred to her to see a doctor. "Psychiatry was for those who had nervous breakdowns, and I did not break down." She admits that what probably saved her sanity was her habit of writing her diary almost daily: "brought to the aseptic light of the diary's white page, the giant toadstools withered." Here she wrote that on her (only?) New York subway ride she thought, "Horrible-horrible-looking people: I wanted to say 'And which one of you killed my boy?'"

She could wonder: "What *is* there about the English? You seem to be talking openly . . . when snap, the blind goes up (or down), actually, in your face and they have shut themselves in for good." She is enchanted with Greenlanders' country dancing: they have pattern and design and rhythm.

In east Greenland, the pack ice is just offshore stretching out to the sea. "Only a flimsy airplane between us and the ice age." In the Faroes, the natives drive herds of small whales into a fjord and then harpoon, "and all the sea is blood." In Copenhagen, "we pay calls on the Prime Minister." She is 26 and there, at a party, longs to dance, but C. is right in forbidding it, there was a flashlight reporter in the hall. Next day: "Damn, damn, damn, I am sick of being this 'handmaid to the Lord.' They think they can wangle *me*, if they can't get at him."

The trip seems endless—after Paris, then Amsterdam and a ghastly flight towards Geneva. "We plow around for about two hours . . . the dark ground slipping under us beneath wisps of fog. . . . I was in sheer physical terror the whole time. . . . I look at the map—Ostend—a nice reservoir to land in. We circle, weather is worse. . . . He circles and goes on, up the coast." Then Spain, and Portugal, and at Porto Praia, by contacting Sayville, Long Island, she establishes a record (over 3,000 miles) for radio communication between an airplane and a ground station.

Back at her mother's house, writing comes to mean more and more. She is "in book" and "I care about it more than anything else. But never, never let anyone know it . . . how terribly you feel when you've given your secret self away. Nothing is worth it." Living with her mother is hard for them both, especially for her after Elizabeth's death. "I must not cry," she complains. "I must finish the book [*North to the Orient*]." And there is continually "that eternal struggle of what I must be for C., and what I must be for Mother, and what I must be for myself."

—Anne Fremantle, "Let Us Now Praise Famous Women," *America* (20 April 1974): 31

EMILY HAHN

Nothing, it seems, cools off so completely as dated political passion and anger. "The Flower and the Nettle" harks back to an old, furious controversy and makes us wonder sadly what it was all about. Why did we attack our erstwhile hero so savagely?

Like its predecessors, the fourth volume of Anne Lindbergh's memoirs is composed of portions of her diary and letters, in this case from records spanning the period from January 1936 to April 1939, when she and her husband lived abroad. 〈. . .〉

〈. . .〉 They chose England, where Anne had family connections, and arrived there in 1936.

The book opens at this point. "I think we did the right thing, and even temporarily in this quiet garden I feel the difference," wrote Mrs. Lindbergh at her brother-in-law's house in Wales. "No fear of the press trespassing on the grounds, or eavesdropping. No fear at night while putting Jon up to bed and then running up to see if he is all right. . . . We have been bothered very little and seem to be left quietly alone here, both by people and press." Lindbergh, always referred to as "C.," seems content studying mathematics and "plunging ahead through calculus," an interest that makes Anne marvel. She herself majored in English at Smith and quotes rather a lot from the classics. She has already published one book, and hopes to write another if she can find the time, though what with the demands of housekeeping, it does not look at first as if she ever will.

Sometimes she walks up and down the garden "for hours," she says, pondering her thoughts. "Should a woman be satisfied to be 'just a mother' and wife, etc.!" But she seldom feels rebellious. A few pages later she tells us that when C. asked her what she wanted in life she answered that she didn't want anything except to have a home—quietly, anywhere, a home with him and Jon. Even so, she looks back wistfully at the few journeys she made by herself, back in the short period between college and marriage: "mostly I remembered the heady excitement of that independent feeling." 〈. . .〉

〈. . .〉 To a friend in America she writes that she hasn't been working hard enough at her book.

"Isn't it possible for a woman to be a woman and yet produce something tangible besides children, something that stands up in a man's world?" No, she concludes, it isn't. Deep down in her heart she doesn't want to do it, she says, because success involves sacrificing things she is not prepared to sacrifice. In order to compete with men, women must concentrate their energies into a narrow line, "and I think in doing that they deny themselves the special attributes and qualities of women."

Home from a flying trip to India she writes on July 10, 1937, "Where does my day go—what have I to show for it . . . I feel hopelessly inefficient not to do the baby, C. and Jon as a matter of course—'on the side,' so to speak—like those women C. is always talking about who cook, take care of the house, a large family, do the sewing, washing, and some of the farm work, etc." ⟨. . .⟩

⟨. . .⟩ ⟨T⟩he American press too was turning on the Lindberghs, complaining about those trips to Germany, the Göring medal and the fact that the couple were actually thinking of taking up residence in Berlin. Naturally, our intelligence people were not about to explain their part in all this, and matters worsened. As relations between Germany and the United States deteriorated, the outcry grew louder and louder—until the imminent approach of war caused editorial comment to cease abruptly. Suddenly it all seemed unimportant. Lindbergh was needed at home, and Washington summoned him. Anne followed with the children, embarking on April 20, 1939. Two French reporters tried to interview her at the dock but, true to tradition, she brushed them off with a chilly "No comment."

It is easy to sympathize with this reaction. No Lindbergh, one supposes, could ever learn to love the press in any country. All the more praiseworthy, then, is Mrs. Lindbergh's honesty: she's been a scrupulous reporter herself. While selecting from her writings, she has not given in to what must have been a temptation to embroider or alter what she set down years ago. "The Flower and the Nettle" is simply the record of conditions as they seemed to her at that time, a portrayal of what it was like before World War II, without the light of later knowledge. Her few afterthoughts have been lumped into the introduction and the footnotes.

This is an interesting story. Why, then, does it seem to move so slowly, so stodgily? No doubt the admirers of Mrs. Lindbergh's many books will tear this reviewer limb from limb for saying so, but the fact remains that in spite of the material the book is pedestrian. Perhaps it is the method of presentation that is at fault. Diaries and letters, however worthy, can also be wordy.

—Emily Hahn, "The Flower and the Nettle," *The New York Times* (22 February 1976): 3

JOSEPH P. LASH

The splendid quality of this diary ⟨*War Within and Without*⟩ emerges at the start. It is early August 1939. The Charles Lindberghs and their two children have recently returned from a two-year self-imposed exile in Europe. He hands her a letter and introduction to the French edition of her book, "Listen! the Wind." They are written by Antoine de Saint-Exupéry, whose own book, "Wind, Sand and Stars," is a magnificently lyrical statement of the values of aviation. All through supper she reads his introduction, translating its subtleties for Charles. "I am startled by what he has seen in me," she writes shyly. A note from her publisher says that the Frenchman, now in New York, would like to meet her. Charles Lindbergh calls his hotel the next day. "I am rather afraid to meet him," Anne confesses, and shyness turns to fright when her husband, unable to pick up Saint-Exupéry, tells her to do so. "Now *what* would I talk to him about?"

They get along famously, even though her car breaks down, and the furious conversation on the trip out to Huntington on the Long Island Rail Road is symptomatic of the heady weekend that the French aviator-poet spends with them:

"It was very exciting. Perhaps it was only because it was almost the first time anyone had talked to me purely on my *craft*. Not because I was a woman to be polite to, to charm with superficials, not because I was my father's daughter or C.'s wife; no, simply because of my book, my mind, my *craft*. I have a *craft*! And someone who is master of that craft, who writes beautifully, thinks I know enough about my craft to want to compare notes about it, to want to fence with my *mind*, steel against steel."

Lindbergh finally turns up about 10 that first evening, and the conversation "takes on a higher, less feminine tone." "Mr. St.-Ex." hits it off with both of them. They drive him back to New York, Lindbergh chauffeuring (and running out of gas), and, as they leave him at his hotel, Anne hopes they have made a friend. "I hardly know, looking back, which are my thoughts and which his."

They never see him again. She notes sadly in her diary in January 1941 that "St.-Ex." has been in New York and left without making any effort to see them. She cares deeply, ". . . because I keep looking for someone to be left like that from *my*, my world of writing. But there is no one left. I have lost them all this year. . . . It is not my 'time' to see the St.-Ex.'s of this world."

The outbreak of the war had created a fearsome personal dilemma for her, and she had foreseen it: "It is because of C. that I am afraid," she writes two weeks before that fateful weekend. "Can I follow him? How can I follow him? That is the nightmare . . . separated from him." Her answers to those questions give this book much of its poignancy and drama. "War Within and Without," "the fifth and last" of her diaries, covers the years 1939–1944. Because it deals with the 1939–1941 battles between the isolationists led by her husband, and the interventionists who included her mother, sister and sister-in-law, there were rumors it would never be published.

But here it is, and it is fascinating. ⟨. . .⟩ What gives this diary its appeal, however, is its day-to-day account of how a gifted woman solved the basic problems confronting her womanhood, as well as how she came, despite her internationalist upbringing, to support her husband's political position. Public men serve themselves by dying before their wives, especially if the latter lack their husbands' self-righteousness. In the introduction to her book, she writes, "It is, I realize, more personal, more open, and more vulnerable and, because of this, ultimately more honest than any of the preceding volumes." "I can see and admit my own mistakes," she writes, "and those of my husband."

In September 1940, Mrs. Lindbergh explains to her mother that her just-published little book "The Wave of the Future" is her effort to build a bridge between her husband's position and her own. "I *had* to write it." In it she argues for staying out of the war and concentrating on domestic reform because, among other reasons, Italy, Germany and Russia, whatever their flaws, are symptoms of a new world struggling to be born. But people she cared about damned the widely-read book as a plea for appeasement and a condonation of totalitarianism. The latter criticism hurt. "I never said Totalitarianism was the Wave of the Future," she complains in her journal. "In fact, I said emphatically that is was *not* and I hoped *we* in America could be in our way." Two years later she still is lamenting, "It will never be washed away." As a favorite cousin, Richard Scandrett, wrote about the book—Mrs. Lindbergh does not quote his letter—"The Wave of the Future" was "a lyrical and silver-coated exposition of the views expressed by Charles."

Only once did she diverge sharply from Lindbergh, in the fall of 1941, and then in private. He had unleashed his infamous attack on the Jews, warning them of retribution for being, along with the British and the Administration, among the leading "war agitators." She tries to explain to herself her "profound feeling of grief" over what Charles has said, and decides it is "at best unconsciously a bid for anti-Semitism. It is a match lit near a pile of excelsior." But to an old friend she explains her willingness to continue living with him: "We do disagree but I have the utmost faith in his essential goodness of spirit."

Her complete commitment to her husband is the key to her position. Saint-Exupéry can sit in a hotel room and write. "*He can*—but I can't. I am married—more than married—dedicated to marriage. And I care about the man I am married to, I care intensely about his life, our life together. . . ."

Another answer was possible—indeed, had been given by spirited women. Alice James, the invalided sister of William and Henry, asked in her journal, "When will women begin to have the first glimmer that above all other loyalties is the loyalty to truth, i.e., to yourself, that husband, children, friends and country are nothing to that." And Virginia Woolf confessed that to be a writer she had to begin by killing that part of herself which put a man's views before her own ⟨. . . .⟩

"How hard it is to have the beautiful interdependence of marriage," Anne Lindbergh acknowledges late in this book, "and yet be strong in oneself alone."

—Joseph P. Lash, "Faithful Wife," *The New York Times Book Review* VII, no. 7 (20 April 1980); 7

ELSIE F. MAYER

Anne Morrow Lindbergh's fifth volume of diaries and letters, *War Within and Without* is a diary without trivia. The events of World War II from 1939 through 1944 are the background of this volume. Filtered through Anne's sensitive lens, we see how these events affect the Lindberghs, at times causing bewilderment, pain and grief.

The Lindberghs' lives oscillated between involvement and withdrawal. For Charles, her husband, the period brought feverish activity as he traveled around the country, lecturing on behalf of the America First Committee. For Anne the same period is best characterized by the publication of her controversial essay, "The Wave of the Future," which she insisted was "a moral argument for isolationism," not a concession to totalitarianism as her critics claimed. After the United States entered the war, the Lindberghs moved to Michigan, where Charles served as a consultant in Henry Ford's aviation program. The volume ends with the Lindberghs' return east to Connecticut in the fall of 1944 after Charles had completed a testing mission in the Pacific.

The volume clarifies the Lindberghs' stance on the war. Although both were isolationists, each arrived at this position independently: Charles from "a dispassionate conviction" that America should limit itself to its own defense and Anne from the fear that the war would precipitate the destruction of Western civilization. When, however, Charles denounced the Jews along with the British and the Roosevelt Administration as "war agitators," Anne objected to Charles's position, expecting the charge to trigger a wave of anti-Semitism. At times sympathetic with the interventionists, among whom was her mother, Elizabeth Cutter Morrow, Anne admitted that the choice between intervention and isolation was not clear-cut. While Charles emerges from the controversy as politically naïve, Anne demonstrates a capacity for grasping the subtleties of the issue.

Intersecting the war controversy throughout Anne's diary is the dilemma common to the woman-artist: how to balance marriage and career, life and art. Anne saw that they nurtured each other, but the demands of her marriage encroached on art. Nevertheless, write she must because, as she noted, it was a means of letting "my soul catch up." Thus, with almost heroic self-discipline, she kept her diary amidst chaos without and anxiety within her marriage. While living in Michigan, for example, Anne would routinely withdraw to a trailer she had conveniently placed near the house. There in addition to her diary she wrote her short novel, *The Steep Ascent*, based on a harrowing flight she experienced.

Through writing Anne feels the pulse of life. For readers familiar with her earlier diaries this need to discover herself through writing comes as no surprise, nor is the self-portrait of the sensitive woman that emerges from these pages. With this volume the strokes of the portrait grow more distinct. Fading is our impression of a shy, young girl on the arm of America's hero of the 1930's; instead there is a mature woman, now strengthened by the diverse experiences that have befallen her as a public figure.

Not only does *War Within and Without* possess sincerity and candor, qualities we have come to expect in the diary, but it achieves complementarity between form and content. Commenting on the diary, Anne observed it was "my tool for the development of awareness." Herein she has identified the essence of the form, viz., its realism and sense of time. For what the diary reveals, and Anne's eminently well, is the diarist in the process of becoming. We hope this is not her last volume, for interest in her as an artist and woman extends beyond the war years.

—Elsie F. Mayer, "War Within and Without," *America* (25 October 1980): 12

DAVID KIRK VAUGHAN

⟨. . .⟩ It was not until after the death of her baby that Lindbergh returned to the practice of making diary entries ⟨*Hour of Gold, Hour of Lead*⟩. Two important events mark the beginning and the ending of the "hour of lead"; the first is the kidnapping and death of their first son in March 1932 and the second is the birth of their second son, Jon, in August of that year.

⟨. . .⟩ on 11 May 1932, after a lapse of over three and a half years, she once again began to make diary entries.

The first diary entry, which begins "Woke from a dream of the return of the baby . . ." was dated almost two and a half months after the baby had been taken; the baby's body was found the next day. The diary entries that follow reflect feelings of profound sorrow and dull shock. Lindbergh recalls many of the details of her last days with the baby and, by writing about them, begins the slow process of healing and recovery. But even as she gives voice to her sorrow, she engages in a process of self-definition:

> I think . . . women take and conquer sorrow differently from men.
> They take it willingly, with open arms they blend and merge it into
> every part of their lives; it is diffused and spread into every fiber, and

they build from that and with that. While men take the concentrated bitter dose at one draught and then try to forget—start to work at something objective and entirely separate. [9 June 1932]

This early entry illustrates the essential Lindbergh creative process at work; the diary entry first describes the emotional response to an important personal event. Then a process of analysis begins, as Lindbergh assesses the meaning of the event she has described. Out of this analysis comes insight and the motivation to build upon the experience. In an effort to occupy herself after the baby's death she returned to the task of drafting a first version of *North to the Orient*. But more therapeutic than work on her book was the birth of her second child, who arrived on 16 August.

Her diary entry describing the birth of her baby occupies over four pages of *Hour of Gold* and is clearly of major importance. Because she kept no diary at the time her first child was born, this recollection of the pains and pleasures of birth was a new and special experience, and the arrival of the baby seems to signal a true renewal in her outlook:

> I felt as if a great burden had fallen off me. I could not imagine the baby would do this for me, but I felt life given back to me—a door to life opened. I *wanted* to live, I felt power to live. I was not afraid of death or life: a spell had been broken, the spell over us that made me dread everything and feel that nothing would go right after this. The spell was broken by this real, tangible, perfect baby, coming into an imperfect world and coming out of the teeth of sorrow—a miracle. My faith had been reborn.

⟨. . .⟩ The pressure and the uncertainty of the war caused Lindbergh and her husband to engage in a number of discussions about the progress of their work and their long-range goals. One such discussion, which occurred toward the end of July 1940, illustrates Lindbergh's frustrations. She writes ⟨in *War Within and Without*⟩ that Charles had been discussing the progress of her writing: "he goes over the record—nine years, and only two books and wonders why it is. Has he not given me the right kind of environment?" She acknowledges that she is too easily distracted by other tasks because she feels the burden of the writing she should be doing:

> But you ask too much, I want to cry out. I cannot be having a baby and be a good housekeeper and keep thinking and writing on the present times (in my diary) and be always free to discuss anything with you and give to the children and keep an atmosphere of peace in the family (the bigger family which is so scattered and distraught now, all of us disagreeing) and keep my mind clear and open on the present-day things and write a book at the same time.

And then, as she is effectively describing her frustrations to herself, she is caught up in the progress of her own thought. What is the "permanent writing" she should be doing? Not the kind of writing she was doing before the war, she decides; the war has closed that route, practically and philosophically.

> I have the feeling I must begin again, as one has to begin life again
> now, with an utterly new conception, new ideals, new words even.
> But we are just learning them. The new age is just beginning. In fact,
> it is the transition stage. The old world is dying and a new one begin-
> ning, and this is the pain and uncertainty and anguish we all feel.
> How can I write in the new language before that world is born?

This remarkable sequence illustrates the manner in which the materials that contribute to personal tension are transmuted into artistic insight and eventually into finished creative work. The "new language" of the world that will be born of the war, for instance, began to be articulated in *The Wave of the Future*, the brief but controversial work that Lindbergh completed the following month.

Charles Lindbergh encouraged his wife to devote increased attention to her writing and to this end arranged to have her diaries consolidated and typed. Anne Lindbergh was initially not certain that this was a good idea, and the entire project forced her to evaluate the purpose and value that her diaries possess. Dismayed at their youthful naïveté, she at first questions the merit of such an undertaking, but evenually decides that it is absolutely essential that she write them:

> And *now*, am I writing what at fifty I shall think trash? No matter, one
> has to write, one writes not to be read but to breathe—I did even
> then. One writes to think, to pray, to analyze. One writes to clear
> one's mind, to dissipate one's fears, to face one's doubts, to look at
> one's mistakes—in order to retrieve them. One writes to capture and
> crystallize one's joy, but also to analyze and disperse one's gloom.

⟨. . .⟩ The concluding period described in Lindbergh's final volume of diaries and letters extends from April through October of 1944. In April Charles left for the Pacific theater of operations, where he was involved in test-flying the P-38, primarily in demonstrating long-range cruise-control characteristics to the combat pilots of the area who were required to fly long distances across the Pacific Ocean. In his absence Anne Lindbergh was plunged into an emotional and creative limbo, during which she wrote nothing of note, even avoiding making any diary entries. Only when her husband returned in October 1944 did she resume recording her thoughts in her diary. This lack of creative energy confirmed what she had acknowledged earlier, that her creative activity was nourished by her nearness to her husband, even though that nearness often brought a significant increase in traveling and other physical activities.

 —David Kirk Vaughan, "Married Life in America," *Anne Morrow Lindbergh* (Boston: Twayne, 1988), 11–12, 24–26

Elsie F. Mayer

In her desire "to dispel images, both good and bad" associated with herself and Charles, Lindbergh chose "the untouched diaries and letters" instead of autobiography for publication because she perceived the diary to be closer to the truth than biography or autobiography. ⟨. . .⟩

 ⟨. . .⟩ ⟨T⟩he reality Lindbergh creates is not purely mimetic; it is psychological. The life she recreates, both private and public, is transformed through her perception before assuming permanence in language. True to the form, Lindbergh's diaries combine psychological truths and events, the subjective and the objective, into a gestalt. The insights, however, whose worth she underestimates, gives them their vitality. ⟨. . .⟩

 Against [a] background of fame, travel, and war, Lindbergh faithfully kept the diaries. Throughout, the reader witnesses a probing mind attempting to sift through the chaos of life to the inner silence of revelation. At times this mind is clearly visible in the foreground like the froth on the surface of a stream; at other times it is submerged like an undercurrent. But it is always present and always persistent in its search for truth. Although her sensitivity drives her to seek a greater understanding of life, her diffidence necessitates that she experience the approval of those she respects. As a young woman, no approbation is cherished more than that of her mother and sister Elisabeth, both revered models. Later as a flying companion she marshals all the strength of mind and body to satisfy Charles's expectations of her as a member of the crew.

 Two themes, fundamentally private, dominate the diaries and letters. The first arises from the tension between life and art as experienced by the creative artist. From her youth, Lindbergh aspired to become a writer. She later sought to be an exemplary wife and mother. When the two endeavors compete for the same time and energy, anxiety results. Unfortunately, Lindbergh often views them as mutually exclusive, thereby exacerbating her anxiety. Attempts to resolve the conflict, often poignantly expressed, run like a thread through the diaries and letters. The second theme is the sensitive individual struggling to preserve the integrity of her life in the face of a public bent on transforming her into its own image. Hers is a temperament that eschews the artificial in favor of the natural, pretention in favor of sincerity. With the resoluteness of her convictions, Lindbergh defends her right to confront life independently with the resources of her own mind. For Lindbergh the diary assumes significance because it allows her the freedom of thought and expression the public denies.

Lindbergh is always at the center of her diaries. The assertion that writing clarifies experience reverberates throughout their pages. The tension released in the diaries allows her to transform negative energy into a constructive force that moves her forward in life. Like Antaeus who drew strength from contact with the earth, Lindbergh derives strength from the diary. By allowing her to weigh and judge life, it reanimates her for future endeavors. ⟨. . .⟩

Claiming *The Flower and the Nettle* is slow paced and stodgy, Emily Hahn notes that despite its merits, "the book is pedestrian." ⟨*The New York Times* (22 February 1976): 3⟩ The fault, she adds, may be Lindbergh's choice of forms, the diary and letter. Unfortunately, Hahn, in her criticism, overlooks the variety of experience in this volume, which encompasses 1936–1939, years representing the Lindberghs' withdrawal from public life until they moved to Paris. ⟨. . .⟩ In Paris the tempo of life is accelerated by the rich diversity of people and experience. Faithful to the changing circumstances of this period, Lindbergh captures their rhythm throughout this volume in a manner that is true to the naturalistic quality of the diary. In her criticism Hahn underestimates this achievement. ⟨. . .⟩

Supplanting the conflict of the creative woman in marriage throughout the latter portion of *The Flower and the Nettle* is ⟨Anne's⟩ fear of war engulfing Europe. ⟨. . .⟩ ⟨T⟩he Lindberghs feared entering the war: Charles because of the superiority of Germany's air force, Anne because of a philosophical belief that war is evil. Their position was not unique. The prevailing attitude throughout the embassies they frequented was similar; peace by negotiation was urged by many diplomats and intellectuals alike. Nevertheless, in allowing themselves to become involved in controversy, the Lindberghs paved the way for having their position scrutinized and ultimately condemned in the press.

Lindbergh's response to these events in the diary gives them a dramatic quality they otherwise would lack. The impersonality attendant upon a mere record of the facts yields to an emotionally intense narrative in the hands of Lindbergh-the-diarist. Her strong feelings, forthright and sincere, hover on the surface and erupt in anger when Charles is misquoted in the press. The attack on Charles's assessment of German air power, she attributes to "blind stupid hate and fear of jealousy."

In this volume Lindbergh has made great strides towards reaching her personal goals. Although she continues to treasure private over public life, adolescent shyness and fear have faded to mere shadows of their former gargantuan figures. There is more depth of thought in *The Flower and the Nettle*. The dream of personal achievement and the active role thrust upon her as the wife of an international figure have temporarily merged. This she experiences when in February 1939 she reads her early diaries:

> And there is no longer that terrific struggle between the two—that divided self—that was there for years. That old self, suppressed, passionate, insisting to come out—pushed down by that other new self, practical, active, outward, and comparatively efficient.
>
> No; somehow they have fused—at least I think so. At last they are one.

Indeed, the portrait is etched with lines of compassion and humility, lines of sensitivity and insight wrought by responsibility, work, and truth to one's self. The woman coming to terms with her own identity, the artist wrestling with the modern paradox of freedom and responsibility fall more sharply into focus.

—Elsie F. Mayer, "Self-Portrait: The Diaries," *My Window on the World: The Works of Anne Morrow Lindbergh* (Hamden: Shoestring Press, 1988), 11–14, 23, 25–26

BIBLIOGRAPHY

North to the Orient. 1935.
Listen! the Wind. 1938.
The Wave of the Future. 1940.
The Steep Ascent. 1944.
Gift from the Sea. 1955.
The Unicorn and Other Poems, 1935–1955. 1956.
Dearly Beloved. 1962.
Earth Shine. 1969.
Bring Me a Unicorn: Diaries and Letters, 1922–28. 1971.
Hour of Gold, Hour of Lead: Diaries and Letters, 1929–1932. 1973.
Locked Rooms and Open Doors: Diaries and Letters, 1933–35. 1974.
The Flower and the Nettle: Diaries and Letters, 1936–39. 1976.
War Within and Without: Diaries and Letters, 1939–44. 1980.

MARY McCARTHY
1912–1989

MARY McCARTHY was born in Seattle, Washington, on June 21, 1912. While well known for her *Memories of a Catholic Girlhood* (1957), McCarthy's religious heritage was actually quite diverse. Her mother, Therese Preston, was the daughter of an Episcopalian lawyer and Jewish mother. Her father, Roy Winfield McCarthy, a lawyer, was from a wealthy Minneapolis Irish-Catholic family. When moving with their family to Minneapolis in 1918, McCarthy's parents died within a day of each other in an influenza epidemic. This double loss began a bleak period of McCarthy's life, when she and her siblings were relegated to uncaring relatives. McCarthy wrote about these hard years in "Yonder Peasant, Who Is He?" and "A Tin Butterfly," both a part of *Memories*.

In 1923 McCarthy's maternal grandparents in Seattle became her guardians. She was enrolled in the Forest Ridge Convent but spent her weekends at her grandparents' house making her way through their library. There she read Dickens, Harte, Tolstoy, Huxley, and Mencken. After a year in public high school, she attended the Annie Wright Seminary in Tacoma, an Episcopalian boarding school. She graduated in 1929 and entered Vassar in the fall. She graduated with a B.A. in 1933 and began to write short book reviews for *The Nation* and *The New Republic*. In 1936 and 1937, she worked for Covici Friede, a left-wing publishing house. She was an editor and theater critic for the anti-Stalinist *Partisan Review* from 1937 to 1948.

In 1936 she divorced her husband of three years and in 1938 married the critic Edmund Wilson. Their child, Reuel Kimball Wilson, was born that year. Wilson encouraged her to write fiction, and in 1939 Robert Penn Warren published McCarthy's first story, "Cruel and Barbarous Treatment," in the *Southern Review*. This was the first story of the semiautobiographical collection of pieces published as *The Company She Keeps* in 1942. In 1945–46 she divorced and remarried and taught at Bard College and Sarah Lawrence College. In 1949 she was a Guggenheim Fellow and received the *Horizon* literary prize for her utopian philosophical tale *The Oasis*.

During the 1950s she published a collection of short stories, *Cast a Cold Eye* (1950); two novels, *The Groves of Academe* (1952) and *A Charmed Life* (1955); her autobiography, *Memories of a Catholic Girlhood*; as well as two books on art history, *Venice Observed* (1956) and *The Stones of Florence* (1959). She was awarded a Guggenheim Fellowship in 1949

and again in 1959, at which time she moved to Paris. In 1961 she published a collection of essays, *On the Contrary: Articles of Belief,
1946–1961*, and divorced and remarried. She gained a national reputation in 1963 with *The Group*, a best-selling novel about the lives of
six Vassar graduates. In the late 1960s and 1970s she turned to political writing, criticizing the United States for its involvement in
Indochina in *Vietnam* (1967) and *Hanoi* (1968) and investigating the
Watergate scandal in *The Mask of State: Watergate Portaits* (1974).

McCarthy published the second volume of her memoir, *How I
Grew*, in 1987. She died of cancer in 1989 at the age of 77. A final vol-
ume of memoirs—unfinished at her death—*Intellectual Memoirs: New
York, 1936–38*, was published in 1992.

CRITICAL EXTRACTS

ELIZABETH HARDWICK

"Mary McCarthy! 'The Man in the Brooks Brothers Shirt'! That's my Bible!" I
once heard a young woman exclaim. No doubt the famous short story is
rightly understood as a sort of parable representing many a young girl's transgressions, even if it does not concern itself with the steps in the sinner's rehabilitation. It would be hard to think of any writer in America more interesting
and unusual than Mary McCarthy. Obviously she wants to be noticed, indeed
to be spectacular; and she works toward that end with what one can only call
a sort of trance-like seriousness. There is something puritanical and perplex-
ing in her lack of relaxation, her utter refusal to give an inch of the ground of
her own opinion. She *cannot conform*, cannot often like what even her peers like.
She is a very odd woman, and perhaps oddest of all in this stirring sense of the
importance of her own intellectual formulations. Very few women writers can
resist the temptation of feminine sensibility; it is there to be used, as a crutch,
and the reliance upon it is expected and generally admired. Mary McCarthy's
work, from the first brilliant *The Company She Keeps* down to her latest collection of essays, *On the Contrary: Articles of Belief 1946–1961*, is not like that of
anyone else and certainly not like that of other women. ⟨. . .⟩

In a writer of this kind there is an urgent sense of the uses to which a vivid
personal nature may be put by a writer's literary talent. There is very often an
easily recognized element of autobiography and it is in autobiography that
Mary McCarthy excels—that is, of course, if one uses the word in its loosest
and largest sense. *The Company She Keeps* and *Memories of a Catholic Girlhood* are

richer, more beautiful, and aesthetically more satisfying than, say, *A Charmed Life* or *The Groves of Academe*. The condition that made *The Oasis* somewhat still-born was that it was more biography than autobiography. In autobiography, self-exposure and self-justification are the same thing. It is this contradiction that gives the form its dramatic tension. To take a very extreme case, it is only natural that critics who find importance in the writings of the Marquis de Sade will feel that the man himself is not without certain claims on our sympathy and acceptance. In Mary McCarthy's case, the daring of the self-assertion, the brashness of the correcting tendency (think of the titles *Cast a Cold Eye* and *On the Contrary*) fill us with a nervous admiration and even with the thrill of the exploit. Literature, in her practice, has the elation of an adventure—and of course that elation mitigates and makes aesthetically acceptable to our senses the strictness of her judgments.

> —Elizabeth Hardwick, "Mary McCarthy" (1961), *A View of My Own* (1962), excerpted in *Twentieth-Century American Literature*, ed. Harold Bloom (New York: Chelsea House Publishers, 1986), 2361–62

BARBARA McKENZIE

⟨A⟩ major theme that runs through *Memories ⟨of a Catholic Girlhood⟩* concerns the contrast between outward appearance and internal reality. Like the recognition of hypocrisy (with which it is closely allied), this awareness has also affected Miss McCarthy's method as a writer. In "To the Reader," she recounts the first instance of her acknowledgment of the need to sustain outwardly acceptable behavior at the expense of inner truth. On the morning of her first Communion, she unthinkingly took a drink of water. To take Communion after having broken the fast would be, she knew, to accept the Holy Sacrament in a state of mortal sin. Not to take Communion, however, would incur her guardians' anger, the sisters' disapproval, and her classmates' disappointment. "So it came about: I received my first Communion in a state of outward holiness and inward horror, believing I was damned . . ."

Subsequent moral crises in her life, Miss McCarthy affirms, have followed "the pattern of this struggle over the first Communion; I have battled, usually without avail, against a temptation to do something which only I knew was bad, being swept on by a need to preserve outward appearances and to live up to other people's expectations of me" (20–21). On that Communion morning, when she supposed herself damned, Miss McCarthy admits that in actuality she was fated "to a repetition or endless re-enactment of that conflict between excited scruples and inertia of will."

This recognition of the difference between external and inner reality, or between the way things *seem* and the way things *are*, provides the disposition and subject matter of irony. The fiction (and for that matter, most of the non-fiction) of Mary McCarthy employs irony, which is to say that the form of her writing depends not only upon a need to expose and to ridicule, the objective of satire, but upon a deep and consistent awareness of the contradictions of human experience. In her fiction, Miss McCarthy often abandons the exaggeration and distortion of satire in favor of a level-headed, precisely worded presentation of the incongruities of what it is to be human. Irony, in other words, is seldom absent from Mary McCarthy's writing even though it does, at times, get lost amid the less profound trappings of satire. Resting on an awareness of the multiple levels and purposes of life, the ironical vision is, by definition, the result of a mature but resigned wisdom that counteracts the moments of self-indulgent contrariness that have made critics charge Mary McCarthy with precocity.

—Barbara McKenzie, *Mary McCarthy* (New York: Twayne Publishers, Inc., 1966), 31–32

DARREL MANSELL

"Artists in Uniform: A Story by Mary McCarthy" appeared in *Harper's Magazine* (March 1953). The piece describes an encounter in the club car of a train, and later in a station restaurant, between a woman and an anti-Semitic air force colonel. In 1954 McCarthy published an essay, "Settling the Colonel's Hash" ⟨McCarthy, *On the Contrary*, New York, 1961, 225–41⟩. She discusses various questions, comments, and interpretations of "Artists in Uniform" passed on to her by readers, and goes on to give her own "idea" of the work, its "chief moral or meaning" to her. Here is an author's sincere and genial attempt to set her readers right on what she meant. Such an attempt always raises fundamental issues concerning the nature of art, and below I want to explore one of them.

According to McCarthy, her readers have been misled from the beginning. For it was the editors of the magazine who were responsible for the subtitle that refers to "Artists in Uniform" as a "story." "I myself," she says, "would not know quite what to call it; it was a piece of reporting or a fragment of autobiography." Indeed, the

> whole point of this "story" was that it really happened; it is written in
> the first person; I speak of myself in my own name, McCarthy. . . .
> When I was thinking about writing the story, I decided not to treat it
> fictionally; the chief interest, I felt, lay in the fact that it happened, in
> real life, . . . to the writer herself. . . . (p. 227)

The fact that the events "happened, in real life" makes all the difference to her. For when her readers asked whether details like the colonel's having hash for lunch were "symbolic" of something in the same way such details might be symbolic in fiction ("a Eucharist or a cannibal feast or the banquet of Atreus" [p. 232]), she felt the correct response was to say that there "were no symbols in this story; there was no deeper level. The nuns were in the story because they were on the train; . . . the colonel had hash because he had hash . . ." ⟨. . .⟩

⟨. . .⟩ McCarthy can claim that the details in "Artists in Uniform" are there because they "happened," but that cannot quite be the case. To say that a detail appears *because* it happened is not the same as saying it *did* happen. She says the former but must mean the latter. For there must have been other details that did happen during the experience but do not appear in the piece. Why are they absent?

Probably because they contributed nothing to, or even detracted from, the author's own sense of what her work ought to be like, a sense that could only be communicated, to the extent it could be communicated at all, by the details she chose (and created?). As for those absent details (the colonel's name, for instance), is it somehow untruthful to the event that they are absent? Certainly not. ⟨. . .⟩

But no matter how much we question the rationale of distinguishing between "autobiography" and "fiction," no matter how thoroughly we convince ourselves that there is no essential difference between the two, the distinction does get made. Somehow an "intention" declares itself to us. So finally we must ask ourselves: what difference should that declared intention make in how we read the book?

McCarthy seems to be claiming it should make all the difference in the world. To the question, "What is the colonel's hash symbolic of?" she answers, "Symbolic of nothing, because what I wrote (*pace* my editors) is not fiction but autobiography." This seems to mean that a detail like the colonel's hash is potentially "symbolic" (in McCarthy's literary sense of referring to some idea beyond itself) or not symbolic according to whether the detail appears in something declared fiction or something declared autobiography. Does that make sense?

At first sight it does. If we get the idea that words on a page are an account of "what happened," we tend to assume with McCarthy that the related details are arrested in something like a literal stage; we assume that hash "means" simply hash. We assume that the details which exist in the work do so primarily, and probably exclusively, because they existed in a reality that is being recorded. Further inquiries into their "literary" meaning, inquiries into what ideas the details might have been contrived to "stand for" beyond themselves, seem almost, if not entirely, stultified. ⟨. . .⟩

But surely this attitude is irrational. Can we really put faith in whatever we can find out about an author's supposed state of mind at the time she wrote— whatever it is she now says she wrote? If she seems to recall that the events in her work somehow derived from what she remembers as "life" to an extent that, even considering omissions, revisions, and other transmogrifications, she now for whatever reason considers significant, does any declaration of this cut off the possibility of the kinds of symbolic meaning there would be if the work had somehow got itself classified as "fiction"? ⟨. . .⟩

In short, should a work have a different status, a different ontology as an artifact, according to somebody's declared guess concerning the relation of "what happened" to words on a page? Can there be any reasonable answer but No?

—Darrel Mansell, "Unsettling the Colonel's Hash: 'Fact' in Autobiography," *Modern Language Quarterly* 37 (1976): 115–18, 124–27

PAUL JOHN EAKIN

Mary McCarthy ⟨. . .⟩ risks violating the convention of the autobiographical pact at the very opening of her *"memoirs"* when she argues that any autobiographer, acting in the best of faith, is going to produce a narrative that will have fiction in it, like it or not. The presence of fiction in autobiography is not something to wish away, to rationalize, to apologize for, as so many writers and readers of autobiography persist in suggesting, for it is as reasonable to assume that all autobiography has some fiction in it as it is to recognize that all fiction is in some sense necessarily autobiographical. The practice of Mary McCarthy provides an ideal opportunity to launch an investigation of this presence, not only because she explicitly addresses herself to this issue but because her performance offers such a distinctly problematical illustration of it. In her case the autobiographer is an established writer of fiction recalling in a series of sketches that look very much like short stories the truth about a self she portrays as a liar.

McCarthy herself dramatizes the ambiguity of the fiction writer turned autobiographer when she observes of one of the chapters of her *"memoirs,"* "*This is an example of 'storytelling'; I arranged actual events so as to make 'a good story' out of them. It is hard to overcome this temptation if you are in the habit of writing fiction; one does it almost automatically*" ⟨*Memories of a Catholic Girlhood*⟩. McCarthy was, in fact, a well-known writer of short stories when she began in 1944 to publish a series of sketches about a character with the same name as her own. There were to be eight of these pieces, and thirteen years later she presented them in a single volume, which she called *Memories of a Catholic Girlhood* (1957). At that time she arranged the sketches in a chronological sequence, adding a commentary or afterword for each one, and providing a long preface ("To the Reader") in which she described the problems and motivation for her autobiographical project. To be sure, autobiographies are frequently many years in the writing, and there are numerous instances where manuscript drafts exist of different versions and revisions; what is unusual in the case of McCarthy's *Memories* is that the form of the text itself, with its alternation of chapters and interchapters, displays the evolution of the autobiographical act as an essential feature of the autobiography, an evolution which is usually masked by the publication of only a final draft.

McCarthy's commitment to autobiography is manifested not only in the structure of the text but in the tenor of her opening remarks in the preface as well. Even though some readers, finding her *"memories"* in a magazine, took them for *"stories,"* even though the author herself often states that she wished she were writing *"fiction,"* she asserts at the outset that *"this record lays a claim to being historical—that is, much of it can be checked,"* and she invites anyone detecting *"more fiction in it than I know"* to come forward with corrections. More fiction in it than she knows, for she is the first to point out the presence of fiction in her enterprise. Conversations, for example, *"are mostly fictional"*; she can only vouch that *"a conversation to this general effect took place."* Again, after the first sketch, the added commentary begins, *"There are several dubious points in this memoir,"* and of one of the scenes she writes, *"I believe this is pure fiction."* Of another sketch she observes, *"this account is highly fictionalized"*; *"the story is true in substance, but the details have been invented or guessed at."* Of the penultimate sketch, however, she states firmly, *"Except for the name of the town and the names of the people, this story is completely true."* And sometimes she is hard put to distinguish fact from fiction, as when she comments on yet another sketch, *"This story is so true . . . that I find it almost impossible to sort out the guessed-at and the half-remembered from the undeniably real."* That a story may be *"so true"* without being *"undeniably real"* offers some measure of the difficulty we face in dealing with the presence of fiction in autobiographical narrative.

Do McCarthy's commentaries on the extent to which she has manipulated her materials—sometimes consciously, sometimes not—discredit the autobiographical nature of her project, or do they confirm it? McCarthy's own position on this score is unmistakable. In collecting the eight *"stories"* she had written about herself since 1944, she clearly believed that she was assembling the material of her autobiography, and all of the framing commentary she added to bind the pieces together as a group stresses the dynamics of the autobiographical process in which she thought she was engaged. ⟨. . .⟩

⟨. . .⟩ ⟨C⟩onflicting impulses of repression and confession govern McCarthy's autobiographical narrative. Confession itself, moreover, as we have seen in the episode of the first Communion, offers an equivocal model for the expression of autobiographical truth, involving as it does in McCarthy's case the partly involuntary, partly voluntary, public performance of a lie about one's self. As far as we know, the history of the autobiography begins with the involuntary recall of the C. Y. E. episode ⟨wherein she is

reminded of a painful childhood nickname); it is equally true, again, as far as
we know, that this beginning is the only part of the history that McCarthy
later cancelled. The cancellation is all the more remarkable given the author's
decision to structure the completed narrative in terms of a counterpart
between chapters and interchapters that explicitly dramatizes shifts in autobiographical perspective. What, then, is the source of her hostility to "C. Y. E.,"
and why did she choose not to speak of it in the interchapter commentaries
whose leading feature is their pretense to candor? It seems safe to infer from
the fact of the initial confession and its subsequent cancellation that some special kernel of truth about the self is latent in the episode of the nickname, a
truth that governs the behavior of McCarthy as a girl in 1923, as a young
woman in 1943, and as an older woman in 1956–1957. In each case, in both
the event and its two retellings, the impulse to reveal is accompanied by an
equal and opposite impulse to conceal. The episode, with its emphasis on public exposure of some secret truth about the self, expresses both the desire for
autobiographical confession and its ultimate defeat, for what "C. Y. E."—hidden or displayed—signifies for all these Marys is the unknowable mystery of
one's inmost identity. What the troubled psychological and literary history of
the nickname suggests is a deeply ambivalent view of the autobiographical act;
whether the revelation of the self to the self and to others is either desirable
or even possible remains unclear.

    —Paul John Eakin, "Fiction in Autobiography: Ask Mary McCarthy No Questions," *Fiction
in Autobiography: Studies in the Art of Self-Invention* (Princeton: Princeton University Press, 1985):
10–12, 34–35

WILFRID SHEED

Miss McCarthy's passion for strict truth, perhaps combined with faint scars left
from The Feud, may weigh a little too heavily on the early, or childhood chapters of her book ⟨How I Grew⟩—a period of life concerning which *everybody's*
memory is as wobbly as Miss ⟨Lillian⟩ Hellman's allegedly was about everything. At this point, the reader is still coping with the self-importance problem endemic to all autobiography (why *her* story and not mine?) and is thus in
the resentful, or who cares? stage—as in who cares when the lady first read
"Rumpelstiltskin" or precisely where?

    Miss McCarthy cares, of course, tremendously, and so the one phase of
life that really calls for some impressionism gets it only in this troubled sense
of a fact-checker with partial amnesia chasing after trivia through a mist. The
effect is occasionally oddly haunting, but only occasionally. (Incidentally,
since this is pre-eminently, and importantly, a psychological biography, this
review will be stingy with the details, which differ from other people's details
mainly in the author's extraordinary exposition and analysis of them.)

Even when real memory moves in on Miss McCarthy and begins to take over, she continues to fret about it, but to much better effect. Anybody cursed with such a fixed, questioning stare at life develops protective screening devices and it is amazing how much such an unblinking recorder can still manage to forget, or else remember all right, but somehow take the curse off.

For instance, her foster parents in Minnesota treated her with Dickensian brutality and she remembers that all right, but not with her *body* the way she remembers their terrible food. When she does think about "Uncle Myers's" descending razor strop, it is mostly to smile over it. "Over the years I have found a means—laughter—of turning pain into pleasure."

Over the years, but presumably not at the time, Honest Mary has simply devised a species of twilight sleep between herself and her past and called it laughter; it is hard to imagine what such laughter is really made of, how you start it and what it feels like. But it works—at a cost. "It does tend to dry one's feelings out a little, as if by exposing them to a vigorous wind. . . . There is no dampness in my emotions, and some moisture, I think, is needed to produce the deeper, the tragic notes."

This, and much more like it, is the kind of harsh but bracing self-judgment that fanatical honesty can extract even out of psychological murk. Reading Miss McCarthy can, in fact, be not unlike walking in that dry wind of hers.

In the matter of personal shame, young Mary contrived a totally opposite kind of medicine to her pain remedy. After her first "unnatural" (in those days) sexual experience, she opted simply to stare the scene down until the shame became meaningless, and finally nonexistent, thus preparing her for what she saucily calls "my adult 'career of crime.'"

Again she feels that something was lost in the transaction—this time not only the very memory of shame, but the sense of what shame had been for in the first place. "Is it right to overcome self-disgust? . . . If, as Raskolnikov learned, the inhibition was really a deep-lying instinct, part of my interior warning system . . . what stupid thing was I doing?"

Again this is confessional writing of an intense order, and one is reminded here of the real confessionals that figured in her earlier book "Memories of a Catholic Girlhood." On a humbler plane of introspection, she also makes a point, as one had to in those confessionals, of reciting as many youthful lies as she can fit into the session, and they are plenty.

Lying must have been irresistibly attractive to a precocious, not particularly saintly child who had been shuttled between families, regions and schools, adopting new personas on the way like baggage labels, and, like many basically truthful people, Miss McCarthy took to it like a duck to water (it helps to know exactly what you're lying about). But those lies now constitute another exasperating scrim between herself and what she so desperately wants to remember. However knowingly and consciously the lie is told, it plants a seed of ambiguity, another version of truth is now at large in the world—which may be why the author was so hard on Miss Hellman. (To a reformed liar, lies are the ultimate menace, as booze is to the alcoholic.)

A small instance of something lost forever behind the scrim of falsehood is a phase she went through at Vassar of pretending to despise the place (brittle and all that) while actually loving it. She knows that in this she was echoing her first husband-to-be, Harold Johnsrud, and presumably trying to please him. Having conquered shame and pain, was she still capable of such little-girl ruses as that? One gathers she wouldn't believe it even today, if she didn't absolutely have to.

But then as she says elsewhere, "I was a case of uneven development . . . rising on one side like a half-baked biscuit." As a description of almost any bright person's adolescence this phrase can hardly be bettered. Thus, on one page she is indeed a little girl, on the next an extremely knowing little woman, and on some pages both at once. ⟨. . .⟩

Such a study of memory—how it works, or pretends to work, or simply decides to take the day off—could only have been undertaken by someone on fire for exact truth, and it amply justifies Miss McCarthy's method. The small price *we* pay is that the laser beam never seems to go off.

Pity, for instance, anyone the author ever met who had a skin defect: she recalls every last pit. In fact, Miss McCarthy puts faces on all her characters, like a child who only doodles faces: and since she is also given to calling off rosters of (to us) quite meaningless names, the faces sometimes seem to crowd into a blur.

And while on the subject of rosters: Miss McCarthy also seems to feel at times (not always) that periodic lists of books read and courses taken do sufficient duty as an account of how her intellect grew: As I stare at these little batches of facts, the first phrase that comes to mind is "cut and dried"; and one wonders again about the missing dampness she talks about earlier as necessary for "the deeper notes."

To understand where all the moisture went, I find it useful to read "Memories of a Catholic Girlhood" alongside "How I Grew." In "Memories" we meet a younger Mary McCarthy who is in process of becoming a Sacred Heart convent-school girl, and to this day her older self still reminds me more of one of those than of any of the other selves latent in this newer narrative. The fixed smile, the unflagging ladylikeness, the Grace Kelly coolness and the mind of a nun forever correcting papers—these were, if not standard issue at Sacred Heart schools, common enough; and if one imagines such a cool customer strolling gracefully (shoulders back, and appear to glide) through the events of this book, it brings them to a vivid and quite startling new life, supplying us with the one missing face and making of the combined memoirs something of an event in itself; that is to say, a genuine artwork as original as any of her fiction, while containing all the facts even a McCarthy could want.

And with all that going for you, who needs dampness?

—Wilfrid Sheed, "How I Grew," *The New York Times Book Review* (April 19, 1987): 5–6

Elizabeth Sifton

Sifton: You imply that most of the stories were distinctly autobiographical ⟨in *The Company She Keeps*⟩.

McCarthy: They all are more or less, except the one about the Yale man.

Sifton: Is this distinction between autobiography and fiction clear in your mind before you begin writing a story, or does it become so as you write? Or is there no such distinction?

McCarthy: Well, I think it depends on what you're doing. Let's be frank. Take "The Man in the Brooks Brothers Shirt"; in that case it was an attempt to describe something that really happened—though naturally you have to do a bit of name-changing and city-changing. And the first story, the one about the divorce: that was a stylization—there were no proper names in it or any-thing—but still, it was an attempt to be as exact as possible about something that had happened. The Yale man was based on a real person, John Chamberlain, actually, whom I didn't know very well. But there it was an attempt to make this real man a broad type. You know, to use John Chamberlain's boyish looks and a few of the features of his career, and then draw all sorts of other Yale men into it. Then the heroine was put in, in an imaginary love affair, which *had* to be because she had to be in the story. I always thought that was all very hard on John Chamberlain, who was married. But of course he knew it wasn't true, and he knew that I didn't know him very well, and that therefore in the story he was just a kind of good-looking clotheshanger. Anything else that I've written later—I may make a mistake—has been on the whole a fiction. Though it may have autobiographical ele-ments in it that I'm conscious of, it has been conceived as a fiction, even a thing like *The Oasis*, that's supposed to have all these real people in it. The whole story is a complete fiction. Nothing of the kind ever happened; after all, it happens in the future. But in general, with characters, I do try at least to be as exact as possible about the essence of a person, to find the key that works the person both in real life and in the fiction. ⟨. . .⟩

Sifton: Getting away from novels for a moment, I'd like to ask you about *Memories of a Catholic Girlhood* if I might. Will you write any more autobiography?

McCarthy: I was just reading—oh God, actually I *was* just starting to read Simone de Beauvoir's second volume, *La Force de l'Age*, and she announces in the preface that she can't write about her later self with the same candor that she wrote about her girlhood.

Sifton: You feel that too?

McCarthy: On this one point I agree with her. One has to be really old, I think, really quite an old person—and by that time I don't know what sort of shape one's memory would be in. ⟨. . .⟩

Sifton: I have something else to ask, apropos of *Memories of a Catholic Girlhood*. There are certain points, important points and moments in your novels, where you deepen or enlarge the description of the predicament in which a character may be by reference to a liturgical or ecclesiastical or theological parallel or equivalence. What I want to know is, is this simply a strict use of analogy, a technical literary device, or does it indicate any conviction that these are valid and important ways of judging a human being?

McCarthy: I suppose it's a reference to a way of thinking about a human being. But I think at their worst they're rather just literary references. That is, slightly show-off literary references. I have a terrible compulsion to make them— really a dreadful compulsion. The first sentence of *The Stones of Florence* begins, "How can you stand it? This is the first thing, and the last thing, the eschatological question that the visitor leaves echoing in the air behind him." Something of that sort. Well, everybody was after me to take out that word. I left it out when I published that chapter in the *New Yorker*, but I put it back in the book. No, I do have this great compulsion to make those references. I think I do it as a sort of secret signal, a sort of looking over the heads of the readers who don't recognize them to the readers who do understand them.

Sifton: If these references *are* only literary ones, secret signals, then they are blasphemous.

McCarthy: Yes, I see what you mean. I suppose they are. Yes, they are secret jokes, they are blasphemies. But—I think I said something of this in the introduction of *Catholic Girlhood*—I think that religion offers to Americans (I mean the Roman Catholic religion) very often the only history and philosophy they ever get. A reference to it somehow opens up that historical vista. In that sense it is a device for deepening the passage. ⟨. . .⟩

Sifton: In reading the Florence book ⟨*The Stones of Florence*⟩, I remember being very moved by the passage where you talk of Brunelleschi, about his "absolute integrity and essence," that solidity of his, both real and ideal. When you write about Brunelleschi, you write about this sureness, this "being-itself," and yet as a novelist—in *The Company She Keeps* for instance—you speak of something so very different, and you take almost as a theme this fragmented unplaceability of the human personality.

McCarthy: But I was very young then. I think I'm really not interested in the quest for the self any more. Oh, I suppose everyone continues to be interested in the quest for the self, but what you feel when you're older, I think, is that— how to express this—that you really must *make* the self. It's absolutely useless to look for it, you won't find it, but it's possible in some sense to make it. I don't mean in the sense of making a mask, a Yeatsian mask. But you finally begin in some sense to make and to choose the self you want.

Sifton: Can you write novels about that?

McCarthy: I never have. I never have, I've never even thought of it. That is, I've never thought of writing a developmental novel in which a self of some kind is discovered or is made, is forged, as they say. No. I suppose in a sense I don't know any more today than I did in 1941 about what my identity is. But I've stopped looking for it. I must say, I believe much more in truth now than I did. I do believe in the solidity of truth much more. Yes. I believe there is a truth, and that it's knowable.

    —Elizabeth Sifton, "Mary McCarthy," *Women Writers at Work. The Paris Review Interviews*, ed. George Plimpton (New York: Viking Penguin, 1989), 176–77, 190–91, 198–99

JANIS GREVE

Given photography's vital role in laying claim to a family history, one can easily see how the camera would have a weighty significance as the autobiographical tool for an orphan; the search for family moves, in this case, much closer to home, and the burden of familial "proof" becomes more immediate. *Memories of a Catholic Girlhood*, Mary McCarthy's chronicle of her life from early orphanhood to young womanhood, reveals photography as a lurking preoccupation in her autobiographical act. Real photographs of family members, references to photography, and a satiric verbal portraiture which aims to create "likenesses" of her life's authority figures, all lend credence to ⟨Susan⟩ Sontag's claim that photography becomes a "defense against anxiety" for individuals who feel themselves robbed of a past. By examining some of the intricate problems of orphanhood and selfhood which McCarthy exposes throughout the chapters of *Memories*, one gains a better understanding of photography's significance in this autobiography. The interwoven themes of memory, language, and class reveal a persistent fear of self-obliteration which begins with the event of McCarthy's orphanhood. Autobiography is the obvious counter to this negative drift; it is the life-opting and ensuring mechanism of the adult. Photography, then, as a part of this life impulse, details the more subtle motives of the autobiography, and exposes a central and troubling conflict for McCarthy as she rewrites and attempts to "set right" her life. ⟨. . .⟩

Given the serious problems of self-definition for an orphan, which McCarthy so clearly delineates, photography, as a form of "filling gaps," has a special allure. The pseudo-family album in the middle of her text attests to her desire to "prove" her past. McCarthy, as we have seen, has reasons to feel as though her life has been somehow "unreal." If memories can never be relied upon unless "verified," the reality of the past is continually questioned. The photographs, then, tell us that her experience of having had parents, brothers, grandparents, and relatives is real. One feels McCarthy's distress when she tells us that she has no picture of Uncle Myers; for a man who was almost evil incarnate, it is vital to demonstrate his flesh-and-blood existence. Particularly for him, but also for other people in the photos, the quality of this-ness—the fact of their living, material presence—is extremely important, and no other expressive mode can provide it in so pure a form as photography. ⟨. . .⟩

McCarthy's family album contains the combatting impulses to protect and destroy not simply particular family members and past times, but the connotations or "stories" of the photographs as well. McCarthy's verbal treatment of the photographs dating from the Minnesota period of her life reveals an understanding of photography as speaking only the "pure deictic language" that ⟨Roland⟩ Barthes describes. The photograph of the four smiling McCarthy children surrounding a pony on a sunny day is a case in point: as McCarthy explains in her aftertext to "A Tin Butterfly," the happy scene is a fake, its cheeriness the product of an itinerant photographer who had a horse for a prop. Similarly, the cozily serene photograph of Grandma Lizzie knitting in her sun parlor, and the snapshots of Mary on her First Communion and dressed as a flower for a school play, we come to find out also tell "lies." The sun parlor scene is darkened by our knowledge of Grandma Lizzie's parsimonious and "sun"-less disposition, and Mary calls our attention to the girlhood photos to make sure we don't misread them: the smile on her face and her body posture signify discontent and oppression rather than the pleasure of an important event. In short, these photographs demonstrate nothing besides the simple bodily and historical existence of the persons whose images they capture; they say only "look" and "here it is," and the stories they might suggest are not reliable. However, McCarthy applies little or none of this critical sophistication to the photographs of her mother and father in the days of their courtship and early family life, and her deconstructive silence fuels the impression that these, by contrast, do *not* contain the possibility of falsifying frames, and *can* speak for themselves. These opposing intentions and assertions involved in McCarthy's photo display show us, among other things, that the "proof positive" offered by actual photographs to the orphan who aspires to recreate a past is severely limited: they may help populate her past, but certainly do not supply memory, and cannot even reliably, and without uncertainty, fortify what is so shakily remembered. ⟨. . .⟩

However, in the course of her portrait-filled autobiography, McCarthy hints that she begins to see a connection between the falsifying and exploitative framing to which she has drawn our attention in the photo album, and herself as author/autobiographer. The tone of the self-interrogating aftertexts which follow each written memory is largely confessional, as McCarthy frequently and apologetically refers to the "framing" hand of the author which rendered "truth" into "fiction." We begin to see that a vital autobiographical problem for McCarthy is keeping the manipulations involved in her own authorial framings separate from, and on a higher moral plane than, the contriving photographer's hand which arranged the children in a false pose, and the dishonest "framing" intentions of Myers and Margaret, who then sent the photo out to the West Coast grandparents as proof of the children's well-being. The brutally funny verbal portraits of Myers and Margaret—which aim to "contain" the tyrannical power of these old guardians, as well as disclaim them as family, in spite of Margaret's blood connection—ironically align McCarthy with these persons in what must be for her a vexing manner because of the "criminal" implications.

"Ask Me No Questions," the final chapter of *Memories*, which focuses on McCarthy's paternal Grandmother Preston, dramatizes a correlative peril to this autobiographer dilemma: if McCarthy aligns herself with those she critically casts off, she also cannot identify herself with those whom she wishes to embrace—a botching of intention and effect aided by the text's photographic modes. In contrast to the apparent ease and absence of scruples with which she lays bare her aunt and uncle, she has difficulty beginning the "likeness" of her Grandmother Preston. Her sense of doing her grandmother wrong by writing about her is so intense that she guiltily images meeting up with her in Limbo, where the old woman waits for her on "some stairhead with folded arms and cold cream on her face."

—Janis Greve, "Orphanhood and 'Photo'-Portraiture in Mary McCarthy's *Memories of a Catholic Girlhood*," *American Women's Autobiography: Fea(s)ts of Memory*, ed. Margo Culley (Madison: University of Wisconsin Press, 1992), 167–68, 175–77, 179–80

ELIZABETH HARDWICK

Intellectual Memoirs: New York 1936–38. I look at the title of these vivid pages and calculate that Mary McCarthy was only twenty-four years old when the events of this period began. The pages are a continuation of the first volume, to which she gave the title *How I Grew.* Sometimes with a sigh she would refer to the years ahead in her autobiography as "I seem to be embarked on how I grew and grew and grew." I am not certain how many volumes she planned, but I had the idea she meant to go right down the line, inspecting the troops you might say, noting the slouches and the good soldiers, and, of course, inspecting herself living in her time.

Here she is at the age of twenty-four, visiting the memory of it, but she was in her seventies when the actual writing was accomplished. The arithmetic at both ends is astonishing. ⟨. . .⟩

Her memoir is partly "ideas" and very much an account of those institutional rites that used to be recorded in the family Bible: marriage, children, divorce, and so on. Mary had only one child, her son Reuel Wilson, but she had quite a lot of the other rites: four marriages, interspersed with love affairs of some seriousness and others of none. Far from taking the autobiographer's right to be selective about waking up in this bed or that, she tempts one to say that she remembers more than scrupulosity demands. Demands of the rest of us at least as we look back on the insupportable surrenders and dim our recollection with the aid of the merciful censor.

On the other hand, what often seems to be at stake in Mary's writing and in her way of looking at things is a somewhat obsessional concern for the integrity of sheer fact in matters both trivial and striking. "The world of fact, of figures even, of statistics . . . the empirical element in life . . . the fetishism of fact . . .," phrases taken from her essay "The Fact in Fiction," 1960. The facts of the matter are the truth, as in a court case that tries to circumvent vague feelings and intuitions. If one would sometimes take the liberty of suggesting caution to her, advising prudence or mere practicality, she would look puzzled and answer: But it's the truth. I do not think she would have agreed it was only her truth—instead she often said she looked upon her writing as a mirror. ⟨. . .⟩

⟨. . .⟩ I don't think Mary kept a diary. At least I never heard mention of one or felt the chill on rash spontaneity that such an activity from this shrewdly observing friend would cast upon an evening. From these pages and from the previous volume, it appears that she must have kept clippings, letters certainly, playbills, school albums, and made use of minor research to get it right—to be sure the young man in Seattle played on the football team. In these years of her life, she treasured who was in such and such a play seen in an exact theater. On the whole, though, I believe the scene setting, the action, the dialogue came from memory. These memories, pleasing and interesting to me at every turn, are a bit of history of the times. Going to *Pins and Needles*, the Federal Theater's tribute to the Ladies Garment Workers Union, a plain little musical with fewer of the contemporary theater's special effects than a performance of the church choir.

The pages of this memoir represent the beginning of Mary McCarthy's literary life. She was a prodigy from the first. I remember coming across an early review when I was doing some work in the New York Public Library. It was dazzling, a wonderfully accomplished composition, written soon after she left college. As she began, so she continued, and in the years ahead I don't think she changed very much. ⟨. . .⟩

I gave the address at the MacDowell Colony when Mary received the Medal and there I said that if she was, in her writing, sometimes a scourge, a Savonarola, she was a very cheerful one, lighthearted and even optimistic. I could not find in her work a trace of despair or alienation; instead she had a dreamy expectation that persons and nations should do their best. Perhaps it would be unlikely that a nature of such exceptional energy could act out alienation, with its temptation to sloth. Indeed it seemed to me that Mary did not understand even the practical usefulness of an occasional resort to the devious. Her indiscretions were always open and forthright and in many ways one could say she was "like an open book." Of course, everything interesting depends upon which book is open.

—Elizabeth Hardwick, "Mary McCarthy in New York," *The New York Review of Books* (March 26, 1992): 3

B I B L I O G R A P H Y

The Company She Keeps. 1942.
The Oasis. 1949.
Cast a Cold Eye. 1950.

The Groves of Academe. 1952.
A Charmed Life. 1955.
Sights and Spectacles: 1937–1956. 1956.
Venice Observed. 1956.
Memories of a Catholic Girlhood. 1957.
The Stones of Florence. 1959.
On the Contrary: Articles of Belief, 1946–1961. 1961.
Mary McCarthy's Theatre Chronicles, 1936–1962. 1963.
The Group. 1963.
Birds of America. 1965.
Vietnam. 1967.
Hanoi. 1968.
The Writing on the Wall and Other Literary Essays. 1970.
Medina. 1972.
The Mask of State: Watergate Portraits. 1974.
The Seventeenth Degree. 1974.
Cannibals and Missionaries. 1979.
Ideas and the Novel. 1980.
The Hounds of Summer and Other Stories. 1981.
Occasional Prose. 1985.
How I Grew. 1987.
Intellectual Memoirs: New York, 1936–38. 1992.

KATE MILLETT
b. 1934

KATHERINE MURRAY MILLETT was born on September 14, 1934 in St. Paul, Minnesota, to James Albert Millett, a civil engineer, and Helen Feeley Millet, a college graduate. After her father left the family, Millett's mother sold insurance to support the family. Millett and her two sisters attended Catholic schools, and she graduated from the University of Minnesota in 1956 with a B.A. in English, *magna cum laude*. That summer she worked in a factory and had her first significant relationship with a woman. In the fall she enrolled at St. Hilda's College, Oxford, where she studied Victorian literature. In 1958 she became the first American woman to earn a postgraduate degree from Oxford with first-class honors.

In 1958 she returned to the United States and taught for a year at Women's College, now the University of North Carolina at Greensboro, and then for a year in a kindergarten in East Harlem. In 1961 she traveled to Japan to study sculpture. Two years later she had her first one-woman sculpture show at the Minami Gallery in Tokyo. While working in Japan she met the Japanese sculptor Fumio Yoshimura, who returned with her to the United States. They were married in 1965.

When she returned to the U.S., Millett had trouble finding a job: she had an "Oxford degree, but couldn't type." This experience was crucial to the development of her feminist politics. After a year teaching freshman composition at Hunter College in Manhattan, Millett was admitted to Columbia to work on her Ph.D. and began teaching English at Barnard. Millett was also involved in the civil rights movement. In 1964 she joined the Congress of Racial Equity. She was a founding member of the New York chapter of the National Organization for Women (NOW) and chaired the Educational Committee from 1966 to 1970. In 1967, NOW published *Token Learning: A Study of Women's Higher Education in America*, a critique of the curricula in women's colleges.

Millett was also a founding member of Columbia Women's Liberation and joined the Downtown Radical Women and Radical Lesbians. Her involvement in campus politics cost her her job at Barnard when she supported and participated in the Columbia student strike of 1968. After these five years of growing political awareness and active political organizing, Millett sat down and wrote her dissertation, *Sexual Politics*, in eighteen months. Published in 1970, the 50th anniversary of women's right to vote, *Sexual Politics* became a best-seller. In this work, Millett expands the concept of the political to include sexual power relations in literature and society. Criticizing the current dominant ideas of the New Criticism, she argued that literature reflects the history and ideology of patriarchal culture and cannot be read in isolation from these forces.

The popularity of *Sexual Politics* caused the media, and in particular *Time* magazine, to adopt Millett as the "leader of the women's movement." Millett hated this because it went against her ideals of an egalitarian and nonhierarchical women's movement. Later that year she was speaking at a Columbia conference on bisexuality when a member of the audience asked her if she was a lesbian. Millett said yes, and *Time* magazine ran another article on the women's movement in an attempt to discredit her, now easily portrayable as a hostile lesbian, and not an objective commentator on literature and society. Her own experience of the personal and political, and the dislocation she felt from her own identity and that of "Kate Millett the media sensation," lead her to explore the concept of "self" in autobiographical writing. During the time she was writing *Flying*, she filmed a documentary, *Three Lives*, in which three women discuss being women in America and compiled *The Prostitution Papers*, a collection of narratives of prostitutes.

In 1973 she moved to California as visiting professor at Sacramento State College and met "Sita," a college administrator with whom she fell in love. That summer Millett went to England to try to save Michael Malik, a Trinidadian civil rights lawyer condemned to death. When she returned to the U.S., her family had her committed to a mental hospital twice in quick succession. She was diagnosed as manic-depressive by the admitting psychiatrist, who prescribed lithium.

When *Flying* was published in 1974 it received almost universally negative reviews, but it established a new genre of autobiographical writing that Millett continues to explore. It breaks with the male-dominated tradition by interweaving the private and public experiences of women, including their sexual experiences. With the publication of *Sita* (1977), Millett left behind the public spectacle of "Kate Millett" and focused on the private obsession of a dying love affair.

In 1978, Millett bought an abandoned dairy farm in upstate New York and began restoring the buildings with the hope that it would be a place where women artists and writers could work on their art. The first summer residents helped Millett work on the buildings and establish a Christmas tree farm. When the farm was almost self-supporting, in 1986, Millett accepted the first artists and residents. In the summer of 1980 while Millett was there with a number of apprentices, she decided to go off her lithium. *The Loony-Bin Trip* (1990) is an account that takes Millett from that moment on the farm to her last incarceration in an insane asylum in Ireland.

CRITICAL   EXTRACTS

ELINOR LANGER

Men repress: women confess. The stiff upper lip versus the quavering one. There are occasions when too much of the latter makes the former seem attractive, and for me reading Kate Millett's *Flying* was one of them. After it, I would cheerfully have settled down with the *Principia*. As it was, I reached for the Kleenex, my sorrow not only for the author of this modern pilgrim's regress, but for its readers.

Confession, under the auspices of the Women's Movement, is getting to be a messy business. This is as good a time as any to bring it up.

Flying is a record of a year of affliction in Kate Millett's life, the year following the publication of *Sexual Politics*, the year she committed the sin of doing something well and receiving recognition for it. It also reports memories from the rest of her life in the no-particular-order her subconscious fished them out for her that year, so in a sense it is autobiography as well. Briefly, the story is this. She was a Catholic from St. Paul, beset by passion, a lesbian before she knew the word. Her father disappeared from their family life. Adulthood came slowly, with it the discovery of art, sculpting, Japan, a steadying relationship with the tender, unusual Fumio. The marriage occurred to prevent his deportation. She returned to academic work, to teaching, and to the thesis, which was her book. Then: fame, a *Time* cover, the public announcement of her gayness, despair, perhaps madness. Now, *Flying*. 〈. . .〉

That was her experience, and it is not the experience that I question. It is what she has done with it in this book. I find *Flying* as pitiful as I found *Sexual Politics* brilliant; a pointless, tangled self-revelation as the other was a genuine intellectual achievement; a grand and wily emotional co-optation in which she has taken up the imagined charges of past and future "enemies" and transformed them into self-hate. She has made criticism of the book's content nearly impossible. Everything one might think of to say about it, she has said herself. Any negative comment, she has anticipated in her own fantasies. Though she says she wants to be seen as vulnerable, she has created a kind of armor: no one can lacerate her any more than she has lacerated herself. ⟨. . .⟩ She has recorded all her impressions, but she takes responsibility for none. Free association has supplanted thought.

Millett's refusal to analyze the political structure in which the personal events she narrates took place is a serious loss. She is a capable woman, the author of one of the best analytical books to have come out of the Women's Movement up till that time, and the fact that she was destroyed—tossed away like a deflated prop by the dance-duo of her sisters-and-the-press—is a fact with meaning. ⟨. . .⟩

Clarification, new ideas, would have more value than a seismographic record of all the orgasms in history. Millett could think it through, but won't. She will only tell how it feels: shitty. "Thinking" for her is no more. It is some-thing she left behind at Columbia with *Sexual Politics*, which she explicitly and repeatedly—and tragically—disowns. *Why* is another matter. I would guess the real reason is that it has brought her too much pain. But that is not what she says. It was not the real Kate Millett that wrote the book in the first place, she claims, but an academic impersonator. This splintered, quicksilvery, suf-fering soul, rushing from meeting to meeting, from bed to bed, from shore to shore, jotting down "everything," is really me.

It isn't. *Flying* is a book, and Kate Millett isn't. Writing a book is a profes-sional activity, like running a dress shop or a kennel. It is a business. A small business, but a business. You decide to do it, pursue it, sign a contract, write it, rewrite it, rewrite it again, edit it, read proof, inspect the jacket copy—and take a long vacation, if you are lucky, on earnings from the book. A book is a work of language, nothing else. It is not flesh and it is not time. It is not life. Long as this book is, it is shorter than Millett's year. It is *not* her year. It is con-scious and contrived, each word a literary choice as much as—even more than—an emotional one. This essay is the same way. ⟨. . .⟩

How does one criticize the sad, true, tragic-comic and egocentric mater-ial that is the heart of most private journals? What is a reader to say? Where is the opportunity for discussing either style or values? It is not so different in the case of a published work like *Flying*. The author protects herself with the covert hope that if she says how much it hurts, no one will judge her too harshly. The critic is silenced or hypocritical. Solicitousness overwhelms objectivity. *It hurts*. How callous to mention style when the tears of our hero-ine drench the pillow. How artificial to demand a subject when the subject is the self.

But the subject ought not always to be that. The confession is not disci-plined autobiography. In autobiography, the writer may use the self to inspect the world; in confession, the self runs rampantly through it, crashing up against everything in its way. Everything is seen through the filter of ego. What turned me against *Flying* was not so much the pornography, or the book's betrayal of personal relationships, as the politics, Millett's refusal to countenance and record the grave events that occur outside her own body. ⟨. . .⟩

I have no wish to prolong the torture of Kate Millett. Other people are doing what she has, and *Flying* should not have to bear the weight of the entire confessional genre. But I think it can remind us of the absence of a genuinely critical tradition in the Women's Movement. ⟨. . .⟩

If Kate Millett had been my friend, I hope I would have told her this: Keep your notebook for yourself, but publish another book—or none at all just now. The cure for being exhibited is not to exhibit oneself. The remedy for exploitation is not self-exploitation. Kate: Not all confessions end in absolution. I think the confession is a cocoon, and the inhabitant of this one is not yet flying, despite her claims. I wish for her book a speedy oblivion, and for herself, other and better books.

—Elinor Langer, "Confessing," *Ms.* 3 (December 1974): 69–71

ANDREA DWORKIN

I do not understand how ⟨Elinor⟩ Langer can say that *Flying* "can remind us of the absence of a genuinely critical tradition in the Women's Movement." ⟨"Confessing," *Ms.* 3 (December 1974): 69–71⟩ If anything, the Women's Movement is distinguished by its critical and analytical writings, and certainly Millett is a major figure in that tradition.

Despite what I have read about *Flying* in various reviews, I find it honest, compelling, full of crucial information on how women relate to each other, technically quite astonishing. I am particularly distressed over Langer's repeated accusation that the work is "pornographic." For a woman to write about erotic meetings with other women in a literal way is not to write "pornography." It is not necessarily to demean women and to pander to male fantasy. The fact is that Millett does not at any point cheapen her own sexuality or that of her sisters. I was unhappy that Millett feels such guilt at being "queer"—not that she writes about it, but that she herself feels it. Many women her age, however, do feel precisely what she puts down before us. She does what an artist, a feminist artist, must do—she vividly creates the conflicts, pains, and joys of a life lived bravely.

I find nothing "pitiful" about *Flying* as a work. Millett does not "[take] up the imagined charges of past and future 'enemies' and transform them into self-hate." There is nothing "imagined" about the charges of her past and future enemies; whatever "self-hate" she delineates belongs to us all and is an active dynamic in the Women's Movement—what Flo Kennedy calls "horizontal hostility," the self-hatred of the oppressed.

I don't think that it is legitimate to use *Flying* as the emblem of the confessional form, and then to repudiate the form. These are two separate questions. The form could be valid, and yet *Flying* could fail. But Langer does not like the *form itself*: she rejects journals and diaries en masse, so long the treasured private writing places for so many distinguished women who could not bear the brutality of the public place dominated by men. Langer wants us to reject this woman's tradition—and *Flying* with it—and do serious work: critical, analytical, hard-headed, serious work—"male" work, that is, using the forms that have a certain kind of male approval. But *Flying* is serious work—it is the study of a particular time in a particular woman's life, and it touches themes that concern us all.

To use *Flying* as an emblem for the rejection of a particular literary form is terribly unfair. Rainer Maria Rilke said that works of art should be critically judged by those who love them. If, before one begins, one has no sympathy for the project itself, then how can one see where it is good, where it is bad, where it is useful, where it is not? Adversary criticism ill serves women: the kind of bludgeoning it requires will destroy those who give us the most. Ask a woman who *loves* the confessional form to write about it: the rest of us will find out more about it that way.

—Andrea Dworkin (letter to the editor), *Ms.* 3 (June 1975): 11–13

ANNETTE KOLODNY

Kate Millett's *Flying* was not kindly received by the reviewers when it appeared in 1974. Although one might be inclined to dismiss René Kuhn Bryant's attack, which appeared in the *National Review*, as motivated by her politics and by her overt hostility towards both Millett and Gay Liberation, nevertheless, her description of *Flying* as only "an endless outpouring of shallow, witless comment" repeated the sentiments of many a more sympathetic reviewer, as did her distaste for the way in which the book documented its subject "minute by remorseless minute, if not second by interminable second." Muriel Haynes, writing in the *New Republic*, for example, made much the same observation when she called the book "a leviathan . . . that demands of the reader an analyst's endurance." But the most surprising response was undoubtedly Elinor Langer's "Forum" article, in *Ms.*, which dismissed the book on the grounds that "confession is not disciplined autobiography" (René Kuhn Bryant, "Drowning in Claustrophobia," *National Review*, (30 Aug. 1974): 990; Muriel Haynes,

"Sexual Energy," *New Republic,* (6 and 13 July 1974): 28; Elinor Langer, "Confessing," *Ms.,* (December 1974): 71〉. 〈. . .〉

With purposes very different from that of the male autobiographer, then, intent upon collecting *all* the "tidbits of thought, memory, grasshopper trivia," and without access to any significant countertradition of female autobiography from which to learn, Millett produced a text which in no way resembles that disengaged, self-critical, self-distanced, and self-scrutinizing brand of autobiography we have been taught to read and critics have come to expect. But then any demand that women write the same kind of formal, distilled narrative we usually get from men implies a belief that women share the same kind of reality as men; clearly, this is not the case. All of which brings into question not only the way in which most critical reviewing is practiced, but the theoretical formulae upon which that practice is based. Treated, however, as an ongoing reading experience, rather than measured against a Procrustean bed of received expectations to which it was never intended to conform, *Flying* reveals its own internal organizing principles, as it explores the many-layered associative intertwinings of consciousness, memory, and image. 〈. . .〉

But the breaking of the personal pattern, and the subsequent recording of it in these pages, however, has larger resonances for the student of American literature. Self-consciously disengaging herself from the traditional view that women who experiment with their lives are either damned or doomed, Millett rejects both the tradition and its imagery and declares herself done, once and for all, with "this last broken-wing story." Replacing it, instead, as this book closes, is the buoyant imagery of birds in flight:

> Gulls so many of them I try to count them but they split and break
> I cannot place and order them in the sky. Flying in a haze of wings
> noises cries. Chaos and serenity together.

As a closing statement, it is also an apt description of the mind we have come to know so intimately in these pages and an apt imagistic rendering of our experience of coming to grips with that mind. In other words, Millett's sense of what her life feels like to her, and our sense of what it has meant to participate in that life through this narrative, are both, like the gulls splitting and breaking, an experience of "order forming itself and then [being] lost again." In pursuit of order, Millett has lived her life and composed this text; but because her experience could or would not easily accommodate itself to ordering, so, too, her story of that experience, like the failed counting and placing of the gulls, similarly resists order, placement, organization—in short, resists narrative form as we have come to expect it in autobiography. Hence, this narrative ends 〈. . .〉 with an insistence that, in some lives, if truth be told, chaos is not always reduced to order, but may exist simultaneously with it: "Chaos and serenity together." ⟨. . .⟩

⟨. . .⟩ Important in the Millett text, and germane to any full understanding of it, are the recurrent references to women writers and their work, the application of film techniques to language, and the comic-book heroics of Wonder Woman and Mary Marvel. Again, however, this is hardly a coherent tradition specifically relevant to the autobiographical genre itself nor, some would argue, a coherent or satisfying tradition in any sense of the word.

The result is a text which, out of necessity, resorted to daring experimentation and sheer invention—attempting to build a "bridge," as it were, "between the voice talking in [her] head and prose as [she'd previously] known it." Not that the experiment was an unqualified success. In her unwillingness to leave anything out, based on her observation that too much had already been excluded from what has been written by and about women, she gives us ⟨. . .⟩ the uncomfortable sense of wading through a "collection of the clutter in [her] mind." The writing is often self-indulgent, the narrative associations too abstruse or too idiosyncratic to be meaningful, and some of the people do indeed come across as only "tin echoes . . . feeble sketches." Little wonder Millett agonized over the book's composition, feared she would never complete it to her satisfaction, and, reluctantly, ended up in "bitter disappointment," admitting "This is not literature."

Not literature in the sense of something that will speak beyond its own time and place, perhaps. But it *was* a necessary literary experiment. In attempting to tell the story of a life in a way it hadn't been told before, and, especially, the story of so unconventional a life as her own, Millett broke many long-standing codes of silence and omission. By "telling certain truths, truths about the media and politics, about psychological and social change as they are lived, about unconventional loves and the struggle for a new ethic," Millett herself realized, "something in the fabric, the old fabric of things, was threatened, was ripped and torn." ⟨"The Shame Is Over," *Ms.* 3, no. 7 (January 1975): 28⟩ To deal with such assaults upon "the old fabric of things," our professional reviewing establishment is too little prepared.

   —Annette Kolodny, "The Lady's Not for Spurning: Kate Millett and the Critics," *Contemporary Literature* 17, (1976): 541, 544, 557–59.

SUZANNE JUHASZ

Millett uses *Flying* to create for her reader (who is in the public world) a Kate Millett who is more than object by relentlessly insisting that her personal self be known and taken into account. She is also performing this service for herself, to exorcise her own fears about self-meaning, self-worth. When *Flying* is over, all 678 pages of it, I think that it has succeeded at this task. The sheer accumulation of detail—detail that is sometimes profound, sometimes trivial, sometimes thrilling, sometimes dull, sometimes insightful, sometimes redundant—establishes a world characterized by its dailiness, and a person living in that world. Immersed entirely in that life, the reader finishes with a sense of knowing who Kate Millett is.

Sita, the next installment of Millett's autobiography, published two years after *Flying*, becomes a total rejection of the public self. It records, with the same painstaking (and painful) attention to the detail of the daily that characterized the first volume, Millett's addiction to a dying love affair. The major symptom of her disease—or proof of her love (in *Sita* these are one and the same)—is the fact that she cannot define herself in any way by her public self, "Kate Millett"; nor does she want to do so.

> Do I cling and pursue this love because I have really nothing else to
> do—or am I unable to write because my slavery to this infatuation
> makes work impossible? The former. No, the latter. The former
> because you have not finished a book in three years. The latter,
> because that is the period of time you have known her.

Reviewers literally hate this book. They hate it because it is so personal. "What bothers me is that Millett has been so overcome by self-seriousness that she thinks her personal doings are important to the rest of us," says Sara Sandborn in the *New York Times Book Review* ⟨May 29, 1977, 20⟩. The underlying assumption here seems to be that "Kate Millett" is interesting or worthy of attention only when she is that public person, that celebrity who does things in the public world. Reviewers hate as well the style that creates this personal quality, that style which we have come to identify with private writing and the private world. ⟨. . .⟩

The major effect of that style is, once again, a sense of immersion. The world of *Sita* is painful, humiliating, anxious, obsessive, also tedious, repetitive, cumulative; it is genuinely depressing, a total downer. One is glad, when the book is over, to be freed from that state and from that state of mind. Yet one has indeed been there in experiencing the book; and "there" is exactly where Millett, too, has been. There is no doubt that she has shared her experience.

Hers it most certainly is. We never get the other side, as one reviewer points out. But why should we? Nor is Millett, in the grip of obsessive love, blessed simultaneously with a high degree of distance, objectivity, and interpretative powers vis-à-vis her situation. So? Our own reading of her text can give us, perhaps, such insight. Again, it is a characteristic of traditional autobiography that the writer possess such perspective on her or his experience; the form of the diary, on the other hand, explicitly denies such distance.

What Millett is self-conscious about in writing *Sita* is the act of writing *Sita*. She begins keeping a notebook about her experience with Sita to "study it, even record, possess it" (p. 60). As she keeps the notebook, she begins to recognize its various and varying functions, and even the ways in which they contradict one another. ⟨. . . .⟩

Millett recognizes the simultaneous power of words to alter experience and to reveal, release it. Ideally, she is seeking a form for her words that will as little as possible impose a pattern upon experience from outside (i.e., her own consciousness of her own consciousness); seeking a form that will permit whatever pattern is within her experiences, albeit obscured by them, to emerge, to float to the surface that her book creates. Hence her insistence on documentation, on honesty, on sheer quantity. Yet she is also aware that her ideal book is forever unobtainable, since words must always select and shape. So that the form she chooses gives the *effect* of verisimilitude; that is its fiction. And to create such an effect, this kind of writing seems to need the length, the looseness, even the carelessness that we have been taught are certain signs of bad writing. "It's too long, it's too much, it's too repetitious," cry the reviewers. Yet try to imagine these books cut and crafted to some spare design. Would they work, as they do now, to immerse the reader thoroughly in a daily life?

Finally, there is the companion question of significance; or, was it worth the telling? "For personal writing to work," says Karen Durbin in her review, "it must become, finally, impersonal" (p. 81). ⟨"The Dangerous Fun of Special Pleading," *The Village Voice* (30 May, 1977)⟩ Earlier, Durbin says that "for the writing to work, it must transcend." Yet the two sentences are not automatically parallel: transcendence need not equal impersonality. We need to remember Lessing's remarks to Millett, that the moments when she spoke most for others were the moments that seemed most hopelessly private. In the Millett of *Sita*, for example, I recognize myself, and it is an uncomfortable lesson, for it is a self whom I would prefer not to be. Watching Millett, I understand something of the needlessness of that sort of pain which I, too, court, and even begin to contemplate some ways in which I might avoid encountering it. Certainly, Millett's telling transcends self-indulgence, as her personal experience confronts and illuminates my personal experience. There are no doubt many more readers who also share that particular "personal." In the process, the process of sharing the personal by means of a book, she is altering our definitions of the personal by giving it a public dimension.

—Suzanne Juhasz, "Towards a Theory of Form in Feminist Autobiography: Kate Millett's *Flying* and *Sita*; Maxine Hong Kingston's *The Woman Warrior*." *Women's Autobiography*, ed. Estelle C. Jelinek (Bloomington: Indiana University Press 1980), 226–30

ESTELLE C. JELINEK

For Millett and her generation, the writing of autobiography was no longer considered an act of reflection in old age but a process engaged in as one lived one's life. In addition, the civil rights movement had left its stamp and the second women's liberation movement was well under way. It occasioned a massive outpouring of personal statements, the end of women's silence for all time. ⟨. . .⟩

The absence of anecdotes in *Flying* is significant because instead of focusing on others, indirectly revealing personal feelings and behavior, Millett focuses directly and intimately on herself. Her aim is not to entertain readers with amusing or interesting stories, which accounts for her earnestness and lack of humor, but to take her audience along with her on a painful voyage of self-discovery. Free association is more appropriate than anecdote for Millett's "search," for defining herself as she writes.

Moreover, Millett uses none of the other typical forms of indirection: omission, camouflage, obliqueness, or understatement. *Flying* is all heart and soul, her affirmation of women's strength. ⟨. . .⟩ Whereas ⟨Doris⟩ Lessing's breakthrough was behind a third-person fictional character, Millett breaks new ground in autobiography in her first-person disclosure of intimacies. ⟨. . .⟩

The intimacy is evident in three areas that are usually restrained or eliminated entirely from other autobiographies. ⟨. . .⟩ Millett boldly exposes the confusion and infighting within the women's movement about the issue of lesbianism. She portrays some movement leaders as heavies, others as warm and sincere people. She treats the lesbian leaders honestly, neither glorifying them nor being overly severe. She also deals directly with two other problems within the movement: the overlapping questions of elitism and the conflict between the individual's creative needs and her responsibility to the collective. About elitism, Millett writes:

> It's a double bind; can't quit and can't stay in there either. All the while the movement is sending double signals; you absolutely must preach at our panel, star at our conference—implying fink if you don't . . . and at the same time laying down a wonderfully uptight line about elitism. . . .

⟨. . . ⟩ In addition to allowing herself to appear vulnerable to the public by confronting controversial political issues, Millett also reveals her personal fears, doubts, and weaknesses. ⟨. . . L⟩iteral and lyrical descriptions of the sex act between women had never been described before in autobiography. The leading predecessors for intimate sexual portrayal are, ironically, the three writers whose works Millett deplored in *Sexual Politics*: D. H. Lawrence, Henry Miller, and Norman Mailer. In her literary analysis, Millett attacked their ignorance and disdain of the woman's point of view and their assumption of the male view as universal. In *Flying* she transforms the power politics of competitive male sex into the passionate affairs of love and friendship of women's experiences. She makes no attempt to interpret the male sexual response in the equally lyrical passages of lovemaking with Fumio, which are entirely about her own positive reactions. ⟨. . .⟩

In the political arena ⟨. . .⟩ Millett fuses seemingly disparate positions: gay liberation combined with women's liberation, the freedom of the artist and the responsibilities of the political leader, the private person and the public figure. In writing this autobiography about finding her self, she also *gives* the book to everyone. Essentially, the reason for the extreme honesty and revelation of her intimate emotional and physical life comes out of her commitment to changing human conduct for that "new life" where patriarchal rule is ended. Her vision of an integrated bisexual world requires her to integrate seemingly disparate elements of her own life, which she sees, therefore, as both personal/sexual *and* political. Her "life" is her sexual politics.

Flying also demonstrates this same fusion in its style. ⟨. . .⟩ Millett sought a new form for her "new life" and created a "new autobiography" from a synthesis of three genre traditions: the historical, the literary/fictional, and the autobiographical.

Millett does not hide her self-consciousness about the style of *Flying* or its new form. In fact, to a large extent, the book is about its own composition, certainly a major motif that runs parallel to the attempts at thematic synthesis. Millett wants the book to document her life as it happens and thus become a new kind of documentary history. At one point, she insists that the book is not literature but a new way of writing about women's experience. In what was originally meant to be a conventional preface but was incorporated after the first hundred pages, Millett writes: *"It had occurred to me to treat my own existence as documentary"* (101; emphasis hers). ⟨. . .⟩ Millett herself writes: "I'm so tired of the old one-dimensional notions of things, the media, even the square historians, they catch nothing at all."

A forerunner of *Flying*'s attempt at destroying the line between the objective and the subjective in nonfiction was Norman Mailer's *Armies of the Night*, an effort to combine history and autobiography. In the journalistic sections of *Flying*, where the narrative is most linear and chronological (her excellent reportage on gay marches and women's conferences), Millett's style most resembles the dramatic writing of *Armies*. But there the resemblance ends, for there is a wide disparity between Mailer's "improvisational" history and

Millett's free-associative narrative, between his third-person character named "Mailer" and her first-person narrator, though the aim of the two writers—to fuse the personal and the historical—is similar, as it is with many writers of the "new journalism." ⟨. . .⟩

⟨But⟩ there is also much evidence that a very conscious process of selection and revision went into ⟨*Flying*⟩. Part One, "Vertigo," takes place entirely in Millett's mind as she free-associates about all the problems that make her feel that she is going mad. This is the most chaotic mixture of past and future associations in the book. ⟨. . .⟩ There is also a great deal of discontinuity in the middle sections of the book, especially whenever she is in New York or London, moving frenetically from one meeting, demonstration, film screening, or friend's house to another. But she also has periods of calm, which are expressed in those linear journalistic anecdotes that provide relief from the chaotic associative narrative. In Part Five there is one last frantic scene when Millett searches for her car in crowded Provincetown, desperate to catch the scheduled flight to the conference on violence. Otherwise, this last part of the book, its most serene section, offers the most linear and chronological narrative of all the five parts. Thus, we see a progression in the narrative style from total discontinuity to relative order, revealing Millett's skill in having the formal elements of the narrative mirror the changing emotional states of her life story. ⟨. . .⟩

Thus, thematically and stylistically, Millett has expanded autobiographical form by fusing the documentary completeness of history with the artistic shaping of literature and the personal truth of autobiography. Her idea of personal truth, however, is a step forward in the autobiographical tradition. ⟨. . .⟩ The women's autobiographical tradition gave Millett a context for writing about herself as a multidimensional woman. What she contributed to the tradition is the affirmation of the "fragmented" woman. She is the New Woman, who can fulfill many roles—filmmaker, writer, sculptor, teacher, literary and social critic, political leader, daughter, sister, friend, and lover—and synthesize them into a New Life, a new way of conducting one's life in a utopian "freer sexual culture." Millett is no longer restricted by the solutions that Stanton and Stein opted for in their struggle with the "feminization of the mind/body problem," ⟨Stimpson, "The Mind, the Body, and Gertrude Stein," *Critical Inquiry* 3 (Spring 1977): 489–506⟩ for she has transcended that dialectic. She has come a long way from the earliest women autobiographers.

—Estelle C. Jelinek, "Political and Personal Autobiography Integrated: The Fusion of Kate Millett," *The Tradition of Women's Autobiography from Antiquity to the Present* (Boston: Twayne 1986) 168, 172–74, 178–81, 183

ANDREA FREUD LOEWENSTEIN

The message Kate Millett gives us in the preface and conclusion that surround her remarkable new book, *The Loony Bin Trip*, is clear. Madness, she tells us, is a social construct, manufactured out of social controls, family disagreements, lovers' quarrels, professional interest, and the state's ambition to control private life. It is relative; what is mad in some circles is harmless eccentricity in others. 〈. . .〉

The Loony Bin Trip itself is an unwieldy package, bound carefully by its wrapping, but threatening to break out of that wrapping into contradictory screaming realities. 〈. . .〉

The Loony Bin Trip remains a text that argues against itself only as long as we keep the wrapping on; when we take it off, though (and the preface and conclusion together are only nine pages long), we find a wonderful autobiographical novel that follows directly and logically from Millett's earlier works in this genre, *Flying* and *Sita*. 〈. . .〉

In *Flying*, in *Sita*, and now in *The Loony Bin Trip*, the narrator and governing persona is always Kate with a capital K. This Kate grows older but remains constant in many ways in all three books. She is egocentric and charming, a storyteller, a boaster, a sexual adventurer, and an outlaw. She makes impossible demands and wants it all, insists on her own way, then gets in trouble and won't be a good sport about it, howling and moaning and shouting instead, forcing us to pay attention. Millett's got the kind of energy that allows her to write it all down and make it into a story right when it's happening, and we identify with her even as we're scolding the woman who would dare to do such an unfeminine thing as to use her own pain as good copy.

The voice is breathless—short and clipped or endlessly running on sentences that are half the time not propelled by the normal rules but instead by the need to get it out, a kind of lyrical speedy barrage that feels like it's being shot out of a cannon by its own urgency. What, if any, relation this character Kate bears to the real Kate Millett is not the issue here. Because what Kate Millett is writing in *The Loony Bin Trip* is fiction—fiction that comes out of a deep place in women's experience is part of a tradition that Kate Millett herself has pioneered and reclaimed.

Don't get me wrong. I'm not using the word fiction here as synonym for the word "lie" or as an antonym for the word "truth." I don't mean that we are not supposed to believe that the events in *Loony Bin Trip* in fact took place, because they certainly did, nor that we need not take the message of *Loony Bin Trip* seriously, because it is serious, and we need to listen to it. *The Loony Bin Trip* is a powerful and compelling work of fiction, and it is also an important work about madness and what happens to you when you are labeled mad. I mean only that once I discarded the wrappings and recognized this book as fiction, as, in fact, the third in a series, I was able to tolerate and even to enjoy its contradictions. I stopped trying so hard to figure out whose reality to choose, and where, if anywhere, the real madness was, and stopped questioning myself about whether I was reacting the right way. I was able to, in short, let it be.

A document demanding civil rights for those labeled mentally ill, which is what the preface and conclusion are, is not meant to offer contradictory, complex, and opposing realities. A novel is meant to, and its contradictions and complexity are part of what make this one work so well. Like any fine novel, *The Loony Bin Trip* leaves us not with certainties but with questions. We are reminded that my reality is not your reality, and reality depends, anyway, on who is telling the story. I am not attempting to deny the painful message of this book, then, when I say that the storytelling here is first rate, and the teller a mistress at her art. As in her other works of fiction, the journal-like ease of *The Loony Bin Trip* is deceptive. This is a book which has been shaped and revised with great care. I've read it three times so far, and each time I've discovered something new.

—Andrea Freud Loewenstein, "A Complex Tale of 'Madness,' Drugs, and Hospitalization," *Sojourner: The Women's Forum* (August 1990): 15

KAREN MALPEDE

⟨*The Loony Bin Trip*⟩ is a harrowing, hallucinatory, heroic book. Harrowing because it tells how Kate Millett was incarcerated against her will in mental hospitals in California, Minnesota and Ireland. Diagnosed as "manic depressive" in 1973, she was put on daily doses of lithium, a drug which damages the kidneys, causes hand shakes and diarrhea and generally slows the mind, thus suppressing manic highs which crash into horrific depressions. During and after periods of incarceration Millett was given other drugs as well: the heavy-duty tranquilizer Thorazine, anti-depressants, and a particularly sinister substance administered in Ireland called Prolixin which drove her into deep, tortured sleep.

Hallucinatory because it is written in the style of vision and rhapsody, the tongue of a super-agile mind spilling out rivers of image and thought, emotion, sexual desire, fantasy, historical or linguistic fact. Witch lore, amazon myths, utopian dreams, lesbian love, the culture of women become the thread Millett follows out of the labyrinth. The book invites the reader to free her/his own mode of perception, to loosen up, take a trip and a chance, give over to one's own free-wheeling personal associations, one's own inner sight. Be surprised, emboldened.

Heroic because though diagnosed as manic depressive, condemned to life on lithium and punished with forced incarceration for having dared go off the drug, Millett fights back. She writes. She exposes the injustice done, the wanton brutality of the mental hospital. She ruminates on the nature of "sanity" and "madness," pleads in favor of the whole expanse of experience open to the human mind. Ultimately she refuses to accept her own "diagnosis." She recovers her life, her art from the horror of what has passed. ⟨. . .⟩

The Loony Bin Trip held out a dual promise: it would be a brilliant exposé of psychiatric abuse *and* a self-confronting journey of the inner life through to another mode of psychic integration. On both these levels I became its avid reader, for on both these levels the book works with an electrifying precision. But at the very end, I found myself beginning to be dissatisfied with the limits to perception implicit in the form itself. From performance art to autobiographical writing, there is a current fashion for the obsessional tale of self. No other person exists in these narratives except as a function of the speaker's memory. Too often, too, the speaker seems "done to" by these hazy others: no relationship is evoked, no sense of different energies flowing back and forth, no inner reality granted to anyone else. For me, the greatest challenge and pleasure of writing is the creation of unique characters in interaction. So it must be the playwright in me that wanted more.

When finally Millett is off the lithium for good, she tells us that "nothing happened." But I wanted to know what life free of drugs, diagnosis and depression was like. I wanted to know how Millett, the no-longer-victim, felt inside, and if her sense of responsibility toward herself and toward the personal, daily life she lives with others had altered. And it's just here, at the very end, that the inquiry seemed to run out of steam, as if all the energy had been spent on vivid excoriation.

—Karen Malpede, "To Hell and Back," *The Women's Review of Books* 8, no. 1 (October 1990): 7–8

JEANNE PERREAULT

Kate Millett's *The Basement: Meditations on a Human Sacrifice* makes her own feminist subjectivity present in part through the paradox of ventriloquism, speaking in an array of frightening agencies and voices that she has both appropriated from the real world and created through her imaginative identification with those figures. Millett speaks here in her "own" voice, familiar to us from her other writing as "I," situating her particular experience in the foreground of a writing that layers the self with horror. *The Basement* is a detailed account of the torture and murder of a sixteen-year-old girl by a woman and a group of teenagers in Indiana in 1965. Millett's book gives us her relationship to the story of Sylvia Likens's death. She uses photographs of the people and the house, excerpts from magazine and newspaper reports, transcript pages of the trial of Gertrude Baniszewski and her followers, and the testimony of Sylvia's younger sister, Jenny, who had been boarding with Sylvia at Gertrude's while their parents followed the carnival. And she enters the minds of the characters, speaking in their voices. It is Millett's relentless drive toward self-inscription and self-exposure from *within* the agents of this narrative that makes her feminist reading of this crime and its "meaning" autographical. "Self" in this text pushes boundaries of fragmentation and multiplicity very close to the "terrifying slide" into psychosis that Jane Flax describes as the real others—Gertrude, Sylvia, Jenny—become metonyms of Millett's interior drama, and projected figures of our own cultural scripts.

The ubiquitous discourse of female evil and guilt and female reparation and expiation internalized by the "characters" determines the logic of Sylvia's death and of Kate Millett's obsession. In order to understand how anyone with a Ph.D., a job, and books published can say, as Millett does, "I am Sylvia Likens," we must engage intimately with Millett's process of making herself (and her reader) into Sylvia and Gertrude and Jenny. In this text we, as readers, are drawn and revised, written as ourselves, with the qualities and capacities of the characters. Millett makes her "reader" a flexible entity. She assumes a common culture, speaking from a cross-class position in which class markers are recognizable, but not fixed. She does not address race (is this a "white" crime?), and she seems to speak to a group of women and men having, for instance, childhood games in common, but strictly gendered roles within them. Only at times is the "we" she uses explicitly, exclusively female. Although the major figures in the "story" are female, the male reader is positioned as "actor" in the court testimony and in the imagined thoughts of the adolescent boys who helped think up tortures. Male readers, then, are offered a parallel reality to their own; they may "identify" with female terror, passivity, or rage, and hear their own cultural scripts echoed in the boys' reactions to Gertrude and Sylvia, or they may read as disassociated "outsiders." ⟨. . .⟩

The hysteric body of this text, inscribed compulsively in Sylvia Likens's torments and Kate Millett's identifications, is not only hysterical. In the interstices of the hysterical speech of rage, guilt, fear, and desire, *The Basement* interprets, analyzes, and integrates. It speaks with the language of the mind as well as that of the body. These languages make an autography that incorporates victim and tormentor, reader and writer, self and other in an interrogation of feminist ethics. With this fragmented mirror of the self and society, Kate Millett takes us into common places of childhood—the games, the teasing, the bullying. She recalls the trying games—the basement games of sexual experimentation—and the excitement of "the waiting in the dark" for the attack, the game that "trains" women for their role as passive victim.

As Millett encircles herself, her moment of first meeting Sylvia Likens, her descriptions getting increasingly personal, specific, the personal embraces a larger being than the merely individual Kate Millett. We see Millett here as she sees herself retrospectively, reading about Sylvia Likens in *Time* magazine, sitting in the canteen at Barnard College, describing her "sick fascination," her "horror," "anger," and fear: "The fear especially, an enormous fear." And the feminist consciousness (not ideological here, but intensely associative) charges the fear with a deep identification: "Because I was Sylvia Likens. She was me. . . . She was what 'happens' to girls. Or can. Or might . . . if you are sixteen, or ever have been or female and the danger is all around you. Women, the corpses of women, surfacing in newsprint." Millett's "I" becomes "you" and then "we," and the personal is exposed as public, and shared. Her assumption is that every woman will identify equally. She says, "We all have a story like this, and I had found mine." The "story" here is the objective correlative for the internalized fear and shame of femaleness in our culture, and it is recognizing that story as a cultural "fable" that is the product (and producer) of a feminist consciousness. The female self/subject here, then, is both subject as agent of selfhood and subject as topic, as passive, as written upon.

Millett anticipates the frustrated, reasoned reactions to the atrocity: "you think, why the hell did they do this?" and echoes an answer the reader is expected to recognize:

> And then you see the line about being a prostitute and you know, though you can hardly think—in the sense of conceptualizing it— you know, it is for sex. That they killed her for sex. Because she had it. She was it. . . . Because nubile and sixteen she is sex to the world around her and that is somehow a crime. For which her killing is punishment. Execution. A sentence carried out. Upon Shame.

The broken syntax here suggests that only a small piece of this knowledge can enter at one time. Millett fragments it for forcefulness, and for particularizing the extended trope of a whole system of justice in action. The paragraph ends on the capitalized "Shame," and her next assertion indicates it is the answer to the question not yet asked. "And shame? The answer to the other question— 'Why did she let them do it to her?' Sure, admittedly she was tied up the last few weeks." Millett traces Sylvia's story as though reading it, as indeed she did, as we do (the authority of the text relied on, while being challenged, in the idiom of newspaper readers everywhere): "But it says here that before that she was still free." Millett asks the logical questions—why did she not tell the teachers, the pastor, why did she not run away? Millett answers the questions, "It was not only the body that must have been broken, but the spirit. And that is the whole meaning of shame." Millett concludes her first chapter with reference to another story: "In Kafka's Penal Colony the sentence is carried out upon the flesh, written thereon so that it will enter into the soul. Here too." In this sentence "here" is multiply ambiguous. "Here," in this text, is Sylvia Likens's body repeatedly undergoing its sentence(s) of death. "Here," in Sylvia's life, was her sentence (in words and in punishments) inscribed on her flesh. "Here" in this culture is sexual shame inscribed on women's lives.

    —Jeanne Perreault, "Kate Millett's *The Basement:* Testimony of the Unspeakable," *Writing Selves: Contemporary Feminist Autography* (Minneapolis: University of Minnesota Press, 1995), 72–73, 76–77

B I B L I O G R A P H Y

Token Learning: A Study of Women's Higher Education in America. 1967.
Sexual Politics. 1970.
The Prostitution Papers. 1973.
Flying. 1974.
Sita. 1977.
The Basement: Meditations on a Human Sacrifice. 1979.
Elegy for Sita. 1979.
Going to Iran. 1982.
The Loony-Bin Trip. 1990.
The Politics of Cruelty: An Essay on the Literature of Political Imprisonment. 1994.
A.D.: A Memoir. 1995.

ANAÏS NIN
1903–1977

ANAÏS NIN was born in Neuilly-sur-Seine, near Paris, on February 21, 1903. Her father, Joaquin Nin, was a composer and musician, and her mother, Rosa Culmell, was a singer of Danish and French ancestry. Both parents were from Cuba. When her father deserted the family, Nin's mother moved back across the Atlantic, bringing her three children to New York City. About this time Nin began keeping her diary. It began as both a letter to her absent father and as a literary and personal exploration of self. Nin attended public schools in New York from 1918–1919 and then dropped out and continued her own course of reading at public libraries.

In 1923, Nin married Hugh Guiler and moved to Paris. Later that year she published her critical work *D. H. Lawrence: An Unprofessional Study*. The American author Henry Miller became interested in her writing and met her while in France, beginning a life-long professional and intimate relationship. In the 1930s they aided each other in their work. Nin's circle also included Antonin Artaud, Lawrence Durrell, and Michael Fraenkel. During this time she also studied psychoanalysis with Otto Rank and practiced as an analyst. Her surrealistic prose poem *House of Incest* (1936), which deals with psychological torment, shows his influence.

After returning to the United States, Nin continued her work exploring the relationship between eroticism and identity. Some members of her circle objected to her self-exploratory writing. She herself saw the diary as a way of establishing and accepting a feminine identity. She launched her own press, Gemor Press, and printed her novel and short stories at her own expense. Her collection of short stories, *Winter of Artifice* (1939), contains three novellas about a daughter's relationship to her father. This was followed by two collections of stories, *Under a Glass Bell* (1942) and *This Hunger* (1945), and by her first novel, *Ladder to Fire* (1946). While her stories and novels received little critical attention, many leading literary figures appreciated and respected her work.

Not until the publication of her *Diary* (1966–1980) did Nin's work become well-known. Taken by the artistry and immediacy of her writing, critics began debating, and still do, the extent to which the diary is the immediate emotional response of Nin, or the studied and well-crafted work of the writer Nin creating the impression of immediacy. The *Diary* was created, after all, by the novelist Nin. The six diaries that Nin compiled cover the years 1931–1966 and were published between 1966–1976. The seventh and last volume of the *Diary* was edited by Gunther Stuhlmann (who had assisted Nin on the other volumes) after Nin's death in Los Angeles in 1977 and was published in 1980.

CRITICAL EXTRACTS

HENRY MILLER

As I write these lines Anaïs Nin has begun the fiftieth volume of her diary, the record of a twenty-year struggle towards self-realization. Still a young woman, she has produced on the side, in the midst of an intensely active life, a monumental confession which when given to the world will take its place beside the revelations of St. Augustine, Petronius, Abelard, Rousseau, Proust, and others.

Of the twenty years recorded half the time was spent in America, half in Europe. The diary is full of voyages; in fact, like life itself it might be regarded as nothing but voyage. The epic quality of it, however, is eclipsed by the metaphysical. The diary is not a journey towards the heart of darkness, in the stern Conradian sense of destiny, not a *voyage au bout de la nuit*, as with Céline, nor even a voyage to the moon in the psychological sense of escape. It is much more like a mythological voyage towards the source and fountain head of life—I might say an *astrologic* voyage of metamorphosis. ⟨. . .⟩

There is a very significant fact attached to the origin of this diary, and that is that it was begun in artistic fashion. By that I do not mean that it was done with the skill of an artist, with the conscious use of a technique; no, but it was begun as something to be read by some one else, as something to influence some one else. In that sense as an artist. Begun during the voyage to a foreign land, the diary is a silent communion with the father who has deserted her, a gift which she intends to send him from their new home, a gift of love which she hopes will re-unite them. Two days later the war breaks out. By what seems almost like a conspiracy of fate the father and child are kept apart for many years. In the legends which treat of this theme it happens, as in this case, that the meeting takes place when the daughter has come of age.

And so, in the very beginning of her diary, the child behaves precisely like the artist who, through the medium of his expression, sets about to conquer the world which has denied him. Thinking originally to woo and enchant the father by the testimony of her grief, thwarted in all her attempts to recover him, she begins little by little to regard the separation as a punishment for her own inadequacy. The difference which had marked her out as a child, and which had already brought down upon her the father's ire, becomes more accentuated. The diary becomes the confession of her inability to make herself worthy of this lost father who has become for her the very paragon of perfection.

In the very earliest pages of the diary this conflict between the old, inadequate self which was attached to the father and the budding, unknown self which she was creating manifests itself. It is a struggle between the real and the ideal, the annihilating struggle which for most people is carried on fruitlessly to the end of their lives and the significance of which they never learn. ⟨. . .⟩

One thinks inevitably of the manifestoes of the Surrealists, of their unquenchable thirst for the marvellous, and that phrase of Breton's, so significant of the dreamer, the visionary: 'we should conduct ourselves as though we were really *in the world!*' It may seem absurd to couple the utterances of the Surrealists with the writings of a child of thirteen, but there is a great deal which they have in common, and there is also a point of departure which is even more important. The pursuit of the marvellous is at bottom nothing but the sure instinct of the poet speaking, and it manifests itself everywhere in all epochs, in all conditions of life, in all forms of expression. But this marvellous pursuit of the marvellous, if not understood, can also act as a thwarting force, can become a thing of evil, crushing the individual in the toils of the Absolute. It can become as negative and destructive a force as the yearning for God. When I said a while back that the child had begun her great work in the spirit of an artist I was trying to emphasize the fact that, like the artist, the problem which beset her was to conquer the world. In the process of making herself fit to meet her father again (because to her the world was personified in the Father) she was unwittingly making herself an artist, that is, a self-dependent creature for whom a father would no longer be necessary. When she does encounter him again, after a lapse of almost twenty years, she is a full-fledged being, a creature fashioned after her own image. The meeting serves to make her realize that she has emancipated herself; more indeed, for to her amazement and dismay she also realizes that she has no more need of the one she was seeking. The significance of her heroic struggle with herself now reveals itself symbolically. That which was beyond her, which had dominated and tortured her, which *possessed* her, one might say, no longer exists. She is depossessed and free at last to live her own life.

Throughout the diary the amazing thing is this intuitive awareness of the symbolic nature of her role. It is this which illuminates the most trivial remarks, the most trivial incidents she records. In reality there is nothing trivial throughout the whole record; everything is saturated with a purpose and significance which gradually becomes clear as the confession progresses.

Similarly there is nothing chaotic about the work, although at first glance it may give that impression. The fifty volumes are crammed with human figures, incidents, voyages, books read and commented upon, reveries, metaphysical speculations, and dramas in which she is enveloped, her daily work, her preoccupation with the welfare of others, in short, with a thousand and one things which go to make up her life. It is a great pageant of the times patiently and humbly delineated by one who considered herself as nothing, by one who had almost completely effaced herself in the effort to arrive at a true understanding of life. It is in this sense again that the human document rivals the work of art, or in times such as ours, *replaces* the work of art. For, in a profound sense, this *is* the work of art which never gets written—because the artist whose task it is to create it never gets born. We have here, instead of the consciously or technically finished work (which to-day seems to us more than ever empty and illusory), the unfinished symphony which achieves consummation because each line is pregnant with a soul struggle. The conflict with the world takes place within. It matters little, for the artist's purpose, whether the world be the size of a pinhead or an incommensurable universe. *But there must be a world!* And this world, whether real or imaginary, can only be created out of despair and anguish. For the artist there is no other world. Even if it be unrecognizable, this world which is created out of sorrow and deprivation is true and vital, and eventually it expropriates the 'other' world in which the ordinary mortal lives and dies. It is the world in which the artist has his being, and it is in the revelation of his undying self that art takes its stance. Once this is apprehended there can be no question of monotony or fatigue, of chaos or irrelevance. We move amid boundless horizons in a perpetual state of awe and humility. We enter, with the author, into unknown worlds, and we share with the latter all the pain, beauty, terror and illumination which exploration entails.

—Henry Miller, "Un Etre Etoilique," *Criterion* (October 1937), excerpted in *Twentieth-Century American Literature*, ed. Harold Bloom (New York: Chelsea House Publishers, 1986), 2835–38

LEON EDEL

Diary-keeping belongs to a curious and special order of literature; it is the imagination held at bay by the self—the individual so preoccupied with personal experience that he must re-rehearse it compulsively on a sheet of paper. It is inevitably an act of self-absorption; in the process it becomes also an act of self-revelation—in spite of all that it attempts to conceal. Its interest for the reader resides in its offering glimpses into private worlds—worlds to which we do not otherwise have access.

Anaïs Nin's diary, kept with consistency (and almost, one might say, addiction) over many years, is thus primarily a document rather than an act of creation, a record of self-contemplation in many mirrors—public rather than private mirrors. She began keeping it as a child. Her father, the Spanish composer Joaquín Nin, had left her Danish mother, and the latter took her children to America. To fill the absence of her father, the young Anaïs began to write down all that happened to her, in the hope that some day she might show it to him. She wrote her diaries wherever she went, carrying them with her as a musician carries his instrument. Her voluminous notebooks of the self thus fulfill many purposes. They were, for Miss Nin, a way of giving herself concrete proof of her own existence. The diary also became, as it were, her father; and we catch in these pages the straight, questioning look of a little girl interrogating life and trying to be well-behaved and dutiful. But there is something more complicated as well: the diary is that of a daughter, living or imagining a life that would be pleasing to the absent parent.

That life is divided (in the more adult years of 1931 to 1934 here published) between bourgeois respectability and a king of anarchistic Bohemia. Miss Nin lived on the edge of Paris, at Louveciennes in the *paysages* exquisitely preserved for us by Pissaro's canvasses. To her orderly home came the literary anarchists of the Depression era, and especially Henry Miller. Thus we have in these pages the double image of an intellectual bluestocking who can also be a haunter of bistros and visitor of brothels. Miss Nin disciplined, logical, a *"petite fille littéraire,"* as one called her, meticulous in thought and dainty in word, self-questioning, busy discovering for herself the discovered world. When she is reflective and philosophical, she is an earnest, papa-pleasing little girl; when she looks up from the pages of her writing, she sees the world as a sensitive observer; when she allows herself to feel rather than reflect, her pages take on the color of life rather than of literature. To the critical reader, seeking a self-portrait between these lines, Miss Nin appears above all as a troubled preadolescent pursuing a dream of reuniting her parents and recovering her father; and this is why so much of this journal is devoted to her attempts to make peace between substitute figures, Henry Miller and his estranged wife.

The present excerpts are important above all for the subjective, and probably refracted, "portraits" of Miss Nin's psychoanalysts. Readers will be particularly interested in her account of her analytic sessions with Otto Rank, Freud's brilliant if erratic disciple. Through the blur of Miss Nin we glimpse Rank expertly unveiling to her the defenses she has created in her life by her diary-keeping, not least the ways in which the diaries prevent her from developing as an artist by making her an annotator rather than a creator. Miss Nin gives the impression that she conducted the sessions as if she were the analyst. By her account both her French analyst René Allendy, and the Viennese Rank become fathers and lovers; the symbolic house of incest (the title of her first novel) is recurrently revived.

Henry Miller, with understandable partiality and consistent exuberance, has described Miss Nin's diaries as destined to take their place beside the confessions of St. Augustine, Petronius, Abelard, Rousseau, and Proust. Whether this is true of the millions of unpublished words we cannot say; but the present "sampling" offers a modulated and lowpitched portrait of the early Depression years in Paris after most American expatriates had fled. The myth of D. H. Lawrence prevailed; and life in the Villa Seurat had not yet become the Miller-Durrell legend. Miss Nin is a child of the Lawrentian revolt and of the Surealists, the phase of the movement which looked inwardly into the distortions of the dream. Literary history will probably place her with that last backwater of Romanticism before World War II.

Her diary contributes much to that history, and one hopes for more of the 150 volumes. But they should be quarried, it might be suggested, with caution, lest they become like Frankenstein monsters, too large for Miss Nin's own childlike, lotus-flower essence.

—Leon Edel, "Life without Father," *Saturday Review* (7 May 1966): 91

LYNN SUKENICK

The diaries of Anais Nin, although revised and intensely compressed, and revised—as Nin has said—by the novelist, are, by their nature, a species of autobiography. Although their excellence has caused them to be ranked with works of imagination, a rank accorded few autobiographies in spite of the current popularity of the genre, they are not novels—one has only to put them next to her novels to feel that—and to ignore that fact is to miss out on the special reading experience which they seem to inspire. Nin's diaries are books of wisdom which have elevated their author to the status of a sage and have had a healing effect on many of her readers, an effect which would be altered if the books were semi-fiction, although, clearly, works of fiction can function as books of wisdom. It is unlikely that anyone has bent to kiss her hem as did one adoring reader of George Eliot, but Nin has evoked in her readers a response similar to the tenacious adulation that surrounded Eliot in her later years, and has joined the company of those great teachers—Eliot, Wordsworth, and the savage but salutary D. H. Lawrence—who had a visionary sense of the healing power of feeling. ⟨. . .⟩

Nin's power to stir us and change our lives is not in direct proportion to the quantity of information in the diaries, not a direct function of how much she tells us. Although Nin places her deepest expectations in the personal and private sphere, the diaries are not confessional works. Nin was a practicing Catholic until her teens and therefore familiar with the ritual of confession; she was a student of psychoanalysis and herself an analyst, accustomed to the recuperative monologues of the analysand, but her diaries are not confessional in the most common sense of the word. She does not seek to unburden herself of material as if that material is an impediment to her freedom, nor does she pay guilty attention to the more ignoble details of her life as if to absolve herself by virtue of her typicality or detestability. If anything, she is herself the priest or lay confessor, confessing to herself by means of the diary, but also, by means of the diary, absolving herself from raw experience by transmuting it into form—not just any form, but conscious and lucid writing which expresses control even when she is discussing her weaknesses. ⟨. . .⟩

Nin's occasional neglect of sincerity and candor in the diaries—the lies she tells to others to make improvements or not to hurt, to maintain harmony and dissolve disruption—is directly related to her desire for perfection. She realizes it as a weakness—this tendency to invent or conceal—and she presents her weakness openly, not only in her own person but in figures who reflect and enlarge the problem, living it out to an extreme degree. Lying— her father's, June's—is a deep concern in Diary I, and is a theme that develops richness in *Spy in the House of Love*, where Nin attempts to find relief from it once and for all, creating a final punctuation in the person of the Lie Detector. ⟨. . .⟩

⟨. . .⟩ Although Nin escapes the mechanical and hypocritical impersonations of social existence in the diary, her pursuit of "transmutation" continues there, and the diary itself becomes both an active force in transforming her life (as when she draws portraits of people and shows them their portraits) as well as a distilled account of her experience. Notable for a grace and certainty of style, Nin's diary is utterly distinct from the current outpourings of confessional journalism, undigested notation encouraged by the general abolition of etiquette and the preeminence of therapies which encourage and value the public revelation of personal material. She does not give herself away in her writings but serves us by remaining intact even after we have devoured her work. ⟨. . .⟩

The advocates of spontaneity, from Rousseau on, have regarded artifice as an offense against sincerity and the spirit of democracy (for a doctrine of equality gives value to and an opportunity for candor). A sisterly relation with the reader is desired, a certain obligation to be no better than the reader. But Nin, by aiming high and extracting noble qualities from her experience, improves herself and shows others the way. Nin's distilled style allows us more space for ourselves than the confessional outpourings which make accomplices of us. Her diary, perfected and sometimes reticent, becomes a mirror into which we can look and, often, find ourselves clearly expressed. Her polished surface reflects the reader. ⟨. . .⟩

Nin's tact, discretion, gentleness and sympathy are crucial to all of her relationships as they are portrayed in the diary, at times, in her own opinion, to excess. Virginia Woolf has stated that sympathy was a concern of laggards and losers, and certainly in the era of modernism it has seemed minor, mediocre, and peripheral. But Nin insists on it—"What makes us human is empathy, sympathy," she says—and she is willing to cry out, "This hurts people!" the kind of objection ordinarily made only by unpublished mothers. The most remarkable thing about Nin is how she revives the wisdom of sympathy in an age which tends to be embarrassed by it.

The spareness and omissions of Nin's diaries result partly from her wanting to ignore—in Virginia Woolf's phrase—the "appalling narrative business of the realist," just as her strategy as a novelist is to wean us from simple curiosity and a hunger for ordinary narrative. But it is more than likely that sympathy and discretion are as responsible as formal considerations for the withholding of information in the diaries. Nin's unwillingness to injure coincides with her doctrine of omission and extends the portrait of her as a woman of sympathy. There is in fact a substitution of sympathy for confessional sincerity in the diaries. Nin relates how she sometimes conceals things from others in order not to hurt them, offering warm comfort instead of cold fact. She writes in the diary to compose herself, literally, to offset her empathic merging with others. Yet even this private act, now made public, offers comfort, now to her readers, who receive insights into and a blueprint for the opening of the heart, solicitude and creative energy. The apex of Nin's tact is that she creates an atmosphere of intimacy at the same time that she refrains from a policy of open disclosure. We feel, somehow, that the diaries reach into our lives, that they are intimate about *us*, intimating to us our own latent potential, the latent life force in us.

—Lynn Sukenick, "The Diaries of Anais Nin," *Shenandoah* 27, no. 3 (Spring 1976): 96–97, 99, 100–102

DUANE SCHNEIDER

The intriguing and engaging narrator of Anaïs Nin's *Diary* has surely earned for herself a place among the great literary creations to appear in this century. Purporting to reveal aspects of her life (and the growth of her sensibilities) in selections from an autobiographical journal, the narrator knows and relates the truth about herself. In a series of volumes covering the years 1931–1966, the reader is allowed to trace the progress of this narrator/persona (called "Anaïs Nin") through a set of experiences that simulates the depth and variety of human life and achievement. The creation and development of this narrator unquestionably attest to the power and skill of Nin, the author, and it is therefore unfortunate that many readers have failed to appreciate the difference between the two.

Such confusion is also difficult to understand, as there would seem to be ample directions in the prefatory material of the six volumes to deter us from assuming that Nin the author and Nin the narrator are uniform; since we are told that the published *Diary* represents only a fraction of the original, and since both the processes of selection and organization have taken place we would seem led to conclude that the published versions (having been revised at least once) are carefully wrought works of literature, regardless of the apparent autobiographical nature of their origin.

In any case, Nin never forgot, even if some readers occasionally do, that it "was the fiction writer who edited the diary" (*Novel*, p. 85), and it ought to come as no surprise to find that the values and techniques she employed in her fiction are finely honed for use in the *Diary*. Psychological authenticity, which lies at the heart of all of Nin's work, is effected in the *Diary* as in the fiction through the manipulation of symbolism, dreams, and other dramatic devices which generate a sense of immediacy. Similarly, the *Diary* reveals a fine sense of timing, character development and selection, which Nin initiated and Gunther Stuhlmann aided; as in her fiction, but frequently with sustained concreteness, characters appear and reappear in multiple contexts, while typical of both the fiction and the *Diary* is the presence of a chief female character who is omnipresent—as a participant or as an observer—and whose development is presented through multiple exposures in a variety of contexts, through her own self-analysis, or through the responses she evokes from the satellite characters around her.

There is, however, one important difference between the material as it is presented in the fiction and as it is presented in the *Diary*: namely, the presence within the latter of a central consciousness—that of the persona—through whose mind all the characters and incidents are filtered, interpreted, and colored. Every detail she affords us tells us perhaps as much about herself as it does about the person or incident described. In contrast to the situation in Nin's fiction, therefore, narration in the *Diary* becomes simultaneously self-characterization. Under the appearance of a journal that records real-life situations and individuals, there have, in fact, been gathered a set of compelling "actors" in accordance with the literary principle of point of view. The result is neither fiction in the traditional sense nor diary in the conventional sense but rather something of a new art form—the journal-novel. ⟨. . .⟩

⟨However,⟩ the strength of Volume I is also its weakness. The character of the persona seems incomplete, unrounded—perhaps unreal. Certainly the narrator is relatively flawless. We soon realize, in fact, that she is depicted as the one who is needed, a kind of savior, and not merely one who needs. ⟨. . .⟩

The narrator of Volume II shares a great deal with that of Volume I, and the time of composition (editing, organizing and selecting) was probably close to that of the first volume, since Volume II appeared only a year later. Many motifs, themes and characters reappear in this volume, which covers the years 1934–1939. ⟨. . .⟩

With an agreeable symmetry, not unlike its predecessors, Volume III begins with difficulty and dislocation (also true of Volumes I and II), but ends with success and acceptance—true in Volume I, but only generally so in Volume II. The dovetailing and interweaving of character and motif continue: in time, part of the Paris circle that Nin regrets leaving—Miller, Gonzalo, Helba—appear on American shores. The persona progresses in a logical fashion: the literary initiate of the first volume, who chooses art in the second, becomes the maverick and determined devotee of her own vision in the third volume. The problem she faces is: how does an avant garde writer establish contact with an American audience in 1940? Answer: with extreme difficulty, and never successfully. ⟨. . .⟩

Volume III, however, lacks a continuity that the first two volumes contain. Most of the characters introduced in this volume hold interest for the reader, but some seem superfluous. The narration seems for the first time broken at times, slightly desperate if not shrill. ⟨. . .⟩ The narrator in Volume III remains a literary creation, not a live human being. The author's defenses, it would seem, are still up.

The fourth volume, covering the years 1944–1947, represents to some degree the legacy earned from the years of the early 1940's. More fragmented than any earlier volume, it is not, however, weak or uninteresting, and contains some of Nin's finest and most poignant observations about life and literature. ⟨. . .⟩

The fifth volume, which covers the years 1947–1955, is far different from the first four, and is more fragmented and less sustained even than Volume IV. Although familiar themes reappear—sympathy, analysis, fiction writing, travel—no clear focus emerges and no clear theme is developed. It contrasts most strikingly with a work like Volume I, with its dramatic and engaging characterizations that are developed in great detail. The incoherence of Volume V in fact mirrors the incoherence of the narrator's life at this time; more than in any other volume, the persona here is less stylized and artificial. Suffering from depression and attendant emotional problems, as well as physical illness, the narrator encounters difficulties of considerable proportions, not the least of which are the details of her parents and a strange kind of hostility on the part of critics and reviewers. For the first time the narrator is depicted as beginning seriously to turn to the diary as her major work, with an eye toward eventual publication. In all its fragmentation, it may well be that Volume V, edited carefully, stands as a masterpiece of organic form, imaging in its structure (with short, undeveloped passages) the disconnected nature of the narrator's life. It may have been at this time that Nin chose to redirect her characterization of the persona toward something less glamorous, less dramatic than she appeared in earlier volumes. ⟨. . .⟩

The sixth volume of the *Diary*, covering the years 1955–1966, contains more pages, deals with more years, and has far more balance and structure than earlier volumes. Some will say that it cannot rival the first two contributions to the series, which detail Nin's relationship with her literary associates in Paris; and yet Volume VI brings to the reader a narrator who is more open and relaxed than before. "I have decided to retire as the major character of this diary," she writes, and from that point on it was to be called *Journal des Autres* (Diary of Others). That the narrator had been the central character in the first five volumes will be readily acknowledged; that the persona herself can admit this fact openly in Volume VI is something new. The openness of the disclosure, however, is characteristic of the tone of the volume: the persona retires quietly in the background and the mood is at times relaxed. The narrator does not have to center the attention on herself, and when she speaks she seems to be candid and confident. The tensions and conflicts of the past have been resolved, she notes, and she now turns to the editing and copying of the diary, preparing it for publication. It might be said, in fact, that the diary itself now acquires the centrality and focus which the narrator is willing to abdicate.

—Duane Schneider, "Anais Nin in the Diary: The Creation and Development of a Persona," *Mosaic: A Journal for the Comparative Study of Literature and Ideas* 11, no. 2 (1978): 9–10, 12, 14–18

ESTELLE C. JELINEK

Anaïs Nin's six-volume *Diary*, her lifework, is both similar to and distinct from the genre created by ⟨. . .⟩ women writers, and its peculiar qualities deserve further examination.

Though Nin's work is actually a hybrid form, alternately functioning as diary, writer's notebook, and autobiography, in its appearance, form, and style *The Diary of Anaïs Nin* follows the general conventions of autobiographical writings (as outlined by Bruss) ⟨in *Autobiographical Acts*⟩. More importantly, Nin's *Diary* also illustrates the structural discontinuity and pervasive thematic concerns which seem to typify women's autobiography in particular.

As is the case in other autobiographies and diaries, here the author is the foundation for both subject matter and structure in the volumes. Although she is often hazy about the appropriate point of view for her fiction ("In whose consciousness does the whole appear?"), Nin herself recognizes that "The diary was held together, was given its unity, by my being at the center." Similarly, in her own *Diary* she quotes what James Leo Herlihy has written about her in his: "Anaïs will never be a mistress of artistic forms. This flaw is the price her novels pay for the perfect integration of art and life achieved in the diary. Where is the form in the diary? The life."

Nin also presents her material as the truth about herself, her experiences, and her perceptions. Though she often notes that memory is faulty, she always discovers (particularly while recopying manuscripts) that the diary entries captured the truth about what happened or what was experienced. Several times while editing, she considers destroying rather than publishing the diary, to protect "human beings it might wound"; however, she soon realizes that to do so would be to kill "a lifegiving creation, to save a few from the truth."

In like manner, even when presenting apparently incredible, unbelievable events or personalities, Nin never suggests that she is being anything but accurate (if subjective) in her treatment. ⟨. . .⟩ The *Diary* also compels the reader to identify with the author's particular truths, opinions, and cast of acquaintances. This is usually accomplished by establishing a value system whereby the reader who is unable to see things the way she does, feels that Nin would place him/her alongside the other bourgeois critics, socialists, bureaucrats, or unimaginative suburbanites she regularly castigates. This creates a problem in the *Diary* because the "true" picture Nin presents of herself (or Henry Miller or Kenneth Patchen or various critics) is often obviously adjusted in accordance with her biases, anxieties, or periodic desires for flattering exaggeration or stylization. Without worrying about verifying the truth concerning people or events, the reader must still worry about verifying the problematic nature of Nin's diary persona.

If Nin's *Diary* exhibits the general characteristics of autobiographical works, many of its techniques are also conventional. In compiling 15,000 manuscript pages, Nin certainly used the diary as an intimate, chronological record of her life. It was her obsession with this personal, daily diary, her "opium," that prompted Rank, Allendy ⟨both her doctors⟩, and others to urge her to abandon it. ⟨. . .⟩

Thus, while the impulse to continue writing in the diary notebooks was essentially personal, the editing process, marked by Nin's desire to present portions first to a limited and then to an extensive audience, reflects the concerns of an autobiographer cognizant of external readers. From her early attempts to charm back her overly critical father with a diary/letter to him, to her increasing willingness to show entries to friends, associates, prospective publishers, and even potentially hostile critics (Henry Miller, James Leo Herlihy, Maxwell Perkins, and Maxwell Geismar, to name only a few), Nin expanded the focus of the diary beyond herself so as to reach a wider and wider audience. Or, rather, as she states toward the conclusion of Volume VI, the *Diary* showed that "if one goes deeply enough into the personal, one transcends it and reaches beyond the personal."

The conflict between writing for oneself and writing for others, between private woman and public personality, is reflected throughout Nin's work. The autobiographical impulse triumphs, but not effortlessly: "The impulse to give and the impulse to hide fought a mighty battle. . . . I would call it a battle between the woman and the creator. The woman, protective, secretive, placing the needs of others before her own, accustomed to her mysteries which man has feared; and the creator, no longer able to contain her discoveries, her knowledge, her experiences, her lucidities, her compiling of the hidden aspects of people so ardently pursued." ⟨. . .⟩

⟨. . . Nin wished that⟩ instead of recalling sometimes painful past events in order to edit the diary, she "could create fiction out of the present, but the present is sacred to me, to be lived, to be passionately absorbed but not transfigured into fiction, to be preserved faithfully in the diary." The formal sentence structure of the *Diary* prose most often conveys ordinary details of everyday life in a conventional manner or captures "the real thing" in complete detail so that later, perhaps, Nin can use the material in the fiction and present it through the patented, lush, stylized, and often fragmented poetic prose for which she is noted. ⟨. . .⟩

The diffuse organization that characterizes women's autobiographies is evident in the lack of even topical or thematic organization in Nin's *Diary*. The fact that the same topics and themes recur at random intervals throughout the six volumes is less indicative of any exterior coordinating principle than it is of her ongoing struggle for emotional and creative maturation. Accordingly, time and time again, she announces conclusions—only to withdraw them, to the frustration of the reader not prepared for such diffuseness. For example, because there is no logical progression or the "summing up" found in the more structured autobiographies of some men and women, one gets situations like that in Volume V, where Nin writes: "My feelings have changed about America. . . . I want to help, to teach. . . . I feel reintegrated into the human family. I have overcome the neurosis at last"—only to harp on the same complaints and exhibit the same psychological problems all over again in Volume VI. It is only fair, however, to observe that Nin herself expressed frustration over this aspect of the diary mode. At times she wishes she could wrest more control over the material, impose more order: "I would love to finish the 1955 diary properly. Being also a novelist, I love to wind up with some sort of climax, as in a novel. To point up a climax and make prophecies. I sometimes have the feeling that the diary is not a finished work and needs filling in."

—Estelle C. Jelinek, "Anaïs Nin's *Diary* in Context," *Women's Autobiography: Essays in Criticism*, ed. Estelle C. Jelinek (Bloomington: Indiana University Press, 1980), 213–17

ALBERT E. STONE

"I am submerged by the enormity of my material," ⟨Nin⟩ exclaims in the sixth volume ⟨of her diaries⟩. In actuality, she did not sink under its weight. Over nineteen hundred pages of a sensitive woman's intimate thoughts, feelings, experiences, and relationships have been reassembled into one continuously flowing narrative. Before her death, her faith and her friends' faith were vindicated in the eyes of a growing circle of readers. Henry Miller's early prophecy in *The Cosmological Eye* ("a monumental confession which when given the world will take its place beside the revelations of St. Augustine, Petronius, Abélard, Rousseau, Proust, and others") could now be considered in the public light which the autobiographer so long shunned.

The ordering and reordering of passing impressions and permanent memories make strenuous demands on Nin's readers and critics. Intuitive empathy and cool, intellectual judgment are equally required to embrace the surprising range of moods, ideas, personalities, ties, and social contexts recorded over thirty-five years of the writer's European and American experience. As the narrative of a richly private life, the *Diary*'s underlying rationale is as thoroughly psychological as Mead's is anthropological, for Nin deliberately organizes her life-story in line with Jung's injunction "proceed from the dream outward." ⟨. . .⟩ Thus her principal task—a more ambitious one than Mead's—has been to find a language adequate to represent the intricate interplay of consciousness and the preconscious as she locates a woman's imagination within the society of men. Though timeless dream images provide the psychic foundation, a thread of historical continuity runs through this story of an unfolding self. Each of the six volumes takes a chronological slice through psychic and social experience. Furthermore, though recurring motifs unify the whole, there is also a perceptible movement in the *Diaries* away from private dream toward history and social involvement. The engagement with the external world never overshadows the private agenda, however. This continues to include the development of the self in *all* its artful femininity, the problem of neurosis and the struggle for mental equipoise, intense relationships with a few individuals at a time, always the attempt to unite conscious art and spontaneous life. ⟨. . .⟩

The editorial act reuniting the young writer in Paris and the older woman in California was a complex and emotional process. "I felt the need to publish the diary as strongly as the snake pushing out of its old skin," she recalls in volume 6. "All evolution had this impulse. The impulse to give and the impulse to hide fought a mighty battle in this quiet office overlooking a garden. I would call it a battle between the woman and the creator. The woman, protective, secretive, placing the needs of others before her own, accustomed to her mysteries which man has feared, and the creator, no longer able to contain her discoveries, her knowledge, her experiences, her lucidities, her compiling of the hidden aspects of people so ardently pursued." ⟨. . .⟩

⟨. . .⟩ The most striking ⟨gap⟩ is the absence of Ian Hugo, Nin's husband, who like certain other relatives chose not to appear in volume 1 of the *Diary*. (He is passingly mentioned later, though never as her husband.) Nin's respect for others' wishes is explained in *The Novel of the Future* as well as in volume 6. "As a diarist I drew my own boundary lines indicating that a respect for the life of a human being is more important than satisfying the curiosity of invaders, violators of human rights. . . . I take delight in the creative possibilities of the intimate portrait, but it has to be with the collaboration of the sitter." Mead, by contrast, assumes the easier task; she preserves the rights of others by refusing to probe or confess. Another of Nin's surprising suppressions, given her marriage and her friendship with Henry Miller, is the taboo about sensual experiences. "It was not in my nature to be explicit in sexual matters because for me they were welded to feeling, to love, to all other intimacies," she explained. Paradoxically, these very silences are meant to support the story's underlying psychological candor. "I had to act according to my own nature," she declares, "or else the diary itself would be destroyed." To disappointed readers and suspicious critics she offers this excuse: "The fact remained that there was so much richness of experience that the exclusions did not matter."

—Albert E. Stone, "Becoming a Woman in Male America: Margaret Mead and Anaïs Nin," *Autobiographical Occasions and Original Acts* (Philadelphia: University of Pennsylvania Press, 1982), 210–14

JOAN BOBBITT

Beginning with the publication of Volume One in 1966, the *Diary of Anaïs Nin* has inspired both popular admiration and critical effusion. Nin offers the story of her life as a celebration of subjectivity and feeling, a self-proclaimed paean to unfettered emotion. From all indications, she has been accepted at her word. Critics have called the multi-volume work "a continuous moment of intimacy" ⟨Zaller, *A Casebook on Anaïs Nin*, 1974, 133⟩, as well as "an attempt to give visible shape and embodiment to human love" ⟨Zaller, 110⟩. The author herself has been heralded as "the closest thing we have to Venus" ⟨Zaller, 152⟩ and "a high priestess in the House of Erotica" ⟨Zaller, 111⟩. Upon close examination, however, the *Diary* reveals a determined self-consciousness of design and content, a calculated artistry which is in direct opposition to Nin's espoused ideal of naturalness and spontaneity. ⟨. . .⟩

Several critics have observed this literary quality in Nin's diaries, noting in particular the similarity between her fiction and nonfiction. Anna Balakian's remark that "at times one has the feeling that the diary has literary structure as

much and even more than the novel" ⟨Zaller, 116⟩ is a typical response to this
similarity. Such recognition, however, rarely moves beyond the presence of
these literary devices to explore their reason for being. Though critics
acknowledge that they are remarkable, they generally credit these techniques
to coincidence rather than conscious plan. When Diane Wakoski comments
facetiously that "there are times reading Anaïs Nin's diaries when I think she
invented them and her whole life" ⟨Zaller, 148⟩, she is actually closer to the
truth. For in fact, the world of the diaries is a carefully contrived and beautifully synchronized artistic creation, a world fashioned and executed by Anaïs
Nin.

At the center of this world is the self Nin devises as persona, the divine
artificer who determines its laws. Duane Schneider argues persuasively that we
must recognize the character of Anaïs Nin "as the artist's conception of herself" ⟨Zaller, 50⟩. Though the diaries are ostensibly about the evolution of the
personality, its development through flux, the character which emerges is
remarkably static. While the first six diaries cover thirty-five years of her life,
Nin never ages. The description of the young woman of twenty-eight who
lives at Louveciennes is virtually indistinguishable from the mature woman of
sixty-three who rejoices over the publication of the very diary which chronicles that earlier period. ⟨. . .⟩

Granting the difficulty of finding an accurate label, the real question
seems to be one of artistic truthfulness, whether the substance of the *Diary* is
compatible with the ideal which Nin espouses. Is her work in fact what she
presents it as being? ⟨. . .⟩

In Nin's hands, the diary becomes an art form, with a structure and language "as exacting as other literary forms" ⟨Zaller, 9⟩. Not only does it resemble fiction, it *is* fiction.

That Nin consciously contrived the *Diary* as art should be beyond question. By her own admission, the *Diary* is a country over which she alone reigns.
When she is writing in it, she feels "joy at the realization that this is not a
sketchbook but a tapestry, a fresco being completed. She is not content to
record, but wants "to fill in, transform, project, expand, deepen . . . ." Nothing
less than "the ultimate flowering that comes of creation" will satisfy her. Yet
the *Diary* presents artistic problems as well. The mechanics for converting the
work into "a Joycean flow of inner consciousness" elude her. ⟨. . .⟩

The truth of art is not always the same as the truth of life, and Nin
promises the truth of life. She professes that sincerity is the very essence of her
diary: "I had put my most natural, most truthful writing in it." Commenting on
her method, she insisted that spontaneity and the preservation of authenticity
were her chief concerns ⟨*A Woman Speaks: The Lectures, Seminars, and Interviews of
Anaïs Nin*⟩. To achieve these ends, she found it necessary to record her impres-

sions at the moment. Memory itself was suspect because it "interfered and intercepted and distorted experience," rearranging and reordering in terms of the present. In several personal interviews, Nin goes so far as to deny having rewritten or polished, though evidence from the diaries themselves clearly proves the opposite ⟨A Woman Speaks⟩. ⟨. . .⟩

⟨. . .⟩ Though Nin assures us that she is "more interested in human beings than in writing, more interested in lovemaking than in writing, more interested in living than in writing," we actually learn very little about the things which are a basic part of any human life, much less a life based on openness and naturalness. Although she talks about psychological changes, nowhere does she tell her own feelings. Though she lauds physicality, the Diary is strangely devoid of sexuality. ⟨. . .⟩

This fact is immediately evident in Diary I where Nin appears as a grown woman without a past except for the stories which embellish the myth of her abandonment by a prodigal father. Near the end of the volume, Nin announces that she is pregnant, only several days before she is delivered of a stillborn daughter. The conception appears to have been miraculous for there is no mention of a husband or lover. Neither the physical nor psychological effects of the pregnancy are discussed, an equally inexplicable omission. Regardless of a woman's attitude toward her pregnancy, it is hardly a condition which can be overlooked. ⟨. . .⟩

⟨. . .⟩ Yet Nin's consistent refusal to discuss personal matters, indeed her suggestion that such concern is nothing more than jaded curiosity, would be understandable had she published any other kind of work. But she chose to publish her diary, a work which she celebrates for its frankness. In doing so, she tacitly consented to make her private life public. Consequently, critical interest in that life does not constitute a violation of privacy nor should it be construed as disrespect for those involved. That she should want to publish her personal diary itself raises some interesting psychological questions, but the primary consideration here is whether, in doing so Nin is a poseur, offering fabrication and evasion in the name of truth. ⟨. . .⟩

⟨. . .⟩ At the end of the diaries, however, the real Anaïs Nin remains elusive. Though she exalts openness, she excises from her work everything humanly important, everything that does not affirm her masks and personal fictions. While she offers her self, she presents only a metaphor of self. Ultimately, emotion is reduced to a mere artifact, and reality becomes indistinguishable from artistic creation.

—Joan Bobbitt, "Truth and Artistry in the Diary of Anais Nin," Journal of Modern Literature 9, no. 2 (1982): 267–72, 274–76

B I B L I O G R A P H Y

D. H. Lawrence: An Unprofessional Study. 1932.

House of Incest. 1936.

Winter of Artifice. 1939.

Under a Glass Bell. 1942.

This Hunger. 1945.

Ladders to Fire. 1946.

Realism and Reality. 1946.

Children of the Albatross. 1947.

On Writing. 1947.

The Four-Chambered Heart. 1950.

A Spy in the House of Love. 1954.

Solar Barque. 1958.

Cities of the Interior. 1959.

Seduction of the Minotaur. 1961.

Collages. 1964.

The Diary of Anaïs Nin. 1966–1980.

The Novel of the Future. 1968.

A Woman Speaks: The Lectures, Seminars, and Interviews of Anaïs Nin. 1975.

In Favor of the Sensitive Man, and Other Essays. 1976.

Delta of Venus: Erotica. 1977.

Waste of Timelessness and Other Early Stories. 1977.

Linotte: The Early Diary of Anaïs Nin. 1978.

Little Birds: Erotica. 1979.

The Early Diary of Anaïs Nin. 1982–1985.

The White Blackbird and Other Writings. 1985.

Henry and June: From the Unexpurgated Diary of Anaïs Nin. 1986.

A Literate Passion: Letters of Anaïs Nin and Henry Miller. 1987.

HEƧTER THRALE PIOZZI
1741–1821

HESTER LYNCH SALUSBURY was born in January 1741 to John Salusbury and Hester Maria Cotton, the first and only of their children to survive infancy. She was recognized as a precocious child and learned to read, write, and use language wittily at an early age. Early on her parents turned her ability to use by having her write letters to estranged wealthy relations. For a while this talent earned her the possible position of heir, first to Sir Robert Cotton, her mother's brother, and then Sir Thomas Salusbury, her father's brother. Thus she learned at a young age to use her speech and writing to garner approval, recognition, and economic well-being. Both these hopes were disappointed, however, and in 1763 she married Henry Thrale, brewer of Southwark, in order to make the financially secure liaison her mother had hoped for her. Ten years her senior, Henry Thrale was never her companion nor intellectual mate.

In 1766 soon after the birth of her first child, Hester met Samuel Johnson. He quickly became a friend and a frequent guest at her home. In fact, Johnson coined her daughter's nickname, Queeney, which she went by all her life. Also a precocious child, Queeney could speak well and repeat lessons by age two. Perhaps because of these accomplishments, Thrale decided to keep a book about her children's development. A unique document, *The Children's Book*, began as what we would now consider a "baby book"; it recorded her children's achievements, illnesses, and deaths. Thrale bore 12 children, several of whom died in infancy. Her favorite daughter Lucy died at four, and her son, Harry, at nine, after an illness of only a few hours. *The Children's Book* evolved into the *Family Book*, as it took on the characteristics of an intimate diary. This transformation seems to have been caused by the continuing crises and deaths of her mother and some of her children. After her mother's death, Thrale asked herself, and the diary, who else she could turn to for comfort and confidence.

In 1776, her husband gave her a set of six leather-bound blank books, each with a red label stamped in gold with the title *Thraliana* emblazoned into it. Thrale's writing in these volumes is essentially the first English *ana*. An *ana* was a French form in which the keeper recorded interesting anecdotes, favorite verses, observations, titles of interesting works, and any observation the writer felt should be written down. It was not meant to be a diary. Thrale's ana begins, indeed, with recording the remarks of Johnson encouraging her to keep such a record. Her volumes are full of Johnsoniana. She had previously recorded his comments on scraps of paper. She now transferred them into her new volumes. After Johnson's death she based her books on the record she had kept.

Thrale's ana does not remain a record of aphorisms, however. When she was midway through the third volume, her husband suffered his first stroke of palsy. Again, family losses deterred Thrale's attempts at keeping an "objective" record, this time of the wit and learning of her circle. After this, her writing took on the character of a diary, recording her responses to the crisis of her husband's ill health and death, and including intimate revelations about her growing affection for Gabriel Piozzi and her difficult relationships with her four surviving daughters.

In July of 1784, Hester Thrale married Piozzi and set out on a three-year tour of Europe. This marriage, which set all London talking, caused an irreparable break with her daughters and many friends. Johnson's letters, however, show that he could have accepted the marriage after first opposing it, but he died within a few months of Thrale Piozzi's departure. After arriving in Italy she began her public writing career, publishing two travel books, *Florence Miscellany* (1785) and *Observations and Reflections Made in the Course of a Journey through France, Italy and Germany*, 2 vols. (1789), and two books on Johnson. The first published after Johnson's death, *Anecdotes of the Late Samuel Johnson* (1786), was derived directly from the records she had kept in her *Thraliana*. For the second book, *Letters to and from the Late Samuel Johnson, LL.D*, Thrale Piozzi had to return to England to collect the letters she had left in her bank for safekeeping. She achieved quite a reputation with these two popular books. Her successes encouraged her to keep publishing.

During the French Revolution and the Napoleonic Wars, she collected many antirepublican pamphlets and wrote *The Three Warnings* (1792) and an anonymous political pamphlet entitled *Three Warnings to John Bull before He Dies—By an Old Acquaintance of the Public* (1798). In 1801 she published her last and least successful book, *Retrospection*, meant to be an anecdotal "Review of the Most Striking and Important Events, Characters, Situations and their Consequences, which the last Eighteen Hundred Years have Presented to the View of Mankind." But the book was misread and attacked for its casual format and for having gaps in its history.

The Piozzis settled in Wales, where Gabriel died in March 1809. Hester retired to Bath and died there in 1821, after throwing herself a huge 80th birthday party. Her *Thraliana* and most of her private writings remained in the family, who did not want them published, despite her wishes. But bits and pieces were published over the next century and began to be sold off in the 1920s. The *Thraliana* was bought by the Huntington Library and was first edited and published in its entirety in 1942. Her letters continue to be published in new collections.

CRITICAL   EXTRACTS

KATHERINE C. BALDERSTON

Mrs. Thrale ⟨. . .⟩, under the triple incentive of Dr. Johnson's belief in the value of saving the fragments of life, Mr. Thrale's indulgent expectation, and her own delight in the French anas, sat herself down to glean her wits, and to create what was almost, if not quite, the first English ana. The reader will discover how faithfully she followed her original intention through the first volume. It is a pot-pourri of curious bits, strung together without plan. The anecdotes relate indifferently to the dead and the living, the great and the unnamed obscure. They are sometimes culled from books, sometimes from life at second or third hand, and sometimes from her own experience, and are consequently of unequal interest and authenticity. She sometimes groups her stories under headings, such as 'Odd medical Stories', or under a common theme, such as stupidity or avarice, as did the French writers. Her interest in word derivations, her frequent citation of literary parallels, and the numerous translations of witty verses from foreign languages into her own—in each of which her mercurial wit delighted—are all to be found in Ménage, Scaliger, and others of her numerous models. ⟨. . .⟩

When she reached the second volume, she turned from scattering her energies to concentrate upon Dr. Johnson, and devoted the first ninety-seven pages to a recapitulation and expansion of the information she had already collected about him. This section, which is perhaps the most interesting and important part of her record, formed the chief basis for her later *Anecdotes of Johnson* (which she published after his death) ⟨. . . .⟩ When she had finished with Johnson in the *Thraliana*, she returned to her former unsystematic jottings, interrupting the unrelated flow only for a detailed account of her own life. But at a point about half-way through the third volume the character of her record underwent a change. Instead of remaining an ana, coloured here and there with the more intimate revelations of a diary, it became primarily a diary, only occasionally lapsing into her earlier manner. The reasons for this are not far to seek. In the first place, even Mrs. Thrale's well of anecdote was running dry. In the second, life for her suddenly became exigent, and remained so for a period of over five years. Mr. Thrale's first stroke of the palsy occurred on June 8, 1779, and its impact stirs the placid stream of the diary, for the first time, with the authentic shock of history recording itself. After that, momentous events and emotional conflicts thickened around her—her own dangerous miscarriage, Mr. Thrale's progressive illness and death, the pressing demands of the brewery and her financial troubles with Lady Salusbury, the torment of the public curiosity about her choice of a second husband, her growing and thwarted love for Mr. Piozzi, the struggle with Queeney and Fanny Burney, and her isolation and illness at Bath. The pressure of these events, and, above all, the compulsion she was under during the later part of this troubled period to keep her own counsel, made her turn to the *Thraliana* for the confidential outpourings of an overburdened mind and heart. This new character imposed itself upon her book, however, against her intention, almost against her will. On November 24, 1779, after Mr. Thrale's second seizure, she wrote: 'The Thraliana will be full of nothing but melancholy matters of Fact if we go on thus, I will write no more such things down if they do happen.' She did not keep to this resolution, but the remark shows clearly the bent of her preference. She distrusted by nature and training, and by virtue of a long tutelage to Johnson, the tendency to dwell on feelings, and to enhance miseries by rehearsing them, and she often turned deliberately, when she found herself indulging in those dubious luxuries, to an impersonal observation on her reading, or to a remembered witticism. This juxtaposition sometimes gives the effect of insensibility, or flippancy; it was, rather, a successful device for throwing off anxiety by resolutely placing her mind on other things. Even the intimate recordings come with a curious detachment and restraint, supervised, as it were, by her wary intellectual censor. In the one section of her diary where that censor frankly abdicates, where she pours out her frustrated love for the absent Piozzi, she seems, indeed, like an ordinary sentimental woman, carried away by emotion, and expressing it without restraint or distinction. ⟨. . .⟩

The dual character of the *Thraliana*, being at once a wit's catch-all in the true ana manner, and a private record of her life, accounts for Mrs. Thrale-Piozzi's vacillating attitude toward the desirability of preserving its privacy. Sometimes she wished for, almost took for granted, its eventual publication; at other times, when the intimate character of its revelations was uppermost in her mind, she felt a genuine horror at the thought that it might be seen even by a friend. ⟨. . .⟩ And in 1789, after speaking about the stir made in the world of art and letters by women, and the old idea that the pen was not for ladies' use, she suddenly exclaims, 'I wonder if my Executors will burn the

Thraliana!'—which seems to express a subconscious hope that, after her death and without her connivance, the *Thraliana* might be published, to enhance the growing reputation of her sex. On the other hand, she wrote in 1780: 'Stranger still that a Woman should write such a Book as this; put down every Occurrence of her Life, every Emotion of her Heart, & call it a *Thraliana* forsooth—but then I mean to destroy it.' This hesitancy to let it survive her was fortified by the increasing bitterness which she felt in her later years over the treatment the world had given her. In 1813, in a letter to John Salusbury Piozzi, her adopted heir, about the disposition she wished him to make of certain personal belongings after her death, she wrote: 'Thraliana should be hers [Cecilia Mostyn's]—or burned—but you may read it first, if t'will amuse You— only let it *Never* be printed! oh never, never *never*.' ⟨. . .⟩

Mrs. Thrale's wide and shifting circle of acquaintance, her powers of shrewd observation, her diverse interests and eclectic reading, offer valuable clues, in many directions, to those who seek to understand English life and culture in the years from 1776 to 1809. Mrs. Thrale after all was, herself, a person worth knowing. Her many-faceted personality, which had power to charm and enthral her contemporaries, still exerts its spell on us. And here, in the uninhibited pages of her diary, her personality finds full expression, in a style at once energetic, easy, precise, and colloquial. Even the parts of her record which are tedious—her vain inclusion of her own unimportant verses, in particular—contribute to the candid mirroring of her mind. ⟨. . .⟩

—Katherine C. Balderston, "Introduction," *Thraliana: The Diary of Mrs. Hester Lynch Thrale (later Mrs. Piozzi), 1776–1809*, (Oxford: Clarendon Press, 1942), xi–xii, xiv–xviii

JAMES L. CLIFFORD

Hester Lynch Salusbury, later the wife of Henry Thrale and Gabriel Piozzi, is remembered largely because of her close friendship with Samuel Johnson. For about eighteen years Johnson spent at least half his time living with the Thrales, and in her remarkable journals kept at this time—"The Children's Book, or Rather Family Book," recently edited by Mary Hyde, and in *Thraliana*, edited by Katharine Balderston in 1942—there is much valuable evidence about the great man. After her second marriage—to the Italian musician, Gabriel Piozzi—and Johnson's death in 1784, Mrs. Piozzi published a volume of anecdotes about him and an edition of his letters to her, as well as a delightful account of her travels on the Continent, and other books. These are what established her reputation as a bluestocking writer of the late eighteenth century.

In her later life she also turned into an avid daily diarist, regularly setting down each day some description of her social life and activities. This was normally written in small yearly pocket books, two of them in the series under the titles of *The Daily Journal* and *The Ladies Own Memorandum Book*, which allowed only about three-quarters of an inch for each day's entry. None of hers has ever been published because the subject matter is not very exciting and the friends she saw constantly were not important people. If only she had kept a detailed daily journal and account book during the 1760s and 1770s! Nevertheless, because a few of these later diaries are now at Columbia University it does appear worthwhile to sum up briefly what we know about their history and what they are like. ⟨. . .⟩

⟨. . . W⟩hen Piozzi's health began to deteriorate, they built a charming house called Brynbella in Flintshire, and largely divided their time between Bath and northern Wales. Her only daily diaries that have survived for these years are those of 1800 and 1802 (at Rylands). For some of these years her husband kept the daily accounts, briefly listing what they were doing, whom they saw, letters received, what food they were eating, and expenses. These were scrupulously kept, with few gaps, except occasionally when he came down with severe gout. But there is never anything witty or sardonic in the entries, and for twentieth-century readers they are deadly dull. Those that have survived are either at the National Library of Wales at Aberystwyth (1797, 1801 and 1802) or at Columbia (1803 and 1806).

It was not until about the time of Piozzi's death in 1809 that his wife took over the job of filling the annual pocket books with entries. From 1809 until her own death in 1821, in her 81st year, she rarely missed a day recording what she did. The entries reflect her ebullient spirit, and are more entertaining than those of her husband. For these thirteen years all but two of the yearly note books have survived ⟨. . . .⟩

Even though the people she was seeing all the time were not as well known to us as her friends during the Johnson period, skimming through Mrs. Piozzi's late diaries can be very entertaining. Her character and wit come through even in the brief entries. Every Monday she had to pay her bills, and depending on how much she paid she would write some descriptive adjective in large letters: "Grey," "Light Grey," "Very Dark," "Black," "Coal Black," or "Lily White." Sometimes she becomes explosive, as when she writes "Black Monday dreadful!" or "Grey, indeed, Black rather," or "Ocean roaring, People raving, H. L. P. paying away her money."

On Sunday she was fond of attending Laura Chapel in Bath, and there was almost always some lively comment on the sermon or the preacher, ranging from the highest praise, such as "Excellent," "Admirable," "Inimitable Grinfield" (the preacher), to such remarks as "a dull sermon," "a string of commonplaces saucily delivered," "a Preacher one could not hear," or "some Doctor drowsy I know not who."

The state of her own emotional involvement is clearly shown in the vary-ing size of the entries. ⟨. . .⟩

Generally her comments merely described what she did and whom she saw, but occasionally she could not resist inserting what somebody else said. Once she noted, "a droll Irish Lady laughed at us for regretting her, & said surely at 74 years old, one may take leave without an Apology." And Mrs. Piozzi clearly showed how she felt. Here are some samples: "Dinner at the Lutwiches—grand but dull," "I went but could not shine at all," "Sate at home sullen, & pouted for want of a Letter," "Visited every body—found no Body but Mrs. Glover and Mrs. George Mathew," "Went visiting and spitting Cards all Morning in a Chair." Her occasional boredom when in Wales showed: "No Newspapers, & no Company; no Books and no Conversation. Sun never shines." Once she noted: "a dull Morning—read old Chambers' Dictionary—could not bear to write or work—or any thing."

Once in a while she would jot down some of her purchases, such as cur-rent jelly, slops, and bath water. She even wondered if she was being too social. When Sir James Fellowes suggested as much, she noted: "I begin to be of his Mind—That I *do* see too much Company—they half distract me." ⟨. . .⟩

Despite all the trivia, reading Mrs. Piozzi's daily diaries can be fun. Moreover, for scholars interested in life at Bath in the second decade of the nineteenth century the experience can be very useful. In their own way these diaries have a genuine historical value.

—James L. Clifford, "The Daily Diaries of Hester Lynch Piozzi," *Columbia Library Columns* 22, no. 3 (1978): 10, 12, 14, 17

EDWARD A. BLOOM, LILLIAN D. BLOOM, JOAN E. KLINGEL

Often too quick to take offence, Mrs. Piozzi never suffered from an excess of humility. Even in admitting mistaken judgements, she rarely denigrated her-self. At the same time that she wrote her letters, she appraised their worth as literary and historical documents, as testimonials of an unrewarded virtue, that cried out—she assumed—for preservation and publication. Writing to John Salusbury on 17 March 1811, she optimistically prophesies, "When the black, deep, dividing Gulph is pass'd by your poor Aunt, you will consider these Pages as her Shadows; and prize them accordingly—not for their Wit, because the Head that has nothing better than Wit in it, is scarce worth a Stroke from a French Guillotine: but for the Heart which dictates every Line. . . ."

Strong-minded and insistent always, she nevertheless suffered frustration in this desire, and in others as well. The relatively few letters that have been printed are either fragmented, viciously bowdlerized, or edited in hit-and-run fashion. We have only to examine those to Samuel Lysons printed in *Bentley's Miscellany* in 1850, or the ninety-four to Edward Mangin—bits and pieces published as *Piozziana* (1833). The important letters to Mrs. Pennington—important because they are personal and singularly feminine—signal the brutality visited upon Mrs. Piozzi's correspondence. These were edited by Oswald G. Knapp in 1914. Some of the most candid, more than forty, were ignored; the remainder purified by ellipses and confused editorial commentary which can suddenly and irrelevantly appear in the middle of a letter. ⟨. . .⟩

The personality of H. L. P. may forever escape full comprehension. It seems to us, however, that her letters, selected, dovetailed, and verified by editorial apparatus, confirm the seeming polarities of her nature. They lay bare a woman's psychology, as does *Thraliana*, but they go beyond her diary in time, in intellectual and spiritual scope; the external woman is as real as the hidden psyche. The letters, then, prove an anger disciplined by reason, an intelligence, an awareness of self and the world about her that has too often been dismissed. Indeed, only her letters can justify her right to literary immortality. ⟨. . .⟩

Between 1784 and 1821 she wrote more than two thousand letters; their precise number cannot be determined. Obviously not all of them can be important or reveal literary excellence. To intersperse the incidental with the substantive in the name of completeness would simply vitiate her eagerness to dramatize a life narrative that she deemed exciting and a good read; we would even thwart her desire to be part of a literary tradition. Those letters, which she meant to be preserved in print, place her squarely in the splendid epistolary heritage of the eighteenth century, along with Lady Mary Wortley Montagu, Lord Chesterfield, Edmund Burke, Horace Walpole and Fanny Burney. Not only do her letters have quality in and of themselves, but they provide, as Professor Clifford points out, "an enduring record of people and events, a kaleidoscopic picture of the age in which she lives. This is her chief claim to remembrance; this her value to the social historian of to-day". ⟨. . .⟩

Clearly she intended a selected body of letters to function as an autobiography, a prolonged chat during which she talked about herself, her family and friends. Anyone who knew her kindled to her delight in bright conversation. ⟨. . .⟩

Moreover, ⟨H. L. P.⟩ visualized her correspondence as documents, colloquial, informative, and admittedly biased, that would capture anyone interested in the events of George III's reign and the Regency: the threat—as she saw it—of the French Revolution and Napoleon's adventures in conquest, the difficulties of maintaining a landed estate in North Wales during periods of depression and political unrest, the state of medicine in her time, the excitement of travel on the Continent and in Great Britain, the intrigues of holding salon-court from Streatham to Bath and places between.

Because she thought of her letters in this dual role, we have to face an inevitable question. How reliable, in literal fact, are they? The answer is not long in coming. When she writes of immediate incidents, soon after they occur, she is accurate in her reporting despite some blur of egocentricity and prejudice. What preserves these accounts from distortion is the very openness of her self-interest and bias. When, on the other hand, she indulges in recollection, she is honest enough in setting down the broad outlines of these earlier experiences. But the great men who played their part in them did not always speak as she remembered the dialogue. It is usually witty dialogue, quite trenchant, but as often as not, it is her aphorism or *mot*, her one-liner with only the flavour of the original speaker. ⟨. . .⟩

If ⟨H. L. P.⟩ seemed to favour one epistolary method over another, she never reined her curiosity or willingness to write on any and all subjects. Her letters, then, become a fascinating autobiographical record, as compelling as any work of realistic fiction told by a fairly reliable first-person narrator. She took pleasure in writing about herself: her birth into an ancient and genteel family, her learning, her two marriages. In response to the *Monthly Mirror's* request for a biographical statement, she tried for modesty and succeeded because she held to facts without overt editorial commentary. At the same time she chose the facts carefully, stressing her social conservatism, her intelligence, and her desirability as a woman. She played many roles, especially those that suggested obedience and defiance, intellectuality and passionate femininity. ⟨. . .⟩

We see her relationship with her daughters: their continual sniping at one another, their enduring correspondence, their presence at her deathbed with her hand reaching out to each of them. It is a portrait that presents her as a woman who can face the world down and as one with glaring weaknesses. She is a lion-hunter ready to exploit the lion and yet able to tear into the person in the leonine skin—Sir Joshua Reynolds, Mrs. Montagu, even Dr. Johnson, for example. Mrs. Piozzi was a professional writer who detested reviewers and even those who offered constructive criticism. She was a wit, whose venom was aimed at children, at "enemies" listed in numerical order, and friends.

Her letters provide us with a laminated understanding of the person, one layer biographical, the other social. We realize that she is a strong *individual*, who took what life offered; and what it offered was sometimes bitter. She was not above terror, but she learned to accept it with calm, accepting its inevitability.

—Edward A. Bloom, Lillian D. Bloom, Joan E. Klingel, "Portrait of a Georgian Lady," *Bulletin of the John Rylands University Library of Manchester* 60 (1978): 305, 310, 312, 314, 330, 338

MARTINE WATSON BROWNLEY

Despite his influence on Hester Lynch Piozzi the professional author, Johnson definitely did not create Hester Lynch Salusbury Thrale the writer. From childhood she had been an incessant scribbler. ⟨. . .⟩ Her anecdotes indicate that the quick wit and verbal prowess which characterized her throughout her life appeared early, and writing was a natural outlet for such abilities. However, her intellectual powers were not exercised simply for their own sake. Her parents' marriage, as she depicts it, was a stormy one; one of the consequences was that her mother "had nursed up her Infant Daughter . . . to play a thousand pretty Tricks, & tell a Thousand pretty Stories and repeat a Thousand pretty Verses to divert Papa". Her irascible father was pleased, and the lesson was clear: "Nature pleads her own Cause most powerfully when a little Art is likewise used to help it forward. I therefore grew a great favourite it seems." It was a lesson which Hester Lynch Salusbury never forgot, whether as Mrs. Thrale or Mrs. Piozzi. Her writing, like her intellectual abilities, was quickly put to use to please other people. ⟨. . .⟩

⟨. . .⟩ the basic reason that only Mrs. Piozzi printed is that not until after Johnson's death did she have the opportunity she needed to establish herself as a professional author. From childhood, her eagerness to write and to show off her writing to the widest audience possible had been clear. In life and in death it was Johnson who finally enabled her to fulfil these ambitions.

In life Johnson's friendship gave her ample materials for a biography; the circumstances surrounding his death made her especially eager to go into print. Probably because of early family instabilities, reinforced after marriage by her alienation from her husband and children, she always remained insecure about her relationships with others and enormously concerned about their opinions of her. In *Thraliana*, for example, she continually gauges how much various associates really care for her. Her characteristic response to these anxieties was to do everything she could to placate others. In 1794 she wearily wrote in her diary: "Life has been to me nothing but a perpetual *Canvass* carried on in all parts of the World—not to make *Friends* neither—for I have certainly found very few—but to keep off *Enemies*." By the time Johnson died, she had felt acutely both the displeasure of former friends and general public disapproval. Her second marriage had outraged society, in part because Johnson's objections to it had ended his friendship with the new Mrs. Piozzi. Their mutual friends blamed her for what they considered her heartless abandonment of a dying man, some claiming that her actions had hastened his end. Abroad on an idyllic honeymoon, she recognized that if her relationship with Johnson had contributed to massive public disapproval of her, it had also provided the means to approach that same public. ⟨. . .⟩

Although many of her contemporaries were outraged by what they considered the "vulgarism" of her relaxed and natural style, to modern readers the conversational elements provide part of the charm of her writings, as long as she employs them consistently. When she occasionally cannot resist inserting Johnsonian phrases, her style is marred by the mixture of two antithetical modes. This stylistic unevenness, apparent in all her writings, is one indication of her inability to break free entirely from Johnson's influence, despite her knowledge that her literary strengths lay in another direction. Similarly, she failed to recognize that the generalizations superbly sustained by Johnson's manner and matter simply weighted down her own lighter work. Both she and Johnson were didactic, but only Johnson was in addition genuinely philosophical. She makes few general remarks in the *Anecdotes*, but in the *Observations and Reflections* their proportion begins to rise significantly, diluting the effects produced by her own literary skills. The "observations," fresh, vivid depictions of scenes and experiences, are usually entertaining and valuable; her "reflections," on the other hand, are too often obvious, gratuitous, and overlong. ⟨. . .⟩

Although the *Anecdotes* have long pleased Johnsonians and the *Observations and Reflections* is an entertaining example of its genre, ⟨Mrs. Piozzi's⟩ lasting literary fame is due to her diaries and letters. In both genres Johnson was a vital influence. Like her other literary abilities, her talents as a letter writer had been recognized early, and in this instance the appreciation she received seems to have been fully justified. Johnson again provided reinforcement, begging her for letters and lavishly praising them. "When you read my letters," he wrote to her, "I suppose you are very proud to think how much you excel in the correspondence". She wrote to him constantly because "it is so exceedingly pleasing to have any one care whether one writes or no" ⟨*Letters*⟩. Similarly, although as a girl she had kept at least one journal, Johnson played a major role in fostering the great diaries which captured for posterity several eras of social history and a fascinating circle of personalities. Her *Family Book*, the first of her major diaries, was begun mainly because of his influence; she opened *Thraliana*, her greatest journal, with his admonition to her to keep a diary. He advised her on how to write it and told her that it would interest posterity. When she hesitated to begin the sixth volume, she decided to continue because "Johnson said that Pleasure might one day be made from such Nonsense, so I'll e'en finish this *last* Volume of Anecdote & store up no more Stuff" (ii. 840). She, of course, did no such thing; Johnson had helped to assure that keeping journals would be a lifelong habit.

⟨. . .⟩ As Mrs. Thrale and Mrs. Piozzi, in her journals and her letters she could show her best self as she wrote. These genres highlighted her abilities— her keen observation of the actual, her wide curiosity and varied interests, her colloquial wit and liveliness, her skill in tailoring tone and content to her audience. They did not demand skills she lacked—the capacity for sustained thought, narrative development and organization, and condensation of expression. If the shadow of Johnson created problems in her books, it is only fair to remember that he also played a central role in encouraging her in the forms in which, totally at ease, she could be liberated from his influence in a way that she could never be in her published works.

—Martine Watson Brownley, "Samuel Johnson and the Printing Career of Hester Lynch Piozzi," *Bulletin of the John Rylands University Library of Manchester* 67, no. 2 (Spring 1985): 623–25, 630–31, 635, 638–40

WILLIAM MCCARTHY

That some women wrote and published in England in the eighteenth century is not news; it has been more or less continuously known ever since they did it. The extent to which women published, however, the sheer number of publishing women, is only beginning to be appreciated now. Here are some suggestive data on the subject. 1. A new *Dictionary of British and American Women Writers, 1660–1800* lists 108 British women writers who published between about 1650 and 1760; for the period 1760 to 1810—the half century of Piozzi's career—it lists 209, or almost double the first number in a period only half as long. 2. A bibliographical recovery project now in progress has counted between 450 and 500 British women writers for the period 1660–1800. This is already more than are listed in the *Dictionary*, and the project is by no means complete; one of the scholars working on it, Sarah English, has estimated that the final number may be 2,000. ⟨. . .⟩

Freud somewhere identifies one form of repression as a form in which the event itself is remembered but its affect is no longer felt. The event seems therefore to have no particular meaning; it and its significance are dissociated. I believe that this form of repression can be seen quite clearly in the history at least of Piozzi commentary, and that it can be inferred from that commentary to have operated on the memory of other early women writers as well. Indeed, it began operating at the time of the events, in reviewers' responses to—or rather, denials of—the women writers' works.

From contemporary descriptions of their practice, as well as from specimens of their reviews, it appears that the reviewers' customary defense against women's writing was a style of lofty banter and genteel belittlement. It is a style which says, "I do not take you seriously; you are a lower order of being, and no threat to me." ⟨. . .⟩

⟨. . .⟩ Ever since her death, as we have noticed, writings by her have been reprinted or newly published: a Piozzi canon has been forming. Editors, publishers and reviewers have all declared by their actions that Piozzi is a writer. But not by their words. I offer herewith a sampling of their words:

"Mrs. Piozzi can never be forgotten . . . were it only because her name is closely connected with that of Johnson, whose reputation will endure as long as the language . . . he adorned" (Edward Mangin, 1833 [4–5], introducing his collection of her letters and poems, few or none of which refer to Johnson). "If she had but died while she was mistress of Streatham, we should have only delightful recollections of her. She would have been one of the most agreeable famous women on record" (Charles Eliot Norton, 1861 [615], introducing an unpublished autobiography by Piozzi, a piece written long after her Streatham years and which, therefore, would not have existed for him to introduce had she died according to his wish). "She appears simply as a cleverish woman . . . full of a pert garrulity that might as well have been shrouded in oblivion at this time of day, however naturally it may once have sat on a Tory, an heiress, and a bluestocking. . . . It is from Dr. Johnson that she derives her celebrity" (the *National Review*, 1861 [377], reviewing—at some length— Hayward's collection of her writings). "As . . . the friend of Johnson . . . [she] will never cease to retain a certain kind of interest . . . though she was herself, with all her wit and learning, a weak, fickle, foolish creature" (*The Athenaeum*, 1862 [169], introducing her letters not to Johnson, but to William Augustus Conway). "As a hostess, and it is in that capacity that Mrs. Piozzi's name will last in our literary history, she was singularly gifted" (J. H. Lobban, 1910 [xxxi], introducing his abridgement of Hayward's collection of her writings). This last specimen surely represents the reductio ad absurdam of the technique, a dissociation so severe that it sees no incongruity in asserting that she counts, in *literary* history, as a hostess. ⟨. . .⟩

I close this survey with two recent samples. The first is from a 1970 essay by Patricia M. Spacks that examines in considerable detail a late Piozzi manuscript notebook. Spacks has written several times on Piozzi; it is therefore a surprise to find her not knowing what to call Piozzi and knowing only what *not* to call her: "Whatever Mrs. Piozzi was . . . she was no poet" (227); "her moments of strong writing seem accidental; she hardly knows what is interesting in her material" (247). On this point it is hard to tell the difference between Spacks, ostensibly a feminist critic, and William K. Wimsatt, who in 1974 delivered this estimate of Piozzi: "She wrote . . . chattery, middling books. . . . What we encounter [in *Anecdotes of Johnson*] is grotesque, even shocking. We encounter Mrs. Thrale-Piozzi . . . trying to catch her impressions and recollections in a deliberate tissue of words—Mrs. Piozzi in short trying to be a writer" (364).

"Trying to be a writer"; "whatever [she] was . . . she was no poet." It is as if the male reviewers in 1794 are still writing, an uncanny effect. We seem to have come full circle; but no, for we never moved from our first position. The rhetorical ploys by which the first reviewers defended themselves against women writers when the women were living remain the ploys by which those women's writings continued to be excluded from Literature. Things that one would not have dared say about Jane Austen or Emily Bronte—or about less known nineteenth-century women writers—could still be said as recently as twelve years ago with impunity about the women writers of the first great wave, the eighteenth-century foremothers of them all. The effect, at least until quite recently, has been to foreshorten canonical literary history, to move forward into the nineteenth century events that really occurred in the eighteenth. Women writers are now canonical, but the originating moment, like a traumatic event, has remained unconscious. ⟨. . .⟩

There would thus appear to have been a downward spiral in the standing of the early women writers, a spiral that perhaps coincided with the rise of professionalism in the study of literature. The first gatekeepers of literature were the reviewers, and although they could bedevil the career of a woman writer they could not usually prevent her work from being read. But as their gatekeeping function devolved gradually onto the Academy, and as literature came to be regarded with "high seriousness" as the monument of the past and an object of formal study, the denigration of the early women writers as "amateurs" or "bright school children" did finally prevent their work from being read. One by one, those writers dropped out of print. The last English edition of More's collected works appeared in 1853; Piozzi's "Three Warnings," a staple anthology piece from its first publication, made its last appearance in 1883. ⟨. . .⟩

Happily, however, this state of affairs is now becoming history. The present generation of feminist literary scholars, whose work is embodied in such basic research tools as the Todd *Dictionary*, is asserting the real historic importance of early women's writing, collecting the bibliographical data that demonstrate its range and extent, citing, quoting, and reprinting its texts, and making them at last canonical. The names of those writers—Finch, Astell, Lennox, Barbauld, More, Piozzi—are entering our discourse; passages from their writings, including some of those I have quoted in this essay, are becoming *loci classici*. And the demand is rising that they be taught in courses, alongside the texts of Pope and Johnson and Burke. ⟨. . .⟩

—William McCarthy, "The Repression of Hester Lynch Piozzi; or, How We Forgot a Revolution in Authorship," *Modern Language Studies* 18, no. 1 (1988): 101, 104–9

FELICITY A. NUSSBAUM

For Hester Thrale, private—even secret—writing becomes an end in itself as she describes her various positionings as wife, mother, intellectual, writer, tradeswoman, and election campaigner, as well as hostess and confidante to Samuel Johnson. The narrative experiments and the commonplace content she adopts do not fit predictable textual strategies or tropes such as the fallen woman, the rebellious child, the spiritual heroine, the familial myth of separation and reunion, or independence accepted and rewarded. Thrale regularly rewrote the subjectivity that was too diffuse to confine to one version, often repeating the same incident, with variations, in sequential accounts to represent her own identity as defying easy categorization. Thrale's autobiographical writings set her firmly within the ideologies of gender, genre, and class; yet like women's spiritual autobiographies and the scandalous memoirs, they also make available an oppositional space.

⟨. . .⟩ Throughout her life she simultaneously kept voluminous private journals and notes that were not published in her lifetime. ⟨. . .⟩ From 1776 until 1809 she regularly made entries in a multivolumed diary of anecdotes, personal history, and noteworthy stories. These various notebooks afforded a safe secret place to accumulate the commonplaces of her life, a record of her subjectivity, and the thoughts and events that gave "meaning" to her existence. Of special interest here are *Thraliana*, among the very first English ana, and the "Family Book," the original and unusual document that records the details of her children's early lives. All this material offers a textual ground for the contest over the privatizing of "woman," the production of a consciousness formed at the behest of men, and the questioning of the generic limitations inherent in such autobiographical activities.

In addition, within these texts Hester Thrale rehearses with conviction the conventional expectations of women. The female tradition of private writing, the verbatim transcription of wise sayings from Johnson and other "great men," and the burgeoning publication of medical and educational works directed at mothers make up some of the diverse and discrepant discourses that Thrale adopts to define her own experience. ⟨. . .⟩

The "Family Book," first published in 1976, is extraordinary and original, and the editor Mary Hyde writes of it, "Since the undertaking was so unusual, one wonders how the idea came to Mrs. Thrale" ("Family," vii). Hyde accounts for it through Johnson's influence, Queeney's precocity, and Mrs. Thrale's inexplicable predilection for diary keeping. Thrale's journals are less expressive of her self or of a female voice than an intersection of discourses about "woman," especially "mother" and "wife," that are effective in reproducing class and gender divisions. Thrale's "Family Book" shows the ways that education through the mother is a process that instills culture, makes it intelligible, and imbues the children with class ideology—a crucial task that is both idealized and denigrated within the discourses of the period. Thrale regulates herself and her children within recognizable categories of identity, but she also finds her way in a new genre to record a "mother's" private subjectivity as well as contribute to an emergent genre, the "ana," as she forwards new hierarchies that value woman's domestic and reproductive labor. To the extent that she possesses a whole and unified identity, Thrale defines herself as mother and daughter, as producer, educator, and sustainer of children. ⟨. . .⟩

At other times Hester Thrale remarks that her brand of diary keeping is an unprecedented oddity: "that a Woman should write such a Book as this; put down every Occurrence of her Life, every Emotion of her Heart, & call it a *Thraliana* forsooth—but then I mean to destroy it" (which, of course, she did not do) (*Thraliana*, 464). 〈. . .〉 Occasionally she dismisses what she writes as mere trash, nonsense, or trifles—a view she cannot reconcile with her devotion to the task: "But when the last [volume] comes as near to ending as this now does—my fingers will shake lest I should be near ending as well as my Book. [M]y heart tells me that he [Henry Thrale, her husband] said something when he presented me with the Volumes, as if—I don't know as if: but this I know, that fifteen Years have elapsed since I first made the *Thraliana* my Confident, my solitary Comfort, and Depositary of every Thought as it arose." She characterizes the volumes as "poor foolish wild—confused," the keeping of anas "a silly desire." Several times she indicates that they are "a good Repository" for her "Nonsense." Failing to find satisfying precedents for her manner of writing, she lacks confidence in her achievement. 〈. . .〉

As a writing woman, Thrale replicates her second-sphere status and reflects the prevailing definitions of the female. Her diaries do not so much "express" the essential female voice as they reinscribe the heterosexual division that the culture required to reproduce itself. By containing the imagined alternatives within the private sphere, Thrale sets up a cycle of self reading self, of woman reading woman, of complicity in restraining female transgression. She offers us a paradigmatic instance of the failure of a new paradigm—a woman's account of her family life—to prevail in the public domain. In short, she succeeds in reproducing a bourgeois gendered subject, a woman who manages and is managed.

But the "Family Book" and *Thraliana* also contest cultural assumptions about women's identity. Located in asymmetrical positions as a privileged upper bourgeoise but also a characterless and contradictory "woman," Thrale's tangle of subjectivities at one level embraces oppression as it repels it at another. Though she writes privately, Thrale thinks of her work within the female journal-writing tradition; she opens a space, albeit a private one, for a collective female subjectivity in writing the new genres of the "Family Book" and *Thraliana*. In addition, Thrale's writing offers an alternative organization to the dominant values. Both the "Family Book" and *Thraliana* put the "important" next to the "unimportant" without assigning relative value, thus suggesting that each insertion is equal to the next. In fact, we may argue that the texts place bits and pieces together as if they held equal power and rank in order to interrogate the usual assignment of value to them. For Thrale, and perhaps for other eighteenth-century women, diaries and journals are a commonplace to hold together the commonplaces of female experiences, even those judged trivial by the cultural hegemony, and to grant them parity with those given

higher value by the culture. If some of the bits and pieces seem significant to
the larger culture (such as Johnson's witty sayings), their removal to private
text to be placed alongside the newly valued daily lived experience holds the
disarming potential to force their reevaluation, though her resistance stops
short of explicitly criticizing that which constrains her.

—Felicity A. Nussbaum, "Managing Women: Thrale's 'Family Book' and *Thraliana*," *The
Autobiographical Subject: Gender and Ideology in Eighteenth Century England* (Baltimore: Johns
Hopkins University Press, 1989), 203–5, 213, 218–9, 222

JANICE THADDEUS

⟨. . . In 1783 Hester Lynch Piozzi renounced Gabriel⟩ Piozzi so forcefully he
returned to Italy, but she was so miserable that she called him back. She com-
plained then that she had always acted only so as to please others, and that
such passivity lacked dignity. William McCarthy remarks that this
"epiphany"—for all its power and lucidity—was not really representative of
H. L. P.'s point of view, that she did not consistently recognize that the social
values of her society repressed her dignity. ⟨*Hester Thrale Piozzi* (Chapel Hill:
University of North Carolina, 1985), 37⟩ Thus, although H. L. P. on occasion
deliberately offended against good breeding, she did not systematically revolt.
She knew what it was to be well-bred; without even being aware of her internalized strictures, she attempted to behave as her mother and her society had
taught her. If she did not show her feelings, this did not mean she was cold or
dispassionate. Intensity of feeling was her personal forte, but she always held
back something. As ⟨Philippe⟩ Ariès argues, the shift that occurred in the eighteenth century was not in the *amount* of affection, but in its "quality, intensity,
and objects." ⟨*The Hour of Our Death* (New York: Vintage, 1982), 472⟩ ⟨. . .⟩

Both Hester Lynch Piozzi and Frances Burney d'Arblay wrote about the
daily, exhausting sorrow of caring for their dying husbands, experiencing the
woman's clotted intensity of feeling at this domestic moment; but their ways
of expressing themselves about this fearful experience were different not only
from men's expressions of grief, but also from one another's. Part of the expla-
nation for this second difference lies in H. L. P.'s and Burney's divergent—even
antipathetic—personalities. More importantly, the fact that H. L. P. was
eleven years older than Burney meant that the two women balanced on either
side of that great shift in feeling and in family relationships, the romantic indi-
vidualism that historians are at the moment so disputatiously defining.
Though this shift was underway by 1776 when Harry Thrale died, the old-
fashioned Thrales rushed to Bath, thus incurring the indignation of G. B. Hill.

Besides the general shift in the "quality, intensity, and objects of affection,"
Ariès notes a more specific eighteenth-century shift in attitudes toward death.

Death, once a public and didactic scene, has become a private and emotional event, and in the second half of the century, there is a

> desire for simplicity in the things connected with death. At first, this desire expresses, but with more conviction than in the past, the traditional belief in the fragility of life and the corruption of the body. Later, it reveals an anxious sense of nothingness, which finds no solace in hope of the beyond, although this hope continues to be expressed. ⟨The Hour of Our Death⟩

H. L. P. expressed the traditional religious belief; Burney revealed the anxious sense of nothingness. ⟨. . .⟩

In H. L. P.'s case, the suppression of grief seems to have erupted in the apprehension that she would lose her other children. She fell into near-hysteria whenever one of them had a headache, for fear if would develop into a mastoid infection like the one that killed her favorite child, Lucy. The echo of her grief drove her wild.

Since the distractions of the business world were not available, H. L. P. used a variety of rituals to control grief and potential grief. Some were rather usual, then and now, and require no particular comment. As one might expect, she was always searching out new friendships among both men and women, and she lost herself in reading (though not always novels). She indulged the tendency Ariès has noted in the eighteenth century to emphasize "the fragility of life and the corruption of the body." She tended to anticipate death, and in her poems and autobiographical writings to name death clearly and frequently so as to render it familiar and manageable. Another technique was to write full and agonizing descriptions of the body in pain, descriptions of a type rarely found in any of the acceptable kinds of discourse of the period. ⟨. . .⟩

The lives of H. L. P. and Burney, then, reflect a changing concept of grief, a redistribution of emotional attachments, an increasing concentration on individuals, irreplaceable and unique. That they were women adds another complexity to this change. As Nancy Armstrong has argued, for women the changes that Ariès discusses hinge largely on another great shift. The new domestic woman who appeared in the novel and in life at the end of the eighteenth century represented the replacement for the woman who was defined by her birth, title, and status. Her position as representative of the family meant that she was determined by her emotional qualities. H. L. P. fashioned herself in the old tradition, calling both of her husbands "Master."

—Janice Thaddeus, "Hoards of Sorrow: Hester Lynch Piozzi, Frances Burney d'Arblay, and Intimate Death," *Eighteenth Century Life* 14, no. 3 (1991): 112, 114–15, 125

B I B L I O G R A P H Y

Florence Miscellany. 1785.

Observations and Reflections Made in the Course of a Journey through France, Italy and Germany, 2 vols. 1789.

Anecdotes of the Late Samuel Johnson. 1786.

Letters to and from the Late Samuel Johnson, LL.D. Ed. by Hester Lynch Piozzi. 1788.

The Three Warnings. 1792.

Three Warnings to John Bull before He Dies. By an Old Acquaintance of the Public (1798).

Retrospection. 1801.

Autobiography, Letters and Literary Remains of Mrs. Piozzi (Thrale). Ed. by A. Hayward. 1861.

The Queeney Letters: Being Letters Addressed to Hester Maria Thrale by Dr. Johnson, Fanny Burney, and Mrs. Thrale-Piozzi. Ed. the Marquis of Lansdowne. 1934.

Thraliana, the Diary of Mrs Hester Lynch Thrale (later Mrs. Piozzi) 1776–1809. Ed. by Katherine C. Balderston. 1951.

The Thrales of Streatham Park (which includes the complete *The Children's Book, or rather Family Book* by H. L. T. Piozzi). Ed. by Mary Hyde. 1977.

Mrs Piozzi's Tall Young Beau: William Augustus Conway (including Piozzi's letters to Conway). Ed. by John Tearle. 1991.

The Piozzi Letters: Correspondence of Hester Lynch Piozzi, 1784–1821 (Formerly Mrs. Thrale), I: 1784–1791. Ed. by Edward A. Bloom and Lillian D. Bloom. 1989.

The Piozzi Letters: Correspondence of Hester Lynch Piozzi, 1784–1821 (Formerly Mrs. Thrale), II: 1792–1798. Ed. by Edward A. Bloom and Lillian D. Bloom. 1991.

The Piozzi Letters: Correspondence of Hester Lynch Piozzi, 1784–1821 (Formerly Mrs. Thrale), III: 1799–1804. Ed. by Edward A. Bloom and Lillian D. Bloom. 1993.

MAY SARTON
1912–1995

ELEANORE MARIE SARTON was born on May 3, 1912, in Wondelgem, Belgium. She memorialized the Edenic location of her birth and early childhood in her first memoir, *I Knew a Phoenix* (1959). In a forerunner to this, a piece entitled "Autobiography of Moods," written at age 16, she explains that her "sober" name was replaced with May, "the month of gladness." Her father, George Sarton, was an intellectual and scholar who became a professor of the history of science at Harvard after the family emigrated in 1916. Her mother, Mabel Eleanor Elwes, was a painter and furniture designer. Following the expectations of her parents, Sarton was a highly successful student at Cambridge High and Latin, winning several awards her senior year. She did not, however, enter Vassar as had been planned, but rather joined the acting company of Eva Le Gallienne. She remained with this group, the Civic Repertory Theater, until 1933 and then formed her own troupe, the Apprentice Theater, which survived for three seasons. Throughout this period of her life, Sarton was also reading extensively—French and Russian novels, English Romantic poets, Virginia Woolf, D. H. Lawrence, and Katherine Mansfield.

Throughout the 1930s, and through much of her life, Sarton spent long summers in Europe. There she met Virginia Woolf, Elizabeth Bowen, and Vita Sackville-West. It was during this time that Sarton resolved to be a poet, and her first collection of poetry, *Encounter in April*, was published in 1937. Her first novel, *The Single Hound*, followed the next year. By 1940 her work was popular enough for her to begin annual lecture and poetry-reading tours. Also in 1940 she began her correspondence with Louise Bogan, poetry critic for the *New Yorker*. Although they did not meet until 1953, their extensive letters discussing poetry and its critical reception had already established their friendship.

By the time she published her first memoir in 1959, Sarton had published six collections of poetry and six novels, along with a couple of plays. She continued to write in all these forms and began publishing her journals in 1973. These are not journals written over a lifetime and then compiled for publication, but rather journals specifically written over short periods of about a year. The first, *Journal of a Solitude* (1973), was written to help her overcome the depression caused by the end of a love affair. The journals, as opposed to the memoirs, are for confronting and shaping the present. They are, Sarton writes in *At*

Seventy (1984), "to record a mood as it comes, as exactly as possible, knowing that life is flux and that the mood must change." The journals record her daily life, the weather, the music she listened to, and her thoughts on the writing process and the different forms writing can take. Sometimes she writes about the process she is immediately engaged in and sometimes about other writing she is working on. She contemplates the nature of poetry and the poet. She confronts her own illness and mastectomy and contemplates its meaning.

Journal, according to Carolyn Heilbrun is a "watershed in women's autobiography." It details women's anger and pain as well as women's relationships in new and honest ways. In 1965, with the publication of *Mrs. Stevens Hears the Mermaids Singing*, Sarton confirmed her homosexuality. She also talked about her sexuality and women's lives in her journal *Recovering* and in numerous interviews.

May Sarton died in 1995, just after completing her eighty-second year and her last journal *At Eighty-Two*. This last work differs from the rest in that Sarton reread it and annotated it before sending it to the publisher, thereby melding the forms of memoir and journal for the first time. It adds depth and contrast to the body of work of this prolific and flexible writer.

CRITICAL EXTRACTS

SUZANNE OWENS

Sarton's 'private' writing offers a continuity of form and idea that clearly deserves consideration as literary art apart from its relationship to her substantial body of fictional prose and poetry. It is particularly evident in two subjects which inform her memoirs and journals: the creation-recreation of "home" and the nature of solitude. As literary explorations, the Sarton journals and memoirs record a life-philosophy working out through daily experience filtered through a particularly sensitive and attuned consciousness. ⟨. . .⟩

For Sarton, events remembered in *I Knew a Phoenix* (1959) take on a certain legendary quality through memory, particularly as she recalls scenes from childhood. It is in this volume that we begin to read of her intense identification with houses as homes and as constructs of remembered family life. ⟨. . .⟩

The sketches of *I Knew a Phoenix* move freely between the very distant past (her parents' lives) and her childhood, each chapter reading as a portrait of one person or of an event. *Plant Dreaming Deep* (1968) is a sequential narrative-memoir of Sarton's move to rural New Hampshire and of particular interest to the later journals for the development of the central presence of the house as character. We immediately recognize that "home" and "house" are, naturally, metaphors of particular importance to Sarton's life as an artist, thus continuing a thread from the sketches. ⟨. . .⟩

As a memoir of that first year in Nelson, *Plant Dreaming Deep* details the typical daily chores and responsibilities Sarton took on as householder, but there is always attention given to even the most physical of experiences as philosophical or metaphorical keys to understanding the artist's life. In choosing to purchase an old, run-down house in need of rehabilitation, Sarton notes that she "saw the house as becoming my own creation within a traditional frame, in much the same way as a poet pours his vision of life into the traditional form of the sonnet." But her analysis is not just a truth recognized in hindsight; the point of the entire memoir seems to be the documentation of a life consciously constructed as an expression of the writer's *work*, that is, of literary work. ⟨. . .⟩

The memoir is important in relation to the later journals because it is the beginning of Sarton's conscious and detailed exploration of that "metaphysical frame" and, most important, of "self." Indeed, the title of the first journal, *Journal of a Solitude* (1973), follows from a comment we read in *Plant Dreaming Deep*: "People often imagine that I must be lonely. How can I explain? I want to say, 'Oh no! You see the house is with me. And it is with me in this particular way, as both a demand and a support only when I am alone here.'" Sarton's sense of self, of the physical-metaphorical nature of house and home, of even the condition of solitude are expressed most clearly in *Plant Dreaming Deep*. The memoir sets up conditions and questions which the later journals meet head on. Solitude as a literary subject really grows out of her earlier consideration of the environment of "home" at Nelson:

> . . . there are inner reasons for being highly tuned up when one lives alone. That alertness is also there toward the inner world, which is always close to the surface for me when I am here. . . . The climate of poetry is also the climate of anxiety. And if I inhabit the house, it also inhabits me, and sometimes I feel as if I myself were becoming an intersection for almost too many currents of too intense a nature. . . . No, it is not fear, but an exceptional state of awareness that makes life here not exactly a rest. ⟨. . .⟩

Journal of a Solitude (1973) is a brooding work, but as readers we should be aware that the daily and scrupulous recording of life through journal writing may be a much darker work than the memoir softened by memory. The mem-

oirs had not been entirely untrue, of course, but the screen of memory can filter out the harshest of details, even when the writer does not intend to.
Sarton's choice of the journal as the next form for her private writing was, in
a sense, a means of 'correcting' herself, of altering the 'false' image of her life
which she was afraid she had created in *Plant Dreaming Deep*:

> The anguish of my life here—its rages—is hardly mentioned. Now I
> hope to break through into the rough rocky depths, to the matrix
> itself. There is violence there and anger never resolved. I live alone,
> perhaps for no good reason, for the reason that I am an impossible
> creature, set apart by a temperament I have never learned to use as it
> could be used, thrown off by a word, a glance, or rainy day, or one
> drink too many. My need to be alone is balanced against my fear of
> what will happen when suddenly I enter the huge empty silence if I
> cannot find support there.

Sarton had taken solitude to be the subject of her journal and it is through
an examination of her episodes of depression, anger or frustration that she
believed the "true" image of her life would become clear. ⟨. . .⟩

In 1973, May Sarton moved from Nelson to York, Maine, where she took
up residence in a house on the coast. Two journals have been published since
that time: *The House by the Sea* (1977) and *Recovering* (1980). While the dark
period in Nelson heralded a need for change, Sarton found her new proxim-
ity to the sea inspiring as a clear break from old associations and sorrows. The
new home and land required special attention, particularly gardening. A new
landscape (the rocky shore and sea) required new perceptions. The first of the
Maine journals is a "happy" book overall as new beginnings and new hopes
shape the writer's work. *Recovering* is a far different record—quite literally the
account of a mental and physical recovery from life-threatening illness. Taken
together, these journals do not so much 'complete' a story as bring it full circle. ⟨. . .⟩

Recovering is not simply a book of revelations, nor is it entirely a "success"
story. Sarton confronts the fact of her physical "mutilation" as evidence "that
the door has closed forever on passionate communion with another human
being"; at the same time, she "would like to believe when I die that I have given
myself away like a tree that sows seeds every spring and never counts the loss,
because it is not loss. . . ." Whatever failures she was experiencing that year as
a lover (a relationship was ending) and as a woman stricken by cancer, her
writing continued to connect her to something beyond and outside the self—
her readers certainly, but more importantly to the larger conception of literary identity. It might be true to say that Sarton's desire to "give herself away"
in work was a kind of intentional self-effacement to counter physical deterio-

ration. There was still anger to deal with, and fear, but the focus of the journal was on gut-level pain, so that various issues were forced out in the open that remained shadowy in the earlier works. The journal becomes an attempt to resolve the past or at least clear away patches of old grief. ⟨. . . .⟩

—Suzanne Owens, "House, Home and Solitude: Memoirs and Journals of May Sarton," *Woman and Poet*, ed. Constance Hunting (Orono: University of Maine, 1982), 53, 55, 57–58, 61, 66

CAROLYN G. HEILBRUN

The Sarton memoirs are in three volumes, of which two, *I Knew a Phoenix* (1959) and *A World of Light* (1976), are collections of discrete pieces, while the middle volume, *Plant Dreaming Deep* (1968), is a unified narration of a single extended experience. ⟨. . .⟩ In *Plant Dreaming Deep* Sarton achieved something close to a new form for female writing: she transformed the genre, even as she reported a new female experience.

But one must begin with an analysis of the earliest memoir, *I Knew a Phoenix*. In this collection of short pieces, Sarton excelled in the use of a form already well established. That most of these memoirs were published in *The New Yorker* confirms this point. *The New Yorker*, certainly at the time these pieces appeared, and for many years before, was the cloister of polished writing. To achieve publication in its pages was not only to have written well; it was also to have acquired fame and money without the price of corruption and sinful success demanded by less exalted journals. *The Atlantic* might offer esteem, *The Ladies' Home Journal* riches; only *The New Yorker* bestowed both. ⟨. . .⟩

Sarton herself, in the memoir of the Belgian home where she and her parents lived for a few years before the First World War, offers a different metaphor for the memoir: my mother, she writes, "had lifted out of a pile of rubbish a single Venetian glass on a long delicate stem so dirty it had become opaque, but miraculously intact. How had this single object survived to give us courage? It went back with us to Cambridge and it was always there, wherever we lived. And now it is here, in my own house, a visible proof that it is sometimes the most fragile thing that has the power to endure. . . ." ⟨. . .⟩

The uncertainty of youth, however mildly extended, is rarely described in the lives of women. Even less often are we shown the uncertainties and risks of female middle age. *Plant Dreaming Deep*, extraordinary in many ways, is not least so in being the account of a woman between forty-five and fifty-five; indeed it is unique among what few examples there are. Those women who have published accounts of their middle years have usually written of their lives as wives or mothers (and perhaps as something else as well), or at least, like Simone de Beauvoir, of an existence anchored in another person. Not so Sarton, whose memoir deals with the extraordinary possibilities of solitude. ⟨. . .⟩

What makes *Plant Dreaming Deep* unique and uniquely important, is that Sarton has written a memoir of the possibilities of the solitary female life, but without negatively defining the condition of those who are *just* women. Indeed, as we shall see, she was naively astonished that married women should read into it that negative meaning. Her friends, too, could not escape the analogy to marriage. "My friends," she has written, "realized that my whole relation to the place was a little like that of an old maid who suddenly gets married." It was in fact, very little like, as one can see, for example, by comparing the life of Mary Wilkins Freeman, an "old maid" who married late: she was later to deny all the passionate assertions of her lonely years. For Sarton it was otherwise: the buying of a house where she would live alone was in Unamuno's words, "the effort of [her] past to transform itself into [her] future." The move from solitude to marriage is an escape from what is perceived as incompleteness. Sarton's move, on the other hand, was an effort to crystallize her female autonomy. Once she had written *Plant Dreaming Deep*, had created thus the account of a woman's making of the solitary life, the need to remain in the house slackened and finally disappeared. Within a few years of publishing the memoir, she would move, retaining the solitude but not the drama of that first, hard assertion of selfhood. ⟨. . .⟩

Ultimately, what is celebrated in the memoir and indeed created by it, is not the house itself, nor its lonely occupant coping with the harshness of nature, and the inevitable rush of all earthly things toward deterioration; what is celebrated is the survival of the solitary female artist in the face of the inevitable pain of life, and the need to rage alone at that pain. ⟨. . .⟩

Ironically, but not unnaturally, Sarton did not wholly understand this heartening of others. In *Journal of a Solitude* she agrees that women devalue their own powers, but goes on to assert that "there is something wrong when solitude such as mine can be 'envied' by a happily married woman with children." Hers is not, she feels sure, the best human solution. Is there a best human solution? The point is that the creation of the narrative about a woman's working solitude is so rare that, inevitably, it must be envied by a "happily" married woman, or by any woman less original or less creative than Sarton, who feels less than herself. If Sarton's is not the "best" human solution, neither is there a "happily" married woman. There is only the struggle, and the fiction of that struggle, which we call a memoir, for which Sarton has given us the form.

What Sarton did was to write a new plot for women, a new script. In *Journal of a Solitude* she was to speak of her fears that in *Plant Dreaming Deep* she had not sufficiently rendered her anger, her rage, her sense of isolation, both physical and artistic, nor the agonies of love. Had she led some woman astray by idealizing her lonely struggle? The answer is emphatically, "No." ⟨. . .⟩

I suspect that Sarton does not know in these media-centered days how profound her effect has been in the academic world as well as among those who read only for love. Certainly, she has been remarkably unlucky in her reviewers, especially in the powerful *New York Times*. Yet her life and work have had effect far greater than many of those who have been more grandly praised. Every genre she has taken up has contributed to that effect.

—Carolyn G. Heilbrun, "May Sarton's Memoirs," *Writing a Woman's Life* (New York: W. W. Norton & Co., 1988), 43–44, 46–49, 51

ELIZABETH EVANS

⟨. . .⟩ Particularly in *I Knew a Phoenix* Sarton produces autobiographical writing that is at once vibrant and controlled. Nowhere else in her entire oeuvre does she quite equal again such skill as here where she recounts her life with sure detachment. From the security of middle age she can afford to call up the aspirations of youth, knowing now both the pleasure and the price of being young. ⟨. . .⟩

Sarton has relatively little to say about the memoir as a distinct form, but she has much to say about the journal as a form. She has written five: *Journal of a Solitude* (1973), *The House by the Sea* (1977), *Recovering* (1980), *At Seventy* (1984), and *After the Stroke* (1988). For Sarton keeping a journal has meant keeping a record that will be published, a different task from the traveler's journal or from the individual who writes in his journal or diary those thoughts destined only for the writer's eyes. ⟨. . .⟩

Sarton's journals have been unusually popular; responses come from all ages, not just from middle-aged women. Her journals, however, are risks simply because they invite familiarity from readers who experience the day-by-day routines of the author's life—making beds and meals, filling birdfeeders and shoveling snow, receiving wanted and unwanted guests, exulting in love and despairing in love lost. As Sarton notes in *The House by the Sea*, the journal process remains a very personal record. The journals may well have provided therapeutic value to Sarton; they have also spoken the unspoken for women who could not express anger, deal with regret, welcome the love of women, risk passion in middle or in old age. A role model for younger women and for her own generation as well, Sarton has maintained the balance of a well-written journal and a very personal record, has done so by heeding Elizabeth Bowen's dictum: "One must regard oneself impersonally as an instrument."

Within her journals Sarton refers to the actual writing process. In *The House by the Sea*, for example, she describes the journal as a good way to sort out and shape experience "at a less intense level than by creating a work of art as highly organized as a poem, for instance, or the sustained effort a novel requires." Sustained journal writing, however, makes its own demands. Travel, even a short two days away, breaks the thread and makes picking up difficult. Long trips can interrupt the daily recording altogether, as can the disruptions of illness, holidays, guests. Because each journal entry is dated, the literal turning of the calendar creates pressure to get the work done. To achieve its sense of freshness, the journal is written, Sarton frequently says, "on the pulse" and "must be concerned with the immediate, looking back only when the past suddenly becomes relevant in the light of the present moment." ⟨. . .⟩

A theme recurring in the memoirs and the journals is the figure of the writer who must write, first since that is her calling and second because that is her means of livelihood. A college professor, Sarton says, can connect with her class, can spark interest, cause reactions, and thus stimulate her own work. "The writer, at his desk alone," she argues, "must create his own momentum, draw enthusiasm up out of his own substance, not just once, when he may feel inspired, but day after day when he often does not." Key parts of Sarton's life and work, explored in the memoir and journal pages, converge in this passage. There is the reality of a woman alone making her living in the difficult and uncertain role of writer. Sarton has not gained financial security through inheritance or by producing best-sellers. Her reality is that of a single income that depends upon her steady production. And her first love, poetry, could not provide adequate income nor be produced at will. Whatever the progress of the pattern of the poet in America, few if any have made their entire livelihood by it. (The poetry circuit of readings about the country—"Poe-bis," as Maxine Kumin calls it—supplements poets rather than fully sustaining them.) For Sarton, the success and popularity of the memoirs and journals have made a financial difference, an important fact for one who has not had a tenured teaching post. She has produced steadily because she has had to, generally a book a year. She must be mindful of the New England winters and the heat bills they cause and mindful as well of yearly income taxes—facts of life she often mentions within the journal pages.

Both in *Plant Dreaming Deep* and in the journals Sarton records her anxiety over reviews. An entry in *The House by the Sea* notes that *A World of Light* will be published in a few weeks, and Sarton says that event will bring a week or so of pleasure until the reviews appear and the inevitable shredding begins. When *Kinds of Love*, her New England novel of love in old age, was published in 1970, Sarton admits in the journal entries that she was almost overcome with the hope that this novel would make the best-seller list. Although many reviewers praised the novel, it did not make the list and suffered in fact at the hands of a critic like Richard Rhodes who reviewed it for the *New York Times* ⟨29 November 1970, 56⟩.

In an alarming way the memoirs and the journal entries contain Sarton's expectation that reviews will be unfavorable. In *Plant Dreaming Deep* she declares that the ghost of failure brings increased anxiety when one reaches middle age simply because there is so much less time to recover and to try again for success. In this memoir she cites four causes that have kept her work from gaining a wide critical reception: her divided loyalty between poetry and fiction, self-indulgence, laziness, and an aspect of failure "written into my very bones" (*PD*, 88). These causes are real to her. It is difficult for one writer to excel both in poetry and in fiction, and her divided loyalty has also meant a division of creative energy. The matter of self-indulgence may account for the coolness some critics have shown when that self-indulgence led to a style that draws attention to itself or allows for too much self-exposure. Laziness cannot be taken seriously since Sarton's impressive list of titles denies the trait in her. Her feeling that failure is written in her bones reveals a despair that anticipates disappointments and unfavorable reviews. In *Journal of a Solitude* she attributes the "repeated blows" from critics and the lack of serious critical attention to her own destiny: "I am not meant for success . . . in a way adversity is my climate." ⟨. . .⟩

Most of all in Sarton's journals the strength lies in her forthrightness as a person and in her skill as a writer. She is especially effective in descriptive passages of the garden, the sea, animals, light, as well as in rendering vivid accounts of events in her life. She has literally shared her deepest experiences with the reader. She has demonstrated the rich, full lives of women who never married, and she has willingly given herself away in these journals. ⟨. . .⟩

Finally, the journals record a balance often thinly held and present a remarkably frank account of a difficult, fragile, and fascinating personality. Sarton has followed her own advice: "Keep busy with survival. Imitate the trees. Learn to lose in order to recover, and remember that nothing stays the same for long, not even pain, psychic pain. Sit it out. Let it all pass. Let it go." Because she has written these journals, Sarton has made it possible for herself and for many of her readers "to keep busy with survival."

—Elizabeth Evans, "'By This Familiar Means': Memoirs and Journals," *May Sarton Revisited* (Boston: Twayne, 1989), 24, 26–27, 30–31, 41

KAREN SAUM

Saum: You've spoken of the novel. Earlier, you spoke of the body of your work as a whole. Would you talk about how the different parts fit together?

Sarton: The thing about poetry—*one* of the things about poetry—is that in general one does not follow growth and change through a poem. The poem is an essence. It captures perhaps a moment of violent change but it captures a moment, whereas the novel concerns itself with growth and change. As for the journals, you actually see the writer living out a life, which you don't in any of the other forms, not even the memoirs. In memoirs you are looking back. The memoir is an essence, like poetry. The challenge of the journal is that it is written on the pulse, and I don't allow myself to go back and change things afterwards, except for style. I don't expand later on. It's whatever I am able to write on the day about whatever is happening to me on that day. In the case of a memoir like *Plant Dreaming Deep*, I'm getting at the essence of five years of living alone in a house in a tiny village in New Hampshire, trying to pin down for myself what those five years had meant, what they had done to me, how I had changed. And that's very different from the journals. I must say, I'm not as crazy about the journals as some of my readers are. I get quite irritated when people say the journals are the best thing. God knows, I've struggled with certain things in the journals, especially about being a woman and about being a lesbian. The militant lesbians want me to be a militant and I'm just not.

But as for the vision of life in the whole of my work, I would like to feel that my work is universal and human on the deepest level. I think of myself as a maker of bridges—between the heterosexual and the homosexual world, between the old and the young. *As We Are Now*, the novel about a nursing home, has been read, curiously enough, by far more young people than old people. It terrifies old people to read about other old people in nursing homes. But the young have been moved by it. Many young people write me to say that they now visit elderly relatives in these places. This is the kind of bridge I want to make. Also, the bridge between men and women in their marriages, which I've dealt with in quite a few of the novels, especially in the last one, *Anger*. ⟨. . .⟩

Saum: How was it that you began to write the journals?

Sarton: I wrote the first one, *Journal of a Solitude*, as an exercise to handle a serious depression and it worked quite well. I did have publication in mind. It wasn't written just for me. I think it's part of the discipline. It keeps you on your toes stylistically and prevents too much self-pity, knowing that it's going to be read and that it will provide a certain standard for other people who are living isolated lives and who are depressed. If you just indulge in nothing but moaning, it wouldn't be a good journal for others to read. I also found that by keeping a journal I was looking at things in a new way because I would think, "That—good! That will be great in the journal." So it took me out of myself, out of the depression to some extent. This happened again with *Recovering*.

Saum: You write for publication; do you have an imagined audience?

Sarton: It's really one imaginary person.

Saum: Would you talk a little about this imaginary person?

Sarton: Well, I don't mean that when I sit down I think, "Oh, there is that imaginary person over there I'm writing for," but . . . yes! Somebody who sees things the way I do, who will be able to read with heart and intelligence. I suppose somebody about my age. It used to be somebody about forty-five; now it's somebody about seventy. But then *Journal of a Solitude* brought me a whole new audience, a college-age audience. That was very exciting because until then my work had appealed mostly to older people.

Saum: Isn't it true that lately you have been embraced by the spiritual establishment?

Sarton: Yes, this has happened only recently and has been extremely moving to me. I have come out as a lesbian. And although I have no shame about this at all, I still feel it's quite extraordinary that religious groups would be so receptive to me, as the Methodists were, for instance. They asked me to be one of the speakers at their yearly retreat for pastors. The other speakers were religious in a way that I am not. Then, the Unitarians gave me their Ministry to Women Award last year and I was touched by what they said . . . that I'd helped women by my honesty. The Methodists also talked about honesty.

I must say it was quite brave of me to come out as I did in *Mrs. Stevens*, in 1965. At that time it was "not done." When I spoke at colleges I would never have stated, "I'm a lesbian." But this all changed in the seventies. It's marvelous now that one can be honest and open. At the time *Mrs. Stevens* was published, it was sneered at in reviews and I lost a couple of jobs. They weren't terribly important jobs but I did lose them. Now I don't think that would happen. It might if you were a professor in a college, but coming as a visiting speaker you can be absolutely open. Women's Studies have helped me enormously, there's no doubt about it. This is one way my work is now getting through.

I know of no other writer who has had such a strange career as I've had. When I started writing, the first novels were received with ovations. In 1956, I was nominated for the National Book Award in two categories, fiction and poetry. But after my fifth novel, *Faithful Are the Wounds*, the one that was nominated, this never happened again and I began to have bad reviews. I was no longer in fashion. I can't think of another writer who has had as hard a time with reviewers over a period of twenty years as I have but whose work has been so consistently read. It's word of mouth. It's people . . . every day I get letters saying things like: "I loved such and such a book and I'm buying five copies to give to people." That's how books get around. And then the public libraries. Without the public libraries, serious writers, unfashionable serious writers like me, really wouldn't have a chance. Again, I hear from people, "I was wandering around the library and saw the title *Plant Dreaming Deep*. It caught my attention . . . now I'm reading everything you've written." It's wonderful to have this happen at the age of seventy. ⟨. . .⟩

—Karen Saum, "The Art of Poetry XXXII: May Sarton," *Conversations with May Sarton*, ed. Earl G. Ingersoll (Jackson: University Press of Mississippi, 1991), 111, 116–17

JEANNE BRAHAM

A similarity of method also marks the journals, a method derived perhaps primarily from Sarton's other modes of artistic expression: fiction and poetry. Sarton casts herself as a character in her own story, recreating significant life experience, pondering its shape, discovering its outcome. Much like the novelist who discovers her characters beginning to exert wills of their own, Sarton sets her "plot" in motion, discovering its significance in the retelling. Simultaneously, she deepens "meaning" by concentrating on a few repeated images (home, animals, significant friendships) that function as poetic metaphors shimmering with collective content. Her awareness of audience widens from the reader-over-the-shoulder peepsight of *Journal of a Solitude* to full, front, direct address in *After the Stroke*. ⟨. . .⟩

At Seventy balances the anxieties of old age (an irregular heart beat, a cancer scare, the death of "dearest love" Judy Matlack) with the celebrations of growing into age and its rewards: a huge and appreciative audience, excellent book sales, and the financial security to support worthy friends and projects she deeply believes in. In this journal, May Sarton's most vital values resonate: balance, commitment, connection. As the journal opens, she assesses seventy years of life experience.

> If someone else had lived so long and could remember things sixty
> years ago with great clarity, she would seem very old to me. But I do
> not feel old at all, not as much a survivor as a person still on her way.

⟨. . .⟩ Surely much of what Sarton knows about attachment comes from her relationship with Judy Matlack, always a presence in earlier journals but fully fashioned in *At Seventy*. Judy first appears in a wheelchair, the victim of Alzheimer's disease, reduced to a baby "for whom food is the only real pleasure." Although Sarton visits her in a nursing home in Concord and bravely arranges short trips for her to York, most visits carry a high price.

Only after her death, when Judy begins to live again, can Sarton remember.

> —Judy was the precious only love with whom I lived for years . . .
> only Judy gave me a home and made me know what home can be.
> She was the dear companion for fifteen years, years when I was
> struggling as a writer. We were poor then. . . . But strangely enough
> I look back on those years as the happiest ones. And that is because
> there was a "we."

Although Judy is the primary example of a "we," Sarton's inventory of her life is packed with "connections." Friends of her youth, visiting artists, Mr. Webster (who fixes the pipes), Eleanor Perkins (who cleans the house), Nancy (who makes order out of the chaos of the files), and Sister Lucy (who plows and builds at the commune H.O.M.E. in rural Orland, Maine) crowd the pages. In *At Seventy*, Sarton clearly acknowledges the growing community of readers who buy and read her work, queue up for book signings, send her pounds of mail monthly, and turn out in staggering numbers at her readings. This community of response leads her to write, "the answer is not detachment as I used to believe but rather to be more deeply involved—to be attached." The "self" in *At Seventy* is defined by connection to others, and values become luminous in "the company of others attended by love."

After the Stroke, a darker record than *At Seventy*, records not only the effects of a stroke Sarton suffered shortly before her seventy-fifth birthday but also the more incapacitating side effects of a fibrillating heart and diverticulitis, conditions that complicate and delay recovery time. The journal chronicles nine months of excruciating pain, of the anxiety that builds when one cannot depend on ever feeling wholly well, of the grief that wells up when Tamas— the Sheltie she brought to York fifteen years earlier—dies, and Bramble—the "last of the wild cats tamed at Nelson"—must be put to sleep. It is as if the sustaining metaphors of home and family have deserted her and the most vital ingredient, the concentration that solitude provides, has been replaced by grinding loneliness.

Difficult as these entries are to read, they form a convincing case study for those struggling with life-threatening illness. She documents the particular terror of memory loss, memory she acknowledges as so vital to the writer, and the special fear of losing the ability to make connections and critical judgments—a deterioration Sarton saw at close range in Judy's long bout with senility. She also records the more universal fears of the old or the infirm, prisoners in their own deteriorating bodies, at the mercy of their own thoughts and feelings.

> . . . I lie around most of the afternoon, am in bed by eight, and there
> in my bed alone the past rises like a tide, over and over, to swamp me
> with memories I cannot handle.

The strange displacement of seeming a visitor in one's own home—watching others do the gardening, care for pets, bring in or prepare food—also plagues Sarton: "I look and admire but am not *connected.*" Speaking for herself and for those who have experienced this unwelcome dependence, Sarton says that she must "curl up deep down inside" herself and wait for things to change.

Visitors come, other doctors are consulted, a new cat is given to her by her friend, Carolyn Heilbrun, a new dog is promised if recovery permits, but Sarton finds her own responses merely polite or ritualistic. "I feel so cut off from what once was a self. . . . Everyone I know must be as sick and tired of this illness as I am." ⟨. . .⟩

Accepting an "unearned gift" becomes the key to renewed energy and her leitmotif of the final entries in *After the Stroke.* As Sarton concludes, she reminds herself and her readers that "one of the things old age has brought me is being able to receive gladly and with joy, whereas, young, I only wanted to give . . . ." Although she learns to rejoice in the "life recaptured," as readers of *After the Stroke,* we are never far from the consciousness of death and the precious, fragile gift of health. It is the precariousness that lingers. If Sarton knows now that she makes a myth of her life, it is not a hoax of the perfect artistic retreat the Nelson memoir invented. Instead, it is a consciously chosen, uniquely inscribed metaphor, in Heilbrun's phrase, a new script that has been consciously and unconsciously appropriated by many as a model.

The "new script" empowers on a variety of fronts, for not only does it speak to those who wish to take control of their lives, to tend their talent even when it means risking hostility or isolation or self-doubt, but it also targets issues central to women's creativity: the courage to love other women, the celebration of female friendship in both the private and public spheres, the identification of the creative "Muse" as female.

—Jeanne Braham, "'Seeing with Fresh Eyes': A Study of May Sarton's Journals," *That Great Sanity: Critical Essays on May Sarton,* ed. Susan Swartzlander and Marilyn R. Mumford (Ann Arbor: University of Michigan Press, 1992), 155–56, 159–63

Barbara Frey Waxman

By positioning herself in the middle of friendships with women of 30 or 50, on the one hand and 80 or 90 on the other, Sarton can present women's diverse attitudes toward elders and the aging process, including her young friends' views of her and her reactions to her older women friends. In particular, her discourse enthusiastically celebrates the richness and intensity of very old women's lives such as those of Eva Le Gallienne, Elizabeth Roget, Lotte Jacobi, and Camille Mayran. Sarton relishes her relationships with such elders: "I take strength and joy in the friendship of someone older than I. It is a rest to be with someone who has made her peace with life and enjoys everything so much" ⟨*At Seventy*⟩.

Here Sarton speaks of her relationship with 83-year-old Elizabeth Roget, about whom she also says: "It is a pleasure to be with someone who says that the eighties are her happiest years . . . ⟨.⟩" In such portrayals of women older than herself, as well as in her passages of self-reflection about her 70th year, Sarton attempts to deconstruct myths of aging which have been barriers to intimacy between older and younger women: of aging as deterioration of identity, increasing helplessness, fading joys, and loss of love.

Sarton says she is more comfortable with herself and more relaxed about her life at age 70 than she was earlier:

> I am far better able to cope at seventy than I was at fifty. I think that is partly because I have learned to glide instead of to force myself at moments of tension. . . . I realize that seventy must seem extremely old to my young friends, but I actually feel much younger than I did when I wrote *The House by the Sea* six years ago. . . . And that . . . is because I live more completely in the moment these days, am not as anxious about the future, and am far more detached from the areas of pain, the loss of love, the struggle to get the work completed, the fear of death.

In a journal entry that is a written transcription of an earlier oral text (which occurs frequently in this book), Sarton describes how she had reached out to an audience of college students at a poetry reading by expressing her vision of old age as a time of empowerment; at 70 she is surer of her identity and of what her life means:

> "I am more myself than I have ever been. There is less conflict. I am happier, more balanced, and . . . more powerful . . . better able to use my powers." I am surer of what my life is all about.

Sarton at 70 feels less of a need to be who she is not. She celebrates the integrity of the older woman, an unvarnished integrity that rejuvenates her:

> Now I wear the inside person outside and am more comfortable with my self. In some ways I am younger because I can admit vulnerability and more innocent because I do not have to pretend.

At the same time that she extends herself into relationships with younger and older women, she refuses to blur the distinctions between age and youth; proud of how aging has transformed her, she says:

> . . . for someone of forty to say to someone of seventy "We are exactly alike" is ludicrous and an underestimation of what life itself does to force us to maturity.

Such hard-won maturity is precious to Sarton. ⟨. . .⟩

In ⟨. . .⟩ passages about reunions with old friends, Sarton points out the essence of these relationships and emphasizes the importance of in-person sharing of lives. However, she also teaches readers that these long-term relationships have been sustained and nurtured by other forms of communication, especially letters. Sarton's journal reveals how much of the fabric of her social and emotional life is woven by these letters from friends, acquaintances, and readers of her poetry and fiction. Although she sometimes grumbles about the burden of maintaining her extensive correspondence because it keeps her from her other writing projects, Sarton acknowledges that even letters from strangers "have enlarged my heart." Many of these fan-letters "are precious, each in a different way," bringing her such a "renewed sense of how remarkable human beings can be and are that I felt overwhelmed to be the receptacle of so much love and to be allowed into so many lives." ⟨. . .⟩

One leaves *At Seventy* feeling more knowledgable about aging and better informed about some ways of building and sustaining satisfying intergenerational friendships. Perhaps even more than the fictional journals discussed in this essay, *At Seventy* is optimistic about ending the isolation of elderly women in our society and about tapping their wealth of spiritual/philosophical maturity by encouraging contact between older and younger women. The healing tenderness of these intergenerational women's friendships is also apparent on every page of Sarton's journal, as well as in the passages of *As We Are Now* that deal with Anna and in Jane Somers's entries about Maudie Fowler. The journals of Sarton and Lessing and the letters embedded in them demonstrate in different ways how the goals of socially reclaiming old women and making intergenerational companionship desirable are furthered in a purposeful written discourse. This discourse of aging simultaneously records and shapes emotions, attitudes, and values that make women (and probably men too) more receptive to intergenerational relationships. This discourse shows, once again, how language creates desire, because we can see how it intensifies existing intergenerational friendships. Lessing and Sarton's texts on aging, with their passionateness, meditativeness and self-reflexiveness, are responsive not only to a literary intertextuality that grows exponentially with the graying of

America, but also to the needs of aging readers and of a society in search of a
visionary plan for its increasingly elderly populace.

—Barbara Frey Waxman, "Linking Women Across Generations," *Communication and Women's
Friendships: Parallels and Intersections in Literature and Life*, ed. Janet Doubler Ward and JoAnna
Stephens Mink (Bowling Green: Bowling Green State University Popular Press, 1993),
38–41, 43

Hazel Hunley

In her second memoir, *Plant Dreaming Deep*, May Sarton tells of how she stood
among her unpacked belongings, listening to the "immense" silence and solil-
oquizing about her "crazy decision" to move to the village of Nelson, New
Hampshire, at age forty-five. Hard questions pelted her like the rain against
the windows that bleak October day in 1958. As she waited for the movers to
arrive, she asked herself, "Would the house turn out to be a lunatic asylum for
a single lunatic?" Had she "taken on more than [she] could cope with?" Did she
have "the inner resources to live [there] at all?" Would it "turn out to be a dis-
astrous escape into nowhere?"

Sarton would re-enact this scene of self-doubt about living and working in
solitude more than once at Nelson and later at her house by the sea in Maine.
In spite of considerable mental and material risk, however, May Sarton turned
her back on the predominantly male literary establishment that had rejected
her and went off to a remote New England village to continue her work of
twenty years; moreover, to do it her way. While she lacked critical acclaim,
letters from readers had assured her of an audience so that she could continue
to publish. In retrospect, Sarton said,

> I really went to Nelson . . . out of despair. At that point, I had
> published ten or twelve books. I felt devastated by the lack of
> recognition. I decided to go there and bury myself and work. I felt
> that eventually *they* would come to *me*, which is what happened
> . . . It was out of rejection of the whole establishment and everything
> it represented that I went away. ⟨*Plant Dreaming Deep*⟩

Thus, when she signed the contract for an eighteenth-century farmhouse and
thirty-six acres in June 1958, she took possession not only of her new home
but also of her own life and the way she would subsequently live and write it.
Such a step had far-reaching implications in the Sixties for women who were
beginning to establish their own identities, if not find rooms—or even
houses—of their own. Her move from urban Cambridge to a small country village took place even as the curtain was rising on the second act of the women's
movement. ⟨. . .⟩

In her self-imposed solitude at Nelson, Sarton tapped her elemental creative powers because she had learned that "revelation rises up slowly if one gives it space" (*House by the Sea* 253). In a quieter setting, she found her "real life" and learned how to replenish the psychic energy drained off by public appearances and many personal relationships, not to mention the blessed burden of answering letters from readers. She came to covet her uninterrupted solitude for the renewal of her very being, not just for herself but to continue to give generously of herself to the work and to the people in her life. Such is the real or psychological space many women wish for in their own lives, even envy in Sarton, according to many letters she receives. One such letter from a woman who simply finds it difficult being a woman, taking second place in marriage, to children, and in society, asks, "Can one *be* within the framework of a marriage? I envy your solitude with all my heart, and your courage to live as you must" (*Journal of a Solitude* 122). Especially empathetic to married women, Sarton replies:

> It is not irresponsible women who ask that question, but often . . .
> women with children, caring women, who feel deeply frustrated and
> lost, who feel they are missing their 'real lives' all the time.

Part of the answer to women's needs, Sarton thinks, is to draw the "warm nurturing powers out of men" and to divide marital roles according to the needs and abilities of partners. But still, she finds women's powers undervalued and that "women, no doubt, equally devalue their own powers."

In the journals she weaves in excerpts from many women's letters or comments about their lives, as in *At Seventy*:

> This, the third letter, is in recognition of the part you have
> unknowingly played in launching me into a new phase of my life.
> [The reader reassessed her own environment after reading Sarton's
> description of how hers influenced her work.] I saw that I had no
> place to call my own in this big house. I saw that I had never dared
> ask for either time or space that was inviolate . . . From the corners of
> the house I gathered together [into a storage room] the parts of me
> that I had hidden away. I hung the pictures, shelved the books,
> unpacked my cello, and sat and waited for the fusing to begin. It did
> . . . Had I not had this private space and had I not begun to demand
> private time for myself, I never would have dared to do something as
> 'selfish' as going to school.

Sarton replies in her journal, "I found this letter extremely interesting. There must be so many women who have not dared to demand 'a room of their own,' who have not realized how closely bound up one's identity can be with the frame in which one lives."

—Hazel Hunley, "Homeward to 'Self': May Sarton Planting Her Dreaming Deep, Women Reaping the Blessings," *A Celebration for May Sarton*, ed. Constance Hunting (Orono: Puckerbrush Press, 1994), 13–14, 18–19

Angeline Goreau

Now Margot Peters, whose biography May Sarton authorized three years before her death in 1995, tells us that the writer's lengthily celebrated love affair with aloneness was, for the most part, a delusion. According to Ms. Peters, Sarton was quite "incapable of spending more than a few consecutive days in her own company." Cataloguing a frenzy of comings and goings that would make a traveling salesman wilt, Ms. Peters convincingly debunks Sarton's claim that she lived in the old house in Vermont "with solitude for my domain." There are other truths revealed here as well. According to Ms. Peters, the May Sarton devotees saw as "courageous, independent, in harmony with nature, warm, loving, frank about her shortcomings" was in fact a pill of the first water. People who had the misfortune to become her intimates almost universally came to regret it. On the slightest of pretexts, Ms. Peters has it, Sarton subjected them to "terrible scenes, nights of weeping, rages, blowups." She was expert at emotional blackmail, and behaved badly in restaurants. Self-absorbed and insensitive, May Sarton wooed others with extravagant attentions, only to betray and humiliate them later—"with scant regard," Ms. Peters observes, "for the chaos left in her wake." ⟨. . .⟩

But Margot Peters is constantly pointing out May Sarton's fondness for cliché, her flatness, her tendency to wax sentimental. If only May had tried harder, Ms. Peters frequently implies, she could have been a much better writer. "She should have taken accusations of trite and imprecise language with dead seriousness," the biographer scolds. Sarton's publisher, Norton, should have edited her more carefully; Sarton herself should have taken more time.

But who is to say that the writing would have been better? It might even be argued that the fondness for cliché that weakens Sarton's poetry was in fact the great strength of her autobiographical work, lending it a simplicity and homeliness that leaves one with the impression of having had a long chat with a good friend. And mixed with the banalities about what color she chooses to wear on a given day are indeed wisdoms and truths worth keeping.

One suspects that May Sarton may have had the last laugh when, in the final entry of "Encore," she noted: "People often think that I give myself away in these journals written for publication. They do not realize apparently that large areas of my life are never mentioned." For the "important" side of her life, she observed, the intimate side, "readers have to go to the novels."

—Angeline Goreau, "Late Bloomer," *The New York Times Book Review* (6 April 1997): 8

B I B L I O G R A P H Y

Encounter in April. 1937.

Inner Landscape. 1938.

The Single Hound. 1938.

The Bridge of Years. 1946

The Lion and the Rose. 1948.

Shadow of a Man. 1950.

A Shower of Summer Days. 1952.

The Land of Silence and Other Poems. 1953.

Faithful Are the Wounds. 1955.

Joanna and Ulysses. 1955.

The Birth of a Grandfather. 1957.

The Fur Person. 1957.

In Time Like Air: New Poems. 1958.

I Knew a Phoenix. 1959.

Cloud, Stone, Sun, Vine: Poems Selected and New. 1961.

The Small Room. 1961.

Mrs. Stevens Hears the Mermaids Singing. 1965.

Miss Pickthorn and Mr. Hare. 1966.

A Private Mythology. 1966.

As Does New Hampshire. 1967.

Plant Dreaming Deep. 1968.

The Poet and the Donkey. 1969.

Kinds of Love. 1970.

A Grain of Mustard Seed: New Poems. 1971.

A Durable Fire. 1972.

Journal of a Solitude. 1973.

As We Are Now. 1973.

Collected Poems, 1930–1973. 1974.

Punch's Secret. 1974.

Crucial Conversations. 1975.

A World of Light. 1976.

A Walk Through the Woods. 1976.

The House by the Sea. 1977.

A Reckoning. 1978.

Selected Poems of May Sarton. Ed. by Serena Sue Hilsinger and Lois Brynes, 1978.

Halfway to Silence. 1980.

Recovering: A Journal. 1980.

Anger. 1982.

Letters from Maine: New Poems. 1984.

At Seventy: A Journal. 1984.

The Magnificent Spinster. 1985.

The Education of Harriet Hatfield. 1987.

After the Stroke: A Journal. 1988.

The Silence Now: New and Uncollected Earlier Poems. 1988.

Honey in the Hive: Judith Matlack, 1898–1982. 1988.

Sarton Selected: An Anthology of the Journals, Novels, and Poetry of May Sarton. Ed. by Bradford Dudley Daziel, 1991.

Among the Usual Days: A Portrait. 1993.

Writings on Writing. 1980.

Now I Become Myself. 1992

Endgame: A Journal of the 79th Year. 1992.

Encore: A Journal of the 80th Year. 1993.

At Eighty-Two: A Journal. 1996.

May Sarton: Selected Letters, 1916–1954. 1997.

GERTRUDE STEIN
1874-1946

GERTRUDE STEIN was born in Pennsylvania in 1874 but then moved to Oakland, California, with her family. The last of seven children, Gertrude and her brother Leo were conceived only because two older siblings had died. Perhaps this knowledge contributed to Gertrude and Leo's close relationship. She followed him to Cambridge in 1893, where she studied at Radcliffe College under William James. In Baltimore she studied psychology and medicine at Johns Hopkins University and had an affair with May Bookstaver. She wrote about this experience in her first short novel, *Q.E.D.*, and then "forgot" about it. She and Leo moved to Paris in 1904. There they bought and displayed in their home at 27 rue de Fleurus the work of Cezanne, Manet, Matisse, Picasso, and Renoir. Stein's use of language and form in early works such as *Three Lives* (1909) shows that she, Cezanne, and Matisse were experimenting with the same concepts in different media.

As Stein became closer to Picasso and began experimenting with cubism in *The Making of Americans* (1925), written in 1906–08, tensions developed with Leo. Then she met Alice B. Toklas, a fellow Californian in 1907. Toklas moved into the Stein household in 1909 and lessened Stein's dependence on Leo. Stein's lesbian relationship with Toklas and her continuing innovation in writing, which resulted in *Tender Buttons* (1914), the literary equivalent of Picasso's cubist paintings, led to a lifelong break with Leo.

By the outbreak of World War I, Stein's two publications had led to some recognition, and she was to soon be a major influence on the next generation of American writers. During the war, Stein and Toklas donated a Ford and their services as drivers to the American Fund for French Wounded. During and after the war, Stein influenced writers such as F. Scott Fitzgerald, Ernest Hemingway, Marianne Moore, Katherine Ann Porter, Thornton Wilder, and William Carlos Williams. But Stein did not become a celebrated writer in her own country until the publication of *The Autobiography of Alice B. Toklas* (1932). With this accessible, chatty, even gossipy book, Stein caught the imagination of the American public. As critics explain, the *Autobiography* is not a simple or straightforward text. Stein's innovative use of the narrating Toklas persona makes the lesbian couple the subject of the work while undermining the insistent "I" of traditional autobiographies. At the same time Stein was writing *Stanzas in Meditation*

(1932), one of her more demanding works. Both pieces of writing can be seen as negotiating issues of the relation of self to other, and the relation of language, gender, and genre.

Stein followed the success of the *Autobiography* with a lecture tour of the United States, her first visit in 30 years. In 1934 an abridged version of *The Making of Americans* was published, and in 1936 Stein published *Everybody's Autobiography* about her lecture tour of the previous year. After her tour, however, she experienced writer's block for the first time.

In 1942, Stein and Toklas left occupied Paris for their house in Southern France. Living in Vichy France, they were cut off from communication with the United States for two years. They returned to Paris when France was liberated in 1944. Stein wrote about her experience as a Jewish American in France during World War II in *Wars I Have Seen* (1945). She died of cancer in Paris in 1946.

CRITICAL EXTRACTS

JAMES E. BRESLIN

When *The Autobiography of Alice B. Toklas* was published in 1933, the book soon became, as Gertrude Stein both hoped and feared, a critical and popular success. Stein earned celebrity and a substantial amount of money, both of which depressed her. *The Autobiography*'s subsequent literary reputation might have cheered her up, however, for Stein's critics—with the notable exception of her best critic, Richard Bridgman ⟨*Gertrude Stein in Pieces*, 1970, 209–37⟩—have generally either ignored or rejected *The Autobiography*. B. L. Reid dismissed it as "chitchat," and many readers find it merely anecdotal and gossipy. ⟨Reid, *Art by Subtraction*, 1958, 186⟩ Certainly, readers who approach it with expectations shaped by the revival of confessional writing in the 1960's are apt to reject it as too reserved. Stein herself has somewhat different misgivings about the book, stating in *Everybody's Autobiography* (1936) that the earlier work had dealt with what had happened instead of "what is happening." Yet *The Autobiography*'s charming, playful, anecdotal surface has distracted its readers from its real complexity; it provides not—as Stein seems to have thought—a mere submission to the conventions of autobiography but an intense and creative struggle with them.

In many ways the autobiographical act is one at odds with, even a betrayal of, Gertrude Stein's aesthetic principles. Her essay "What Are Master-pieces

and Why Are There So Few of Them" offers a concise statement of those principles: "The minute your memory functions while you are doing anything it
may be very popular but actually it is dull," Stein warns; her desire to live and
write in a continuous present thus turns her against the necessarily retrospective act of autobiography. But Stein's opposition to the conventions of her
genre runs even deeper than this, because her commitment to a continuous
present forces her to reject the notion of identity altogether. "Identity is recognition," she writes: "I am I because my little dog knows me." Identity, an artificial construction based on the perception of certain fixed traits that allow my
little dog or anyone else to imagine that they know me, stresses repetition,
which is, according to Stein, antithetical to creativity. Identity "destroys creation"—as does memory; both, carrying the past over into the present and
structuring by repetition, are ways we have of familiarizing the strangeness,
the mysterious being, of others. Masterpieces de-familiarize; they derive from
"knowing that there is no identity and producing while identity is not." In part
Stein is warning against self-imitation, and she quotes Picasso as saying that
he is willing to be influenced by anyone but himself; but she is also stressing
that to live in a continuous present, to *be* rather than to *repeat*, one must constantly break down identity. But can there be an *auto* biography in which "there
is no identity"? Or, to put the question somewhat differently: autobiographies
are customarily *identified* as acts of *self* representation, but Stein is challenged to
refashion the form to show that she eludes or transcends the category of self
or identity. ⟨. . .⟩

⟨. . .⟩ Moreover, the book's style blends the domestic particularity, whim-
sical humor, and ironic precision of Toklas with some of the leading features
of Stein's writing—e.g., stylized repetition, digression, a language that continually points up its own artifice. ⟨. . .⟩

⟨. . .⟩ most discussions of *The Autobiography* begin by assuming the character of Stein to be its easily identifiable center, and they proceed to discuss this
character as if it were not mediated for the reader by a perspective that is to
some degree external to it. Yet, even if we proceed along these lines, the character of Stein turns out to be an elusive and enigmatic "center." Stein, Toklas
tells us, sought in her writing to give "the inside as seen from the outside"
(p. 156); that is one reason she creates herself through the external perspective of Toklas. ⟨. . .⟩

⟨. . .⟩ *The Autobiography* gives the inside by way of the outside; it plays down
psychology and sticks to the surface, recording externals (objects, acts, dia-
logues) in a way that clearly manifests deliberate and idiosyncratic acts of
selection and stylization. Such admitted artifice annoys many readers who,
with simpler models of self and autobiography, demand a fuller intimacy and
deeper psychology of their autobiographers. But Stein's stylization of the sur-

face reveals the "you" that Picasso, having looked so long and intently, could no longer see when he looked. *The Autobiography*, in short, gives us Gertrude Stein being. ⟨. . .⟩

⟨. . .⟩ But in this first representation of Stein, as throughout *The Autobiography*, the external perspective of Toklas, sticking to the observable surface, suggests the inside while leaving it mysterious. As a result, Stein is not created as a realistic, psychologically complex character; she is, rather, an abstraction, a deliberate simplification—a mythical figure whose peaceful self-sufficiency allows her to transcend external circumstances.

The *Autobiography* of Benjamin Franklin records the attempt to create an identity through acts of will; *The Education of Henry Adams* records the break-down of a similar attempt and the dissolution of the very idea of identity. *The Autobiography of Alice B. Toklas* takes the process one step further; the book shows us not someone striving to create a self, but someone who *exists* calmly in a world without any external orders. ⟨. . .⟩

⟨. . .⟩ In *Everybody's Autobiography*, Stein admires paintings which move rather than being about movement and which seem to come out of the "prison" of their frames—as if the subject were alive, truly existing. Stein's own aesthetic theory, as we have seen, made her acutely aware that by attempting to incarnate her being in language in an autobiography, she was running the risk of merely fixing, of limiting and deadening, herself. But the pressures of autobiography, among them the pressure of language itself, constitute another set of external circumstances to which Stein calmly responds with a playful sense of adventure. The result is that *The Autobiography of Alice B. Toklas* presents a Gertrude Stein who keeps stepping out of the frame, as if she were alive, truly existing. The "psychology" of her character may be a simplified one, but a reader who tries to delineate this character in a careful way finds him/herself speaking in contradictions; and these very contradictions are what make the character of Stein remain mysterious, elusive—alive. ⟨. . .⟩

⟨To put it another way,⟩ *The Autobiography* continually points up the disparity between actuality and its representation, but it does so without irony, without lamenting the insufficiency of either reality or of literary fictions. The book's narrative method simultaneously acknowledges chronological time and the power of writing to play freely with that time; again Stein does not privilege either one over the other. ⟨. . .⟩

At *The Autobiography*'s close, the narrative catches up with itself or at least with its beginning, as we learn of the genesis of the book and that Stein is its author. In the original edition this final page of the text was followed by a photograph of the first page of the manuscript. *The Autobiography* ends by folding back on itself; and a reader is invited to reread the book in light of the revelation that Stein is its author. Lest this revelation make the reader too comfort-

able, he or she is also, as we have seen, assured of the book's Defoe-like simplicity in a way that warns of its complexity and deviousness. At the end *The
Autobiography* circles back on itself as if it were an autonomous verbal reality.
Yet the book's conclusion also reveals Stein to be on a quest that is not completed; the book's ending is also open. The end of the book closes off and
frames a life at the same time that it breaks out of its frame, its artificial closure, to affirm the ongoing process of the author's life. At its close, as throughout *The Autobiography*, moving is in all directions.

> —James E. Breslin, "Gertrude Stein and the Problems of Autobiography," *Critical Essays on
> Gertrude Stein*, ed. Michael J. Hoffman (Boston: G. K. Hall & Co., 1986), 149–53, 155–56,
> 158–59

ESTELLE C. JELINEK

This literary autobiography ⟨*The Autobiography of Alice B. Toklas*⟩ is a *disguise* autobiography par excellence, a disguise of the self in words rather than in cos-
tume, transforming the exotic tradition of the nineteenth-century
autobiographies by women who masqueraded as men to a twentieth-century
context—the total camouflage of an eccentric personality and an eccentric
life-style. By masking her literary voice in that of her friend and lover, Stein
attempts to perpetrate the ultimate concealment of the self as protection from
judgmental readers. Ironically, it was this pretense at autobiography, this hoax
on her readers, suggested by friends to make money, that made Stein famous.
Had she not written it, she might not have had the recognition she has today.

Born in the nineteenth century, Gertrude Stein was a woman of her era
despite her avant-garde friends and literary experimentation. Although earlier
autobiographers merely omitted indiscretions or intimate revelations in order
to protect their vulnerability to an unknown audience, they were committed,
to some degree at least, to self-revelation. Although ⟨Elizabeth Cady⟩ Stanton
excluded much of her private life and problems within the suffrage movement
in order to protect herself and the cause, she does tell us about her childhood,
friendships, and other domestic subjects, if not always directly at least by
means of personal anecdotes about others. But Stein inverts the autobiographical tradition by writing an ostensibly impersonal autobiography, even
more so than Jane Addams's life study, which was, at least, written in the first
person and is discursive about her professional work. Not only does Stein use
a third-person narrator, Alice Toklas; not only does she omit almost everything about herself until her life in Paris as an adult—from 1903, when she was
twenty-nine, until 1932; but she also camouflages the little that she does present about her personal life.

Such apparent impersonality and the overwhelming distance involved in
such an approach seem to place *The Autobiography of Alice B. Toklas* outside the

tradition of women's autobiographical critics, who see in it an intellectual challenge. Be that as it may, the *Autobiography* does display the usual characteristics of the female tradition. 〈. . .〉

Clearly, Toklas's persona allows Stein to praise her friends without appearing sentimental, to criticize those she disliked without attacking them directly, and to brag about herself without appearing egotistical—all without antagonizing her readers. Less perceptible but more significant is Stein's use of Toklas to represent the "acceptable" voice of a traditional female. Toklas's persona is the closest Stein can come to presenting the personal and domestic aspects of a woman's life, which are expected in a woman's life study. Since Stein tells us nothing about herself as a daughter, sister, or lover, Toklas satisfies the reader's expectations of the traditional female component. She likes gardening and needlework, does the cooking and dusting, types Stein's manuscripts, handles her correspondence and appointments, and sits with the wives of geniuses so that her idol can sit with the geniuses themselves—all the normal duties of a wife or servant of a great man. Toklas provides the "wifely" element in their relationship, Stein's other half.

If Stein had written in her own voice about Toklas's wifelike functions, her readers would probably have been shocked or disturbed. But if Toklas chooses to perform these duties, in her own voice, while the genius worked, then the audience may not even notice. Toklas's presence as the narrator legitimized Stein in a world that expected some information stereotypically associated with women in an autobiography by a woman, just as the geniuses Stein gathered around her legitimized her as a professional, if yet unrecognized, writer.

Writing her life story in the voice of her intimate companion serves yet another function. By placing Toklas in the ostensible center of the autobiography and by making her the narrator, Stein pays homage to their—her and Toklas's—personal success story. Stein makes famous the most important person in her life; she makes famous the "wife" of the genius who will one day be famous for her work. 〈. . .〉

In 1937 Stein published a kind of postscript to *The Autobiography of Alice B. Toklas*—*Everybody's Autobiography*, which reads like a travel book about her six-month lecture tour of the United States, taken after the first book made her famous. As unlike the 1933 work as a sequel could be, *Everybody's Autobiography* is predominantly a straightforward chronological narrative with Stein herself the first-person narrator. There is none of the humor of the first book and no portraits of famous people because Stein no longer needs famous people to legitimize her or her work—*she* is now the famous person. In addition, there is only an occasional human interest story or anecdote.

In place of the anecdotes of the first book, this one is strung together by endless abstract and intellectual dissertations; most focus on comparisons between France and America, but also between many other subjects. She compares American and French architecture, street patterns, cars and taxis, road signs, and women and men. She also comments on the differences between painters and writers, nineteenth- and twentieth-century writing, failure and success, armies and dancing, poor people and rich people, public and private schools, speeches and lectures, quickness and slowness, moist food and dry food, the efficiency of planes and armies, mothers and fathers, publicity and audiences, and much more. Some of the comparisons are striking and insightful; others appear trivial, even stupid. One can imagine Stein chuckling to herself as she writes "Well, anyway" or "However" after some of these comparisons, indicating her awareness of their meaninglessness, and also her scorn for popular tastes. ⟨. . .⟩

A significant theme in *Everybody's Autobiography* is Stein's concern that fame will change her identity. She needs to reassure herself that she is the same person by repeating that if her little dog knows her, then she must be the same person. But she is not the same person she was in *The Autobiography of Alice B. Toklas*. Writing in Toklas's voice to celebrate her lover, Stein produced a book with a strong female dimension. Even though a conventional female voice, it makes the autobiography a delight to read. In *Everybody's Autobiography*, Stein writes in her own voice as a successful writer who has made it in a man's world. Projecting the image of what she thinks a man is, she burdens her narrative with endless abstract comparisons to impress her readers with her intelligence. As narrated by a successful "male," her second autobiography is intellectual, self-conscious, and dull. By comparison, it points up how much *The Autobiography of Alice B. Toklas* is a part of the women's autobiographical tradition despite its impersonality. Stein gave her lover of twenty-five years immortality by affixing her name to her autobiography, but Toklas, by providing Stein with the female component to her life and her autobiography, gave her immortality through the one work that is still popular today.

—Estelle C. Jelinek, "Exotic Autobiography Intellectualized: The Legitimation of Gertrude Stein," *The Tradition of Women's Autobiography from Antiquity to the Present* (Boston: Twayne, 1986), 134–35, 143–47

CATHERINE N. PARKE

Shortly before *The Autobiography of Alice B. Toklas* (1933) appeared, Gertrude Stein asked Toklas if she thought the book would be a bestseller. Toklas replied, "no she did not think so because it was not sentimental enough." To both women's surprise and the surprise of the publisher, Random House, *The Autobiography* was a great success. And when this happened, Toklas remarked with comic irony that "well after all it was sentimental enough."

Sentimentality, which Stein defined as the mistaken and dangerous emphasis on human nature over the human mind, was something that she worked very hard to avoid in her writing. There came from this mistaken emphasis, she thought, "all the assertions of the self and all the rhetorical attitudes that," as Thornton Wilder noted in his preface to *The Geographical History of America*, "require the audience—wars, politics, propaganda, jealousy, and so on." In short, from sentimentality comes the violent and destructive politics of melodrama.

Soon after the popular success of *The Autobiography*, Stein experienced for the first and apparently the only time in her life writer's block. Suspecting that she had written a sentimental book and "knowing," as Richard Bridgman observes, "that she now possessed a commercial value," she felt disappointed in herself. This disappointment affected her writing. Four years later, in *Everybody's Autobiography*, she characterized part of what she had learned from this experience: "As long as the outside does not put a value on you it remains outside but when it does put a value on you then . . . all your inside gets to be outside" (*EA*, p. 47). As Stein had come to understand firsthand, we have outsides and insides for a reason—one protects the other—and we tamper with them at our peril. The chief danger of success, like the chief flaw of sentimentality, is the way each threatens, both literally and figuratively, to turn us and our values inside out. As we should fear having our talent turned into a commodity, so we should fear the valuing of human nature over human mind.

⟨. . .⟩ Stein's uneasiness over the thought that her writing might be sentimental and her fear of confusing the "inside" with the "outside," which is to say her fear of confusing self-valuation with her value to others as a commodity, bear upon her understanding of the relationship between writer and audience. By pursuing these issues in her work, we may come to some renewed insights into the chief strength of her work: the way she likes things "simple through complication" ⟨. . . .⟩

This problem of how to tell something to others in a way that does not betray the teller was always one of Stein's chief concerns. How could one, for instance, lecture without sooner or later beginning "to hear yourself talk . . . and you do not hear what you say. You just hear what they hear you say." This danger of confusing inside with outside became of increasing concern to Stein the longer she wrote: "I became interested in how you could tell this thing [reality] in a way that anybody could understand and at the same time keep true to your values, and the thing bothered me a great deal at that time." ⟨Haas, "A Transatlantic Interview," *A Primer for the Gradual Understanding of Gertrude Stein*, (Los Angeles: Black Sparrow Press, 1971), 18⟩ As Stein understood it, these responsibilities were joint means to the same end: the end of writing truly American writing by creating a new language and new literary forms that anybody could understand but that were also distinctively one's own, both based fundamentally on a new notion of time which she called the "continuous present." ⟨Stewart, *Gertrude Stein and the Present* (Cambridge: Harvard University Press, 1967), vii⟩

For her this American project took as its founding assumption that "either nothing is worth writing about or everything is worth writing about." "That," she believed, "anybody can understand." ⟨Stein, "What Is English Literature?," *Lectures in America* (Boston: Beacon Press, 1957), 34–5⟩ Her chief aim in writing, for instance, *The Making of Americans* (1925) was to create for each character a self-conscious existence, a "quality of interest," and a "stake in what happens" equivalent to the ideal politics of universal suffrage—of everybody, including women and children, having the vote (paraphrase from *Transatlantic Interview*, p. 17). For her the key to such an attempt was to approximate the rhythm of the thing one was writing about—the rhythm of a personality if one was writing about other people's lives, the rhythm of an idea if one was writing about mind. It was this project of inventing the right rhythms for biography, fiction, and philosophy (though she would not have distinguished these three as air-tight categories) that occupied the center of her interest throughout a lifetime of creative work. Surely this is the project Stein had in mind when she observed that she liked a thing simple, but "simple through complication." ⟨. . .⟩

⟨. . .⟩ When you have confidence, you can create characters other than yourself "seen splendidly or sadly or heroically or beautifully or despairingly or gently." But when you have no confidence and therefore must hold on to yourself, you can only make yourself "strong or weak or mysterious or passionate or drunk or controlled."

The separation from Leo, twin of her nonbeing and the millstone that weighted down her confidence, and her satisfying union with Alice B. Toklas combined with Stein's lifelong biographical project to create in herself a new and much needed confidence. Her literary program was a genuine and superbly confident pluralism, rich with the traditions which she had inherited from Emerson, Thoreau, Whitman, and James, but also uniquely her own. By taking on in her writings the biographical personae of many different kinds of women and men, by aiming finally to write everybody's autobiography, Stein hoped to spread difference and confidence—difference through confidence and confidence through difference—fearfully, wonderfully through us all. And by spreading these paired qualities she hoped to help us become both distinctly, separately ourselves and at one with each other.

    —Catherine N. Parke, "'Simple Through Complication': Gertrude Stein Thinking," *American Literature* 60, no. 9 (December 1988): 554–7, 574

FAITH PULLIN

⟨In⟩ *The Autobiography of Alice B. Toklas* (1933), she ⟨Gertrude Stein⟩ offers a landmark twentieth-century instance of the way in which an autobiography must establish its own characteristic vision.

For in *The Autobiography of Alice B. Toklas* Gertrude Stein performs an act which verges on a species of ventriloquism. She, as it were, re-enacts Alice Toklas's own style to render a comic portrait of herself, viewing herself from the outside as if an artefact, a moving object in space—in all a stunning mimetic coup. It is a book whose shocking charm derives from the matter-of-fact description of a totally extraordinary life and experience. In this, the contrast with Stein's earlier meditations on personality could not be greater. In *The Making of Americans* (1925), for instance, she had eschewed examination of the individual in favour of 'an exact description of inner and outer reality', an attempt to link the non-individualized self with the outside world. *The Making of Americans* (a none too disguised portrait-gallery of her own family) presents characters as separate units, having little connection with each other, except in terms of their family relationships and as examples of specific classifications; they are defined purely in terms of their modes of being in the universe, whether they attack or resist, are independent or dependent. Paradoxically, although projected as the history of 'everyone who ever was or is or will be living', Stein actually presents a uniquely individualized account of the interior life of a human being. ⟨. . .⟩

⟨. . .⟩ *The Autobiography of Alice B. Toklas* is meta-fictional in that it is a narrative that discusses itself and its own self-reflexivity as well as the identity of its writer. In the final words of the book Stein merges herself as narrator with herself as personality, redefining the categories of autobiographer, novelist and reporter ⟨. . . .⟩

The same position with regard to contemporaneity is arrived at at the close of *Everybody's Autobiography* (1936) in Stein's concluding statement about the nature of identity: 'perhaps I am not I even if my little dog knows me but any way I like what I have and now it is today.' During the course of *Everybody's Autobiography*, Stein makes many retrospective comments on the nature of her achievement in *Toklas*. She now regards the previous work as, in some respects, illegitimate since it was 'a description and a creation of something that having happened was in a way happening not again'. In other words, it was 'history', 'newspaper', 'illustration', but not autobiography. Although Stein claims in the Preface to *Everybody's Autobiography* that 'anything is an autobiography' and 'autobiography is easy', she had, in fact, refused, consistently, to write her own, rejecting the requests of publishers, and it was a profound, traumatic shock for her to find that the 'easy' work *Toklas* was so much more successful and more highly valued than the 'difficult', innovative *Making of Americans*. Even so, *Toklas* is a more overtly sophisticated performance than the later book; Stein recreates Alice's personality as the teller of the tale and at the same time presents a self which is more grandiose and more authoritative than the deliberately naïve and friendly protagonist who traverses and rediscovers America in *Everybody's Autobiography*. It seems that the very success of *Toklas* allowed the relaxation and lack of pretension that characterize Stein's encounters and travels as a celebrity, a celebrity who, paradoxically, is identified with her audience rather than marked out by her superiority as self-proclaimed genius. Her impact as a lecturer comes from the fact that, like the students, Stein does not know the answer: 'I do not even know whether there is a question let alone having an answer for a question' ⟨*Everybody's Autobiography*⟩.

Stein attempts to avoid the essential disjunction between self as object and subject, the internal and the external by the calculatedly ambiguous use of the word autobiography itself. *Everybody's Autobiography* refers both to the book and the life, the fiction and the facts of her actual journey and its events. However, contained within the book's linear structure are meditations on the impact on her life and her vision of her 'self' caused by sudden fame, late in life, after a career of strenuous disappointment. Large areas of *Everybody's Autobiography* are simpl⟨y⟩ picaresque; it is inevitable that Stein's intention of collapsing her audience and herself into one total entity that will be the subject-matter of the autobiography can only be minimally successful. In point of fact, all Stein's writings aspire to the condition of the literary essay since only in this form can she escape the conflicts of character-creation.

—Faith Pullin, "Enclosure/Disclosure: A Tradition of American Autobiography by Women," *First Person Singular: Studies in American Autobiography*, ed. A. Robert Lee (New York: St. Martin's Press, 1988), 126–9

SUSAN M. SCHULTZ

The Autobiography of Alice B. Toklas is one of Stein's most ostensibly accessible works. The second, "Stanzas in Meditation," records the process of telling rather than offering us the tale itself. But the very accessibility of the Toklas autobiography tends to obscure its central sleight of hand, as well as its left hook at literary tradition, for Stein not only writes as her own muse—Alice B. Toklas—but she has Toklas perform a service quite different from that of the traditional muse. Conventionally, the muse has been at once the power behind the text and the text's best audience. But Stein's muse does not so much inspire as advertise her work; her muse promotes the text as a literary, not a spiritual, agent. Even more radically, the work that Stein has Toklas advertise is not the work that she finds herself "writing"; instead, it is the kind of experimental work that we find in "Stanzas in Meditation," work that eschews the muse. Toklas, then, invites us to forget Toklas, just as Stein invites us to become one with Stein. The central subject of the second autobiography, like the first, is the question of audience: for whom is Stein writing, herself or someone else? To what extent can she become her own audience? To what extent does the equation of the artist with her audience obviate or exacerbate the modern artist's problem with audience? She poses these questions in both works, although her strategies are more radical in "Stanzas in Meditation."

⟨. . .⟩ Stein's long poem "Stanzas in Meditation" resists closure only insofar as it resists a muse outside of itself. Stein seeks to find something internal to poetry itself on which to authorize her text. In a poem whose title *sounds* Romantic, Stein deconstructs the Romantic landscape and moves toward a purely linguistic one, which cannot be described because it is a landscape of words, not a place.

This problem is as sexual as it is linguistic. Stein's repetitions bespeak the impossibility of ever actually saying the same thing twice—she is the Heraclitus of modern writers. But they also testify to her ambivalence about the sameness that her repetitions seem to assert. The sameness that Stein desires with her audience is metaphorically like the lesbian union she shared with Toklas. She parodies the homosexual nature of that union of like with like in her conflation of herself with Toklas in the *Autobiography*. She parodies that intimacy again in the first sentence of *Everybody's Autobiography*, published in 1937—"Alice B. Toklas did hers and now anybody will do theirs"—in which she—anybody, everybody—becomes one with all audiences, not just with Toklas. To write everybody's autobiography is both to deny the difference between writer and reader and to assert control over the reader's reception of the text.

Throughout her autobiographies Stein expresses the desire to do away with difference at the same time as she questions the worthiness of her desire to do so. Her text is a mirror in which she perceives herself. But what distinguishes her from other mirror-writers (Renaissance sonneteers such as Sidney, Spenser, and Shakespeare come to mind) is the literalism of her metaphor: Petrarch perhaps saw only himself in the mirror of Laura, but he rerepresented himself as other—as a woman. Not only does Stein look for herself in her text; she is the mirror in which she looks. Thus the lesbian union that she exploits in the Toklas "autobiography" becomes a trope for a far more primary narcissism than that of Petrarch and his followers.

⟨. . .⟩ ⟨T⟩he *Autobiography* is nothing if not a plea for an audience, as well as an extended complaint about the misconceptions of the as-yet-uneducated audience. ⟨. . .⟩ Stein is more ambivalent about her audience in "Stanzas in

Meditation," but only because she fears that her readers will not accept her; she is every bit as anxious for control over her audience. ⟨. . .⟩

Stein's final bow to the audience raises the question of the troubled relation between her desire to find an audience and the obscurity that would seem to deny her such an audience. I would suggest that Stein *uses* such obscurity as an important card in her long career of self-advertisement. The self-effacement of "Stanzas" covers up what is actually the opposite impulse (just as Stein becomes at once everybody and nobody in *Everybody's Autobiography*). The writer who proclaims over and again that she is "the only one," and that she is one of the three great geniuses of the century, displays that genius in works so obscure that even devoted readers of *The Autobiography of Alice B. Toklas* or *Everybody's Autobiography* might turn away from them. The unreadable text is less a text, in the usual sense, than an icon—less an act of communication than of bravado. A work such as "Stanzas in Meditation" becomes a commodity through which Stein can buy the label of genius, and become famous less for what she writes than for the fact that she writes so obscurely. That she recognized the sometimes humorous connection between autobiography and publicity is clear from a passage in *Everybody's Autobiography*: "But now well now how can you dream about a personality when it is always being created for you by a publicity, how can you believe what you make up when publicity makes them up to be so much realer than you can dream. And so autobiography is written which is in a way a way to say that publicity is right, they are as the public see them. Well yes."

"Stanzas in Meditation" forces us to reconsider Stein's use of the word "autobiography," as well as our own. For how can a writer who believes (at least in this poem) in the utter separation of the text from the world write an autobiography, or several autobiographies? What does it mean to tell one's story only "for oneself and strangers," to paraphrase Stein in the opening to *The Making of Americans?* Where are we to find Stein—in *The Autobiography of Alice B. Toklas*, in "Stanzas in Meditation," or in *Everybody's Autobiography?* Perhaps the lesson that Stein teaches us is that the autobiographer makes and remakes herself out of her perceived relationship with her audience. Stein's triumph in "Stanzas"—however uneven—is to show to what extent that relationship defines the writer, even when she tries to write without either a muse or an audience.

—Susan M. Schultz, "Gertrude Stein's Self-Advertisement," *Raritan* 12, no. 2 (1992): 71–3, 86–7

CATHARINE R. STIMPSON

Gertrude Stein began to write seriously around 1903. A decade later, she had a reputation, especially but not exclusively in avant-garde circles. As that reputation expanded to ever larger publics, it divided against itself. In a repetitive binary opposition, two "Steins" competed for attention in an arena that Stein herself could at best partially control. One "Stein" was the "Good Stein," whom the public liked. In 1933, it made a best-seller of her *jeu d'esprit, The Autobiography of Alice B. Toklas.* After passing through the market, *The Autobiography* went on to please a second set of cultural gatekeepers: doyens of the syllabi, denizens of the college curriculum. If Stein appears in the United States classroom, *The Autobiography* or *Three Lives* usually represents her.

The second "Stein" was the "Bad Stein," whom the public hated and ridiculed. The Bad Stein was guilty of a double transgression: first, and more blatantly, she subverted generic and linguistic codes; next, and more slyly, she subverted sexual codes. Both her word and flesh violated normalities. Since the 1970s, a mélange of audiences has inverted Stein's reputations. The Old Good Stein is the New Bad Stein. She is too obedient to convention. The Old Bad Stein is the New Good Stein. Her transgressions are exemplary deeds.

The Autobiography of Alice B. Toklas and a companion text, *Everybody's Autobiography,* mingle the two, pre-1970 Steins. So doing, they undercut, sometimes incisively, sometimes impotently, the binary opposition that her reputation embodies. Skillfully, the Old Bad Stein, the transgressive Stein, is cajoling a potential reader more decorous than she into accepting a story about the Old Good Stein. Indeed, that story will establish the Old Good Stein. In a complex act of deception, confession, and assertion, a misunderstood, under-published author is giving the public what she calculates it can take. Her gift demands that she handle a sub-genre we insufficiently understand: the lesbian lie. This lie insists that no lesbians lie abed here. To imagine erotics is to fall victim to cognitive errotics. The author respects, indeed shares, a reader's sense of decorum. At its finest, such decorum construes all sexuality as private and then begs private things to stay private. At its worst, such decorum is repression's etiquette. Stein's lie, then, is at once manipulative and courteous. The author delicately refuses to stir her readers up too much. Proper manners prevail. So, less fortunately for post-Stonewall sensibilities, will ignorance. ⟨Heilbrun, *Writing a Woman's Life,* 1988, 79⟩ Not surprisingly, the tact that renders sexuality invisible also renders money invisible. *The Autobiography* is genteel about Stein's income. The circulation of her desire and that of her dollars/francs are each veiled.

An effect of Stein's lesbian lie is to permit us to regard the Old Good Stein as if she were both a "character" in the colloquial sense of "What a character!"

and a literary character in an autobiographical gesture. This is an ironic turn
for a cultural analyst who believed that the mass media now spew out personalities (the Duchess of Windsor, for example) in such profusion that these
manufactured personalities have driven the character (Gwendolyn Harleth,
for example) from fiction's dreamy stage. Indeed, *Everybody's Autobiography*
shrewdly meditates on the distinctions among having a sense of personal identity, no matter how momentarily, creating a literary identity, and being a mass
media personality. As character and literary character, Stein is a jolly, bluff,
discreet celebrity who plays with crowds of famous men: Picasso, Matisse,
Hemingway. Each of these attributes—jolliness, bluffness, discretion, fame,
the company of men—is vital to her appeal. She has her anxious moments, but
they test, rather than damage, the bulkhead of her cheer. Moreover, this character exists within a readable narrative. Such readability attracts two audiences
that perhaps would agree only about the readable: a heterosexual audience
generally suspicious of transgression, and a homosexual audience that longs to
celebrate sexual, but not literary, differences.

In brief, Stein's lesbian lie pins up an accessible star, a brilliant amalgam of
democratic openness, spirited realism, and enchantment. Her modulation of
subversion into entertainment both follows and refines a homosexual method
of seeking acceptance in modern heterosexual culture ⟨Leibowitz, *Fabricating
Lives: Explorations in American Autobiography*, 1989, 219⟩. *La Cage aux Folles* is a
commercially triumphant example. Camp is a complex, wickedly self-
conscious extreme. Because this modulation of subversion into entertainment
is often for profit, for financial as well as psychological and physical security,
it is part of the *packaging* of homosexuality. Stein's estranged brother Leo hated
The Autobiography. "God, what a liar she is," he grumped. Leo was wounded
because he thought his sister was being untruthful about him and perhaps
vengeful as well. In his narcissism, he was dully sharpening a real point: *The
Autobiography* does lie. ⟨. . .⟩

⟨. . .⟩ On the one hand, the coda is a tribute to the lesbian couple. Its unity
is at once regressive and a leap beyond individuation and its perils. The
twinned voices of the women are intertwined. The paragraph of their being
merges the sentences of their voices. Indeed, the couple represents a merger-
and-acquisitions policy based on feeling rather than on corporate worth.
Unified, Stein/Toklas assert their rights to love as they please and work as they
wish. Without relying on foundational principles or master narratives, for lesbianism lacks both in any plausible form, they assert the value of their loving,
working presence in the world, their capacities for breath and brain. Their
story, no matter what they leave out, is the proof of their worth ⟨Brodzki and
Schenck, *Life/Lines: Theorizing Women's Autobiography*, 1988, 82⟩. On the other
hand, the coda maintains heterosexual roles. The husband, male-identified

woman, has actually done the work of writing. The wife, the lady, merely speaks. Stein further placates her readers through surprising (but not shocking) them and then giving them something to do. Getting to play "Author, author, who's got the author," her readers swing their attention away from the lesbian couple and onto the game the couple is offering them, rather as if the coda were a party treat or tea cake.

The coda of *The Autobiography* recapitulates mixed messages about sexuality that Stein has tapped out throughout the text. First, the social calendar of Stein/Toklas seems to be largely heterosexual. Heterosexuals need not be monogamous. Ironically, the lesbian couple upholds the principles of monogamy. Hardly Rotarians, the friends of Stein/Toklas live out of wedlock, commit adultery, break hearts, flirt, tease. They practice the conventions of wild Western romanticism. ⟨. . .⟩

However, Stein leaves a paper trail about homosexual realities. Spatially, she sets *The Autobiography* in the houses that Stein/Toklas inhabited, emotionally, in their marriage. The narrative voices are theirs. A lesbian world, the water in which the fish of anecdotes swim, is so fluidly embracing that it seems both invisible and natural. ⟨. . .⟩

Stein's most public autobiographies lack a measure of the pleasure of many of her more radical texts. *Everybody's Autobiography* is often dogged in its descriptions of fun. Neither text has the intricate lyricism and sophisticated engagement with the naive of "A Sonatina Followed By Another." Here, Stein retains traditional marital roles (Stein as husband, Toklas as wife), but transforms the foul into the fowls of a joyous, homey bestiary.

—Catharine R. Stimpson, "Gertrude Stein and the Lesbian Lie," *American Women's Autobiography: Fea(s)ts of Memory*, ed. Margo Culley (Madison: University of Wisconsin Press, 1992): 152–3, 158–9, 162

SIDONIE SMITH

When she came to the scene of autobiography, Gertrude Stein found herself triply discomfited. Neither the old autobiographical "I" of the fathers nor the sexually marked and remarkable "I" she brought to the page nor the conventional narrative itinerary through which the normative autobiographical "I" progressed could do the textual work she wanted to do in *The Autobiography of Alice B. Toklas*. The genre itself, driven by chronology, multiple levels of referentiality, and a normative subjectivity seemed incapable of accommodating her modernist experimentations with time, referentiality, the instrumentality of language, and the erotics of lesbian desire. And so she had a challenge of almost impossible proportions facing her in writing autobiography. How could she displace the center of autobiographical narrative away from a unified subject? How could she keep the identity of the sexually marked subject out of the autobiographical text and keep the celebration of lesbian coupling in the text? How could she keep the materiality of the body and language in the autobiographical text? ⟨. . .⟩ In other words, how could she break the paternal instrumentality of the genre? In grappling with such questions Stein came up with an experimental form through which she both trespassed upon the grounds of the universal subject and restaked its topological and tropological boundaries by engaging in a duplicitous out-of-body ruse. ⟨. . .⟩

⟨. . . We⟩ might say that the autobiographical "I" here is an "I" of two-ness since the voice of the text is not singular. In braiding the voices of Stein and Toklas, the narrator continually forces the reader to equivocate in specifying who speaks at any textual moment. Sentences contain traces of at least two voices as the narrating Stein captures the rhetorical structures, rhythmic cadences, and witty perspective of Toklas as well as her own stylistic experimentations and vision. Thus there is a "we-ness" to the textual "I," ⟨. . . .⟩ And this mixed "we" acts to qualify the promise of coherence and univocity privileged in traditional (nineteenth-century) autobiographical practice. ⟨. . .⟩

⟨. . .⟩ With this shimmering movement of times past, present, and future, movement analogous to the shimmering quality of lines and space in cubist paintings, Stein is effectively able to reorient the reader's time-sense and generic expectations. The anecdotal breaks in chronology, the confusion of past, present, and future, as well as the externalized portrait, subvert the notion of clearly defined developmental stages of growth, of the subordination of time present and future to time past in autobiographical narrative, and the notion of a coherent, unified core of selfhood. ⟨. . .⟩

Sacrificing her own story to Gertrude Stein's story, "Alice" reproduces a very conventional narrative, a "woman's story." In the role of devoted wife to Gertrude Stein's husband, "Alice" seems to embrace her identity as a woman as well as the conventional script of woman's essentialized selfhood by dedicating her text to the enhancement of her spouse, making Stein the entity or artistic genius who inhabits the center of all significant historical and textual activity and relegating herself to the margins of the story. She serves as a virtual host who sacrifices her own life for the life of her spouse. This generic convention traces its roots back to the seventeenth century, when women such as Margaret Cavendish, Duchess of Newcastle, and Ann Lady Fanshawe wrote biographies of their famous husbands, biographies through which they attempted to secure the (sometimes suspect) reputation of their husbands for posterity. ⟨. . .⟩

In fact, in *The Autobiography*, female self-effacement is pushed about as far as it can be pushed. "Alice" sacrifices her very subjectivity to her husband since, in fact, Stein ventriloquizes "Alice." Stein as the author of "Alice" assumes the position of the man who speaks for woman ⟨. . . .⟩

But what does speaking as "Alice" enable Stein to do textually? And what does it have to do with identity practices? If woman is the sacrificial victim of patriarchal culture, what does it mean for Stein to speak as one of the victims? ⟨. . .⟩

By speaking through the voice of Alice B. Toklas, Stein pursues an art of camouflage. ⟨. . .⟩

The camouflaged Stein displaces her "monumental egotism" into the self-effacing voice of "Alice." Through this disembodiment, she can simultaneously present herself as genius and protect herself from the reader's expectation that women should avoid egotistical self-display and self-assertion. Imagine the difference in effect if the following passage contained "I's" instead of "she's": "She realises that in english literature in her time she is the only one. She has always known it and now she says it" (77). The laughter would have been missed for the pretension. Stein uses "Alice" to escape her identity as the patriarchally defined female, even as she herself participates in exacting the sacrifice of "Alice"/woman as wife.

The art of camouflage can also be seen as a strategy for normalizing a culturally abnormal sexual relationship. Assigning "Alice" to the wife position and "Gertrude Stein" to the husband position in the text, Stein reinforces the relationship of self-sacrifice to femaleness and genius to maleness. In doing so she situates in her text a traditionally arranged rhetorical couple that represents the traditional coupling of heterosexuality. Invoking a politics of heterosexism, in order to normalize her "aberrant" sexuality, she appears to be honoring a masculinist hierarchy through which male and female identities are constituted.

But while *The Autobiography of Alice B. Toklas* seems to promote a patriarchal gender hierarchy with its essentialized sexual difference and compulsory heterosexuality, it does so at the same time that it challenges the very bases of that identification.

—Sidonie Smith, "'Stein Is an 'Alice' Is a 'Gertrude Stein,'" *Subjectivity, Identity, and the Body: Women's Autobiographical Practices in the Twentieth Century* (Bloomington: Indiana University Press, 1993): 65, 68, 71, 75–77

BIBLIOGRAPHY

Three Lives. 1909.

Tender Buttons. 1914.

Geography and Plays. 1922.

The Making of Americans. 1925.

Useful Knowledge. 1929.

Before the Flowers of Friendship Faded Friendship Faded. 1931.

How To Write. 1931.

The Autobiography of Alice B. Toklas. 1932.

Operas and Plays. 1932.

Stanzas in Meditation. 1932.

Matisse, Picasso and Gertrude Stein with Two Shorter Stories. 1933.

Portraits and Prayers. 1934.

Lectures in America. 1935.

Narration: Four Lectures by Gertrude Stein. 1935.

*The Geographical History of America or The Relation of Human Nature to the Human
    Mind.* 1936.

Everybody's Autobiography. 1936.

Picasso. 1938.

What Are Masterpieces. 1940.

Paris France. 1940.

Wars I Have Seen. 1945.

Brewsie and Willie. 1946.

Blood on the Dining-Room Floor. 1948.

Two: Gertrude Stein and her Brother and Other Early Portraits. 1951.

Bee Time Vine and Other Pieces. 1953.

As Fine as Melanctha. 1954.

Painted Lace and Other Pieces. 1955.

Alphabets and Birthdays. 1957.

A Novel of Thank You. 1958.

The Making of Americans. 1966.

Lucy Church Amiably. 1969.

Gertrude Stein on Picasso. 1970.

Fernhurst, QED and Other Early Writings. 1972.

EUDORA WELTY
b. 1909

EUDORA WELTY writes lovingly of her parents and childhood in her 1984 autobiography *One Writer's Beginnings*. She was born on April 13, 1909. Her father, Christian Webb Welty, was a schoolteacher from Ohio. While working in West Virginia he met and married another teacher, Mary Chestina Andrews. They moved to Jackson, Mississippi, where Welty's father worked for the Lamar Life Insurance Company, later becoming president. Welty and her two brothers attended the Jefferson Davis Grammar School, where the stern Miss Lorena Duling became the model for many schoolteachers in Welty's fiction. After graduating from high school, Welty attended the Mississippi State College for Women for two years and then studied English for two years at the University of Wisconsin. After graduating in 1929, she studied advertising for a year at Columbia Business School. When her father died in 1931, she returned to Jackson and over the next 10 years she served as social correspondent for the *Memphis Commercial Appeal* and worked at a radio station, WJDX.

From 1933 to 1936 she worked as junior publicity agent for the Works Projects Administration (WPA). As she traveled the state by car and bus, writing news stories and conducting interviews, she took many photographs of WPA projects, such as the rebuilding of Tupelo, Mississippi, after it had been demolished by a tornado. Some of her photographs were displayed in a "one-woman show" at the Lugene Gallery, a small photography shop in New York. She then worked for the Mississippi Advertising Commission, writing copy and taking photographs.

In 1936 her first short story, "Death of a Travelling Salesman," was published in *Manuscript*. Within a year Cleanth Brooks and Robert Penn Warren had published "A Memory " and "A Piece of News" in the *Southern Review*. Soon she was publishing in the *Atlantic Monthly, Harper's Bazaar*, and *Harper's*. Two more stories were published in *Prairie Schooner* in 1937. Katherine Anne Porter read her short stories and became her advocate, writing the introduction to her collection of short stories, *A Curtain of Green* (1941).

The 1940s were a productive time for Welty. Her first two novels were published: *The Robber Bridegroom* (1942) and *Delta Wedding* (1946). Two more story collections were published: *The Wide Net* (1943) and *The Golden Apples* (1949). She also received awards: two first prizes and one second prize in the annual O. Henry Memorial contests. In 1944 she received an award from the American Academy of Arts and Letters. She was awarded a Guggenheim Fellowship for 1942, and it was renewed in 1949–50. With these fellowships she traveled to Italy, France, and England. In 1942 she joined the staff of *The New York Times Book Review*, using the pseudonym Michael Ravenna.

During the early 1950s she continued to publish and travel. Random House reprinted her first collections of stories as *Selected Stories* in its Modern Library Series in 1954. Her third novel, *The Ponder Heart*, was also published that year after being serialized in 1953. Her fourth collection of stories, *The Bride of the Innisfallen* (1955), contained stories about Mississippi, but also about Italy, Ireland, and mythical locales. During the next 10 years, Welty tended to her ailing mother, who died in 1966. While no major work appeared during that time, Welty still traveled, lectured, and received honors. She held the William Allan Neilson professorship at Smith College in 1962, and they published three of her critical essays on fiction. She received the Lucy Donnelly Fellowship Award from Bryn Mawr, the William Dean Howells Medal of the Academy of Arts and Letters for *The Ponder Heart*, and the Ingram Memorial Foundation Award in Literature.

The time spent caring for her mother is reflected in her fiction of the next decade, *Losing Battles* (1970) and *The Optimist's Daughter* (1972). *Losing Battles* was her first work to appear on best-seller lists, and she received the Pulitzer Prize for *The Optimist's Daughter*. Much of her non-fiction, including essays and reviews, was republished in *The Eye of the Story: Selected Essays and Reviews* (1971). Also in 1971 she published *One Time, One Place: Mississippi in the Depression: A Snapshot Album*. In the introduction she reflects on the influence photography had on her writing and her understanding of people and their lives. In 1984 she published *One Writer's Beginnings*, a nostalgic look at her past and her development into a writer.

CRITICAL   EXTRACTS

C. VANN WOODWARD

In her introduction to Eudora Welty's first book, "A Curtain of Green" (1941), Katherine Anne Porter remarked of the young writer that "She considers her personal history as hardly worth mentioning." More than 20 years later, when pressed for biographical information again, she replied, "Except for what's personal, there is really so little to tell, and that little lacking in excitement and drama in the way of the world." In view of this reticence on the part of a major American writer, it is a good thing that Harvard University had the gumption to get Miss Welty to give a series of lectures on her life as a writer and the good sense to publish them in this small volume.

"One Writer's Beginnings" is not a misleading title. It takes two-thirds of the book to bring the author down to age 10, and yet this and the remaining part are all addressed to the origins of a writer and her art. She manages, in her informal and self-deprecatory way, to be quite informative about her real subject. "Children, like animals, use all their senses to discover the world," she writes. "Then artists come along and discover it the same way, all over again." An early interest in painting and in photography, a passion for words and for reading and a precocious gift and eagerness for listening are all relevant here. As a small child she would plant herself between adults and say, "Now, *talk.*" She listened for stories long before she wrote them. "Listening *for* them is something more acute than listening *to* them," she points out. Many of her stories, for example "Why I Live at the P.O.," are told wholly in monologue and many in dialogue. And as she rightly adds, "How much more gets told besides!" in the telling. The telling is done in the authentic idiom of a time and place. 〈. . .〉

But Welty stories are almost entirely filled with Southerners, Mississippi Southerners, as authentically Southern as they come in their idiom, their gestures, their moods, their madnesses, everything to the finest detail. Black and white both, though mostly white. There are no Compsons or Sartorises, no hero with a tragic flaw, no doomed families with ancestral ghosts. With few exceptions—one thinks of "The Optimist's Daughter"—they are unsophisticated and very plain people. Some are as objectionable as the Snopeses, but they are never types, only individuals. They never speak for the author, only for themselves or the community. Miss Welty writes with detachment and sympathy but without identification. She has no fictional spokesman. "I don't write out of anger," she says, for "simply as a fiction writer, I am minus an adversary." It could be said that she is apolitical, nonideological, perhaps even ahistorical. 〈. . .〉

〈. . .〉 Whole families pass in review, several generations of them, trailing no clouds of destiny, no hereditary curse, no brooding guilt or racial complications or torments of pride and honor. They are located in time and place but are never seen as the pawns of historical or social forces. That is not the Welty way. As much as she may admire that way in works of her contemporaries, she has left it to them.

She has her own way, and it would be a mistake to push her into any traditional category. Her fiction is often enigmatic, elusive, elliptical, difficult.

Much is said between the lines or in the *way* it is said. Distinctions between love and hate, joy and sorrow, innocence and guilt, success and failure, victory and defeat are often left vague. So are the lines between dream and reality, fantasy and fact. One critic was brought up sharp by the suspicion that the whole story in "The Death of a Traveling Salesman" was hallucination on the part of the main character. The same sort of suspicion arises in that gem of a story "A Worn Path" or in "Powerhouse" or in "The Purple Hat." The author keeps her counsel. She records but never judges and often leaves enigmas enigmatic and mysteries mysterious.

The rich variety of her characters discourages generalization about them. Some are outsiders, loners, waifs, hitchhikers, restless salesmen, the loveless and the unlovable. In one tour de force, two deaf mutes are made to communicate elaborately, and in another two men with no common language spend a whole day together. The grotesque, the deranged, the deformed, the queer and the brutal all have parts to play, but they do not become a preoccupation. They are no more typical than judges, beauticians, housewives, ageless grannies, preadolescents, music teachers and hired hands. ⟨. . .⟩

In "One Writer's Beginnings," we find that in a turbulent period when authors commonly wrote in anger, protest and political involvement and many of them had reason to do so, one of them led a sheltered, relatively uneventful life, never married and always made her home in a provincial community. The same could have been said of Jane Austen.

 —C. Vann Woodward, "Southerner With Her Own Accent," *The New York Times Book Review* (19 February 1984): 7

Peggy Whitman Prenshaw

Like ⟨Elizabeth⟩ Bowen, Eudora Welty has shied from personal revelation and autobiography. She has written a few memorable reminiscences, most of which are collected in *The Eye of the Story*—"A Sweet Devouring" and "The Little Shore," most notably, in which she writes of her childhood love of books and of her neighborhood in Jackson, two blocks from the Mississippi State Capitol, where she spent her early years. For the most part, though, Welty has maintained a firm reticence about her private life. In a 1972 interview in the *Paris Review*, she told Linda Kuehl that she would feel "shy, and discouraged at the very thought" of a biography about herself, and she repeated her conviction that "a writer's work should be everything. A writer's whole feeling, the force of his whole life, can go into a story—but what he's worked for is to get an objective piece down on paper. That should be read instead of some account of his life." A little later she added, "Your private life should be kept private. My own I don't think would particularly interest anybody, for that matter. But I'd guard it; I feel strongly about that." 〈"Conversations with Eudora Welty," 81〉

Both Bowen and Welty later changed their minds about offering further revelations about themselves. Coincidentally, at about the same age each woman began writing her autobiography, Bowen in her seventy-third year, and Welty during the months preceding her seventy-fourth birthday in April 1983. 〈. . .〉

Welty's *One Writer's Beginnings* and Bowen's *Pictures and Conversations* elucidate one another in many suggestive and provocative ways. Like Bowen, Welty writes of her childhood and its strikingly visual, material world, which remains sharply etched in her memory. Also like Bowen, she seeks to locate the threads of attachment that link her early experiences within the family to the themes and landscapes that she would later create in fiction.

The chapter headings and titles of both books indicate the writers' preoc-cupation with the lessons of listening and seeing they learned as children. 〈. . .〉

Welty's book, which is also an investigation of psychic and artistic origins, also comprises three chapters, "Listening," "Learning to See," and "Finding a Voice." 〈. . .〉

Structurally and thematically, both autobiographies are concentrated upon the people, especially the parents, and places of youth. What marks their sharpest similarity is the writers' emphasis upon the evolution in their child-hood of a bifurcated vision of the world and of themselves, which they attribute partly to the differing personalities of their parents and partly to the division of their "home places." 〈. . .〉

〈. . .〉 Welty locates her dawning awareness of the outside world of appear-ance in the removals from home—for Welty, the dislocating, if beloved, sum-mer journeys to Ohio and West Virginia, the visits to distant grandparents, her hereditary home. In the chapter "Learning to See," she describes the family's trips and her realization that her parents—and by extension she herself—belonged not only to Jackson, Mississippi, but to a land elsewhere. The jour-neys made her understand, she writes, how Ohio had her father "around the heart, as West Virginia had my mother."

For Welty, the trip to another, "earlier" home opened her eyes, taught her to see. Perhaps it was Ohio and West Virginia, Welty suggests, that nudged her toward writing. "The trips were wholes unto themselves," Welty says. "They were stories. Not only in form, but in their taking on direction, move-ment, development, change. They changed something in my life: each trip made its particular revelation, though I could not have found words for it."

In *One Writer's Beginnings*, Welty writes of having early formed an impres-sion of her parents as embodying opposing, if complementary, personalities.

Welty's relationship to her parents casts much light upon certain persistent themes in her fiction, particularly the existence of the mysterious otherness that lies below the surface of self. ⟨. . .⟩

Welty's father read widely for information—there were books in the living room and encyclopedia tables and dictionary stand in the dining room—but her mother's first love was fiction: "she sank as a hedonist into novels," Welty writes. "She read Dickens in the spirit in which she would have eloped with him." It was she who supported her daughter's ambition to be a writer, perhaps partly from a sense of relief, for she thought of writing, Welty says, as offering a "safe" career. From the witness of the autobiography, one sees that the complementarities of her parents have provided Welty with a quite conscious design for patterning and formulating complementarities of great variety and scope in her fiction.

What emerges from reading *One Writer's Beginnings* and *Pictures and Conversations* side by side, proceeding antiphonally, is not the discovery that these writers led parallel lives—they did not—but rather the discovery that they locate the origins of their art, their literary creativity, in similar perceptions of childhood and youth. When as young women they began writing seriously—Bowen in the 1920s, Welty in the 1930s—they sought separation from youth, adult independence, largely through their work. ⟨. . .⟩

For Welty and Bowen the writing of fiction also turns out to be the chief way of maintaining the past, the family, one's youth. For both women, the means and meaning of writing have been the "welding together" of an "inner landscape," a connecting of the past, through memory, with the ever-changing, revealing outside world. ⟨. . .⟩

Welty concludes *One Writer's Beginnings* with the comment that she has led a "sheltered life," but she does not hold her mother's view that the life of the writer is "safe." Rather, the sheltered life can be "daring indeed."

—Peggy Whitman Prenshaw, "The Antiphonies of Eudora Welty's *One Writer's Beginnings* and Elizabeth Bowen's *Pictures and Conversations*," *Mississippi Quarterly* 39, no. 4 (1986): 643, 645, 646, 648–50

RUTH M. VANDE KIEFT

"The events of our lives happen in a sequence in time, but in their significance to ourselves they find their own order, a timetable not necessarily—perhaps not possibly—chronological. The time as we know it subjectively is often the chronology that stories and novels follow: it is the continuous thread of revelation." Thus Eudora Welty summarizes the method of her autobiography, *One Writer's Beginnings*. The voice of memory speaks with an artlessly rambling progress, revealing, celebrating—mostly her beloved parents, to whom the book is dedicated. Personal experience and family history are blended with observations about her development and practice as a fiction writer.

Much is achieved in the hundred pages of this book. Though the comparison may seem absurd for a work so brief and modest in its claims, it is a private odyssey, an inward journey or quest for the self as writer, of the same nature as Wordsworth's *Prelude* or Joyce's *Portrait of the Artist as a Young Man*. It is a compendium of private human insight and wisdom flexible in tone—playful, sorrowful, satirical. It is also something more public, wholly justifying its original sponsorship as a series of three lectures in the History of American Civilization program at Harvard University: a vivid re-creation, over more than a century of places, persons, and experiences remembered and tales told, of the physical settings, manners, customs, values, and beliefs of three independent though, in the writer's life, convergent American types: the educated Appalachian "pioneer" (her mother's roots), the midwestern farmer (her father's roots), and the small-town "New South" Mississippian (her own and her brothers' roots).

Wonderful is her evocation of early twentieth-century American character types. Miss Duling, big brass bell in hand, ringing and summoning all vagrant, unruly children to march to their learning, is the Ur-teacher-principal: self-denying, stern, dedicated, omniscient, controlling the town, "a lifelong subscriber to perfection," the most "whole-souled figure of authority" Eudora Welty ever knew. Other teachers, and there are many, are variants on the type which came to be the most usual "heroine" of her fiction. Miss Calloway, she of the "dragon eye," "a witch," is the Ur-librarian, bastion of petty public morality, insistent on SILENCE except for her own "commanding voice," strict enforcer of rules intended to prevent books and readers, like lovers, from achieving their joyful unions. ⟨. . .⟩

The first two sections ("Listening" and "Learning to See") are concerned chiefly with the writer's preparation; the last ("Finding a Voice"), her performance; but the progression is not chronological. It is spiraling, with overlapping time periods, sense impressions, themes. She proceeds always from the particular to the general, stressing that connections can be made only by the use of hindsight, and that patterns are discovered through memory: to use Richard Wilbur's phrase, only as they are "wrought . . . in the tapestries of afterthought." She speaks of how, in writing about her parents, new connections in their lives became evident to her—perhaps because she is a fiction writer—making her perceive them "as even greater mysteries" than she knew. Writing fiction has given her "an abiding respect for the unknown in a human lifetime and a sense of where to look for the threads, how to follow, how to connect, find in the thick of the tangle what clear line persists." ⟨. . .⟩

⟨. . .⟩ Lyricism affects form, language, subjects, themes, tone, and sound in Eudora Welty's fiction, and it is evident from the first in her autobiography. ⟨. . .⟩

⟨. . .⟩ "Listening" begins with clocks striking, answering each other through the house, ticking in rhythm to her mother's rocker as she reads stories to Eudora before the fire, the cuckoo clock ending the story with "Cuckoo." Her earliest memories of listening include the sound of her mother's song, coming out "just a little bit in the minor key," making "Wee Willie Winkie" seem "wonderfully sad." Next comes the Victrola, offering opportunities for lullabies, marches, and musical comedy hits at her pleasure, with movement (especially dancing) as part of it, for movement is "at the very heart of listening." The observation leads the writer to reflect that from the time of her own earliest reading, she *heard* whatever was on the page, as though a silent voice, "human, but inward," were speaking—"the voice of the story or the poem itself." "The cadence, whatever it is that asks you to believe, the feeling that resides in the printed word, reaches me through the reader-voice." Her awareness of this voice, especially in its unique rhythm and movement within any particular story or poem, seems to be part of the lyrical impulse informing her work—something *heard*, almost musically, the sound and flow of the sentences testing their truth, reflecting the various moods of her fiction. ⟨. . .⟩

Her lyricism may be oblique or direct, dreaming or earthbound, satiric or sober, revelatory or reticent, exaggerated or understated: all these polarities appear in *One Writer's Beginnings* as much as in the fiction. The reticence is most apparent in a passage describing what must have been one of the most devastating experiences of her life, witnessing her father's death when her mother attempted to save his life by giving her blood in a transfusion. The two parents are lying on adjoining cots; her mother looks at her father with a "fervent face" as she hopes to do for him what he once did for her in helping to save her life:

> All at once his face turned dusky red all over. The doctor made a
> disparaging sound with his lips, the kind a woman knitting makes
> when she drops a stitch. What the doctor meant by it was that my
> father had died.
> My mother never recovered emotionally.

The brief visual description followed by an account of the doctor's reaction with a homely comparison of sounds (almost trivializing the great event to his experienced perception), and finally the childlike simplicity of the witness-narrator's interpretation of the sound, is gratefully numbing in its reticence, as though the reader's heart were caught in a still moment of hiatus before the comprehension that brings its soundless shock. Such passages are beyond praise. This lyricism of reserve, of withholding, could not be in greater contrast to the lyricism that is overflowing, as where the sound of "The Merry Widow" running up and down the staircase opens the autobiography. ⟨. . .⟩

Eudora Welty's autobiography shows her view of her *own* life, and life in general, to be all-affirmative. The child so excited and filled with suspense that she had to be put to bed for prolonged rest with a strange illness called "fast-beating heart," the curious and enthralled listener to family stories and local gossip, the hedonistic reader, the rapt dreamer, the mesmerized traveler, the acute observer and sensitive responder to the outside world, the family comic (with her older brother), the devoted daughter, struggling successfully to achieve her independence against unusually protective and self-sacrificial parents—all these speak of an abundant *vitality* and *joy* in existence, which overflows in her fiction. No wonder she chose a musician to convey the passion and intensity she feels for her work and expresses in it. Mystery rushes through this art, or opens slowly as a night-flower, shedding beauty. Or it is caught in a still, rapt moment of revelation.

—Ruth M. Vande Kieft, "A Continuous Thread of Revelation," *Eudora Welty* (Boston: Twayne, 1987), 186–89, 194, 196–97

GAYLE GRAHAM YATES

Yates: In your discussion of those two novels ⟨*Banner* and *Delta Wedding*⟩ and their locations and the need for those locations because of the story you had, you talked about the value of the family in each one, of your wanting to show family values. It seems to me that in *One Writer's Beginnings*, you talk about your own social values and their origins as a basis for your literary values, one of them being respect for the family and joy in the family. And another being cherishing friendships. And another being—well—tolerating eccentricities or diversity among people. [And] abhorring or rejecting cruelty or human unkindness. You suggest in *One Writer's Beginnings* that the origin of those values is in your own family, in where you were brought up or how you were brought up.

Welty: In my case, it was the family life and the way I was brought up that taught me . . . what I wanted. I am interested in human relationships. That is my true core. That is what I try to write about. Certainly it begins in the family and extends out and out. Of course, all these things are hindsight. I never thought of anything like this when I was writing the stories. Not in an analytical way. I was aware of what I was doing, but not analytically. Even what I say about choosing the place. It was just such an instinctive choice, and then it was dropped because I was into the story. I tried to think of that as I was writing this last little book [*One Writer's Beginnings*] because what I had undertaken to do was to try to see what in my life produced certain things. And I thought more specifically and had more scrutiny for it than I suppose I ever did before. I learned a lot from it by doing that.

Yates: I understand from Ross Moore that you were reluctant to undertake that assignment.

Welty: I was. If it hadn't been for Ross I probably wouldn't have done it. I don't know if I ever would have undertaken lectures at Harvard. Still it seems to me amazing that I had the temerity to do that [and] I said I don't know anything to tell graduate students at Harvard—you know, I am not a scholar, I am not anything like that. He [David Donald, the Harvard professor who commissioned the lectures that were then published as the book, *One Writer's Beginnings*] said, "Well, there is one thing you know that they don't, and that is you know about what in your life made you into a writer." And that *is* the one thing that I could have talked about. So . . . they were very receptive and helpful. I am very grateful to Ross for setting the ball rolling for me.

Yates: You enjoyed it when you got started?

Welty: I didn't enjoy it until I had done the first lecture. I was petrified—I enjoyed the *writing* of it. But *delivering* it in the form of three lectures was very frightening because I couldn't imagine whether or not anything I had written would communicate itself to the audience I was reading to. It couldn't change what I was doing, but I didn't know how it would be received. But they were receptive [the audience for the first lecture], and after that I drew a deep breath for the first time! After the first one.

Yates: And then when you gave the second one it was more comfortable?

Welty: It was better then. They were really wonderful young people. They were also from the town. And around. That was good for me—to have a general kind of audience. But the young people were the most enthusiastic and sympathetic of all. Isn't that wonderful?

Yates: And then it [the book] has been number one on the best-seller list for just weeks and weeks.

Welty: Isn't that amazing? Harvard was as staggered as I was!
  —Gayle Graham Yates, "An Interview with Eudora Welty," *Frontiers* 9, no. 3 (1987): 100–4

ROBERT H. BRINKMEYER JR.

In her review of Elizabeth Bowen's *Pictures and Conversations*, Eudora Welty suggests that Bowen is a regional writer not in the familiar sense but in a deeper, more mysterious way. She says that Bowen's regionalism is not of a particular place, but of the mind and heart. Rooted in this mysterious realm of the spirit, both Bowen's fiction and her interior life—the life that both gives birth to her writing and ultimately receives nourishment from it—brim with sensibility and meaning. The growth and development of one's inner region, Welty goes on to suggest, is inextricably tied to the process of writing fiction, and she cites an intriguing sentence from Bowen's book: "Since I have started writing, I have been welding together an inner landscape, assembled anything but at random."

Welty's observations here on Bowen (one of Welty's favorite authors) seem particularly relevant to Welty's own career as a writer. By the terms she establishes in this book review, Welty must certainly be considered a regional writer, for like Bowen, she too roots her fiction in the mysteries of the mind and heart. To an interviewer's suggestion that the most difficult things for a writer to express "would seem to be the hidden reaches of the human heart, the mystery, those impalpable emotions," Welty responded simply: "For a writer, those things are what you start with. You wouldn't have started a story without that awareness—that's what made you begin." Moreover, like Bowen, Welty has forged with her art an inner landscape alive with wonder and suggestive of the wealth of her vision.

Exploring the imaginative vision that both springs from and creates this inner vision is, I believe, one of the best ways to appreciate the depth and fullness of Eudora Welty's mind and art ⟨. . . .⟩

I want to begin by looking at a deceptively simple statement by Welty that is rich in insight. In an examination of the dynamics of fiction in her essay "Place in Fiction," Welty writes that the novelist—and she uses the term to signify all writers of fiction—is blessed with an inexhaustible subject: "You and me, here." These unassuming words work in several ways, all of which are significant to Welty's thought. To begin with, Welty suggests here that the writer's subject is the interior life and growth of the individual—the life of you and me. But the connective "and" underscores a second concern: that interaction with others constitutes not just the human experience but also, at the same time, the means to plumb its depths. Finally with "here" Welty suggests that fiction must also deal with place, and specifically with the charged relationship between people—you and me—and the here-and-now. ⟨. . .⟩

For Welty life's ultimate mysteries and meanings lie with a person's interior life. The world of the mind and heart is timeless and immutable; there is nothing mystical, she likes to say, but everything mysterious about our interior life. ⟨. . .⟩

A person does not achieve a fulfilling interior life, however, merely by turning within and reflecting upon what mysteries he or she finds there. ⟨. . .⟩ Welty counsels instead for people to embrace the life outside themselves—the other—and then to incorporate what they have learned into themselves. Speaking of her own development, she writes in *One Writer's Beginnings* that she possesses a passion to connect with the outside world and that this world "is the vital component of my inner life. . . . My imagination takes its strength and guides its direction from what I see and hear and learn and feel and remember from the living world." Knowledge, then, results from a process that includes exposure to the world and reflection upon that experience. Welty describes this dynamic in the preface to *One Time, One Place* as "the living relationship between what we see going on and ourselves" and suggests in "Place in Fiction" that through cultivating this relationship a person will eventually, "with fortune's smile," transform "the open mind and the receptive heart" into "the informed mind and the experienced heart."

Connecting with the world outside oneself involves for Welty encounters with realms of otherness: with the mysterious meaning found in place and in other people. Both kinds of encounter, which ultimately are integrally related, possess great potential for informing and nourishing one's inner life and for leading a person to his or her supreme fulfillment.

A person's encounter with place, Welty believes, works on several levels. On the basic and surface level, connection with place is significant in that it gives a person a sense of perspective that he or she otherwise lacks. "We tend to understand what's tragic and or comic, or both," Welty says in an interview with Don Lee Keith, speaking of Southerners like herself who live in established communities, "because we know the whole story and have been a part of The Place. Our concept of Place isn't just history or philosophy; it's a sensory thing of sights and smells and seasons and earth and sky as well." ⟨. . .⟩

As this observation suggests, Welty's concern with place goes far beyond a focus merely on location. Indeed, overshadowing its importance in providing definition for a person is the significance of place in opening up a person to profound and mysterious feelings within and without. Speaking of Welty's "sense of place" is perhaps putting it too mildly; for Welty this sense is rather a far-reaching feeling, even a passion. The intrusion of place on the human consciousness can be so great as to overwhelm. Describing what she often feels while walking through a section of old Mississippi River country, Welty writes in "Some Notes on River Country," "I have felt many times there a sense of place as powerful as if it were visible and walking and could touch me."

Opening oneself up to the mysteries of place, letting the light from its eternal flame penetrate into the inner neighborhoods of self, is for Welty a means for deepening one's understanding of the passionate nature not only of one's own inner life but also of the world at large. Place, Welty declares in "Place in Fiction," works not just on a person's emotions but also on his or her genius. In some finally unexplainable way, an appreciation of place gives a person a clarity of vision that, rooted in a passionate love for life and the human experience, unlocks realms of mystery and meaning. Welty describes this achievement of vision as an act of focus. "It may be that place can focus the gigantic, voracious eye of genius and bring its gaze to point," she writes. ⟨. . .⟩

For all place has to offer, however, an open relationship with it cannot usher a person to his or her fullest growth. That can occur, Welty believes, only through interactions with other people. Though the mysteries of place often are crucial in establishing and nourishing these human relationships, the relationships themselves are finally what carry a person beyond himself or herself to new levels of awareness. Without an effort to communicate and reach communion with others, Welty believes, a person remains locked inside his or her own way of seeing things. Such a state is limiting and potentially destructive, for imaginative vitality can waste away from disuse. Rather than actively searching out truth, a person who is not actively engaged with others is prone to live by inertia and self-deception. Blame for such a condition lies not with some universal force of Evil but with the individual. ⟨. . .⟩

⟨. . .⟩ "Writing fiction has developed in me an abiding respect for the unknown in a human lifetime," Welty writes in *One Writer's Beginnings*, "and a sense of where to look for the threads, how to follow, how to connect, find in the thick of the tangle what clear line persists." As patterns emerge, the writer's own life opens up before him or her with new significance and meaning. "Like distant landmarks you are approaching, cause and effect begin to align themselves, draw closer together," she writes in *One Writer's Beginnings*. "Experiences too indefinite of outline in themselves to be recognized for themselves connect and are identified as a large shape. And suddenly a light is thrown back, as when your train makes a curve, showing that there has been a mountain of meaning rising behind you on the way you've come, is rising there still, proven now through retrospect."

—Robert H. Brinkmeyer Jr., "An Openness to Otherness: The Imaginative Vision of Eudora Welty," *Southern Literary Journal* 20, no. 2 (1988): 69–73, 75–76

CAROLYN G. HEILBRUN

In 1984, I wrote in an article in the *New York Times Book Review* that, since 1970, I had added seventy-three new biographies of women to my library. That number has certainly doubled by now, and yet there are countless biographies of women that I have not acquired. In 1984, I rather arbitrarily identified 1970 as the beginning of a new period in women's biography because *Zelda* by

Nancy Milford had been published that year. Its significance lay above all in the way it revealed F. Scott Fitzgerald's assumption that he had a right to the life of his wife, Zelda, as an artistic property. She went mad, confined to what Mark Schorer has called her ultimate anonymity—to be storyless. Anonymity, we have long believed, is the proper condition of woman. Only in 1970 were we ready to read not that Zelda had destroyed Fitzgerald, but Fitzgerald her: he had usurped her narrative.

I call it the watershed not because honest autobiographies had not been written before that day but because Sarton deliberately retold the record of her anger. And, above all other prohibitions, what has been forbidden to women is anger, together with the open admission of the desire for power and control over one's life (which inevitably means accepting some degree of power and control over other lives). Nor have those born earlier than Sarton honored the watershed, or deigned to notice it. No memoir has been more admired and loved in recent years than Eudora Welty's *One Writer's Beginnings*. Yet I think there exists a real danger for women in books like Welty's in the nostalgia and romanticizing in which the author, and we in reading them, indulge. Virginia Woolf remarked that "very few women yet have written truthful autobiographies." ⟨. . .⟩

⟨. . .⟩ I do not believe in the bittersweet quality of *One Writer's Beginnings*, nor do I suppose that the Eudora Welty there evoked could have written the stories and novels we have learned to celebrate. Welty, like Austen, has long been read for what she can offer of reassurance and the docile acceptance of what is given; she has been read as the avatar of a simpler world, with simpler values broadly accepted. In this both Austen and Welty have, of course, been betrayed. But only Welty, living in our own time, has camouflaged herself. Like Willa Cather, like T. S. Eliot's widow, she wishes to keep meddling hands off the life. To her, this is the only proper behavior for the Mississippi lady she so proudly is.

As her interviewer noted in the *Paris Review*, Welty is "extremely private and won't answer anything personal about herself or about friends." Michael Kreyling reported that Welty prizes loyalty and gratitude and disapproves of critics who approach writers with "insufficient *tolerance* and *sympathy*." There can be no question that to have written a truthful autobiography would have defied every one of her instincts for loyalty and privacy.

But why should I criticize Eudora Welty for having written the only auto-biography possible to her? From what I know and have heard, she is the kind-est, gentlest person imaginable. What then do I want from her? Would life not be preferable if we were all like Eudora Welty?

It would. Yet, since we are not, her genius as a writer of stories rescues her and us from her nostalgia. But it is that nostalgia, rendered with all the charm and grace of which she is capable, that has produced this autobiography, that same nostalgia that has for so many years imprisoned women without her genius or her rewards. Nostalgia, particularly for childhood, is likely to be a mask for unrecognized anger.

If one is not permitted to express anger or even to recognize it within one-self, one is, by simple extension, refused both power and control.

—Carolyn G. Heilbrun, "Introduction," *Writing a Woman's Life* (New York: W. W. Norton & Co., 1988), 12–15

GARY M. CIUBA

The structure of *One Writer's Beginnings* repeatedly violates chronological frame-work to portray the integral, elusive self as the confluence of past and present. "It is our inward journey that leads us through time," Welty explains, "forward or back, seldom in a straight line, most often spiraling." Her allegiance to the dynamics of inner time typifies the increased appreciation of subjectivity in modern and postmodern autobiographies. Paul John Eakin sees traditional examples of the genre as encouraging the reader to believe that "the play we witness is a historical one, a largely faithful and unmediated reconstruction of events that took place long ago." But Welty rejects such documentary drama for what Eakin calls the play "of the autobiographical act itself, in which the materials of the past are shaped by memory and imagination to serve the needs of present consciousness." *One Writer's Beginnings* makes the process of recollec-tion as revealing as the recollections themselves. Welty does not remember and then write, as if her life were a finished pageant that simply needed to be chronicled by an objective and anonymous observer. Rather, Welty writes as she remembers. ⟨. . .⟩ Living out the writing, Welty shows how personal and family history are always flowing together in the consciousness of the story-teller. ⟨. . .⟩

Yet despite its highly individual course, the structure of *One Writer's Beginnings* is not haphazard. Welty shuns what is merely amorphous, much as does the designing narrator of "A Memory." Hence, her reminiscences are ordered by the same insight that guides her fiction. Writing stories and nov-els, Welty asserts, has given her a "sense of where to look for the threads, how to follow, how to connect, find in the thick of the tangle what clear line per-sists." Her memoirs pursue a strand of discovering affinities and continuities between apparent disconnections. "The events in our lives happen in a sequence in time," she recognizes, "but in their significance to ourselves they find their own order, a timetable not necessarily—perhaps not possibly—chronological." ⟨. . .⟩ If *One Writer's Beginnings* does not follow a straight line, it does pursue what Lewis Simpson has called the "southern aesthetic of mem-ory" to discover the plot strands of Welty's life.

At the end of *One Writer's Beginnings*, Welty finally names the temporal design that has organized the stream of recollections from the start. As if the preceding hundred pages were a prelude, she writes, "I'm prepared now to use the wonderful word *confluence*, which of itself exists as a reality and a symbol in one. It is the only kind of symbol that for me as a writer has any weight, testifying to the pattern, one of the chief patterns, of human experience." *Confluence* provides an image for both the content and the flow of Welty's memories, for the self formed by the various tributaries of her past and for the formal structure of Welty's autobiographical essays. *One Writer's Beginnings* pursues this primal pattern by showing the connections between apparently different times in Welty's life as well as the intersections between obviously different lives and Welty's own time. All of these crossings coexist in memory, "the greatest confluence of all." ⟨. . .⟩

From the first paragraph of "Listening," time is ticking, but its typical sequence is undermined because incidents from various points in Welty's life are always "subject to confluence" in memory. Welty views past events from the perspective of the present and joins these episodes with others unrelated in time to disclose the larger pattern of how she began as a writer. In writing her memoirs Welty rewrites her life so that she reveals not just how the past seemed to her but how it seems to her now as autobiographer. As she recalls listening to songs, sermons, conversations, monologues, lessons in school, her own and her mother's reading, Welty shows how she heard her way to becoming a writer. All the earmarks of her fiction—her attention to dialogue and narrative voice, her pleasure in the sounds of words and cadences of sentences, her sense of story and dramatic scenes—begin in her youth. The child crafted the writer, but Welty the writer also crafts the child. She brings all the author's resources, which she began to discover in her early years, to capture her photographs of the artist as a young woman. Eudora is one of Welty's own best characters. And as her narrative skill in the present shapes her account of the past, the events in her life often follow the pattern of a short story. ⟨. . .⟩

As Welty reviews her childhood train ride, it becomes a circuitous passage that reconnects her with the origins of her life and art in her parents. On the journey Christian Welty saw the vanishing scenery by memory rather than through fantasy, for he had passed its landmarks during the course of many trips. But his daughter never learned exactly how customary was this route until years later. Throughout *One Writer's Beginnings* Welty continually calls attention to what she did not know and to when she later found it out. She does not present herself as the eternally omniscient narrator of her own life who reads back into the past what she only discovered in the future. Rather, Welty shows how she has learned the whole of her own story only in time. Memory discovers the confluence hidden in personal history. Welty remembers learning after her father's death that he used to travel the thousands of miles from Mississippi to West Virginia by train to court Chestina Andrews.

And when he could not afford the trip, the couple wrote daily letters. Kept over the years by Welty's mother in an attic trunk, these pages "brought my parents before me for the first time as young, as inexperienced, consumed with the strength of their hopes and desires, as *living* on these letters." The writer read her beginnings in the fervent writings of her parents. Welty's initial memory of a childhood train ride leads her to recall a later discovery of an earlier time, a revelation of her parents' passion before she was ever born. Their letters, which once bridged space, now bridge all of these overlapping times—especially those sent by her father. "Annihilating those miles between them—the miles I came along to travel with him, that first time on the train," they were "so ardent, so direct and tender in expression, so urgent, that they seemed to bare, along with his love, the rest of his whole life to me." Retrospect turns into prospect as Welty recovers a proleptic image of her father's life journey.

Since Welty's memory makes the recent and distant past into contemporaries, *One Writer's Beginnings* holds all of these times together—the memoirist as imagining young daughter and discovering adult, Christian Welty as parent and future husband. By seeing her father as a fiancé, a role that she could never have envisioned when only a girl herself, the much older writer at last understood how Christian Welty must have seen the landscape on her childhood train ride. She arrived at the truth of the past only by way of what was then the future. And as an artist, the daughter of Christian Welty eventually came to share his passionate vision. Welty recalls a final confluence with her father when she began writing seriously in her twenties, for then she found the world as revealing as the countryside that he had passed on the train. Conflating tenses, superimposing her later discovery on her girlhood recollections, Welty explains that she achieved this new perspective "because (as with my father now) *memory* had become attached to seeing, love had added itself to discovery," and she felt the desire to connect herself to the outside world. Welty's father knew the train route not just by heart but with his heart—with the tender recollections of all the journeys before his marriage. Writing repeats the same interior progress for Welty because it involves not just vision but revision, not just insight but intimacy.

—Gary M. Ciuba, "Welty's *One Writer's Beginnings*," Southern Literary Journal, 26, no. 1 (1993): 80–82, 89–90

EKATERINA STETSENKO

In the twentieth century, southern writers preserved the heightened interest in their history and mythology, but in the context of a new situation in which the process of the unification of American culture and the attention to the inner

world of a human being became stronger and stronger and the experience
of social events acquired a more personal, intimate and psychological character. ⟨. . .⟩

The recollections of Eudora Welty in *One Writer's Beginnings* are notable for
the specific selection of material and some particular motifs. Living, by her
own confession, a solitary life in the Deep South and being by vocation the
artist-psychologist, Welty pushes historical and political problems into the
background and reflects them in her family story only indirectly. "I am a
writer," she writes, "who came of a sheltered life. A sheltered life can be a daring life as well. For all serious daring starts from within." As in her stories and
novels, Welty depicts in her autobiography the inhabitants of the southern
region, their morals and manners and, as in her stories and novels, she is
mostly interested in the psychological, ethical and aesthetic aspects of the
southern world. The social environment serves mainly as a factor which helps
to form a human character and imagination. For Welty, her own biography is
a way and means of a writer's formation.

One Writer's Beginnings consists of three parts and every part corresponds to
a consequent stage of her perception and knowledge of life. The titles are:
"Listening," "Learning to See" and "Finding a Voice." It is in this order, Welty
insists, that southern writers learn to write: through oral and then visual perception of reality. The southern tradition of storytelling trains future literary
artists to be especially sensitive to speech and to write as "listeners," hearing
the words and trusting their inner voice. "It is human, but inward," she writes,
"and it is inwardly that I listen to it. It is to me the voice of the story or the
poem itself." Welty almost physically feels the accordance of a subject with its
word equivalent. "In my sensory education I include my physical awareness of
the *word*. Of a certain word, that is: the connection it has with what it stands
for." For example, she imagines the word "moon" to be round as grapes in the
mouth. "The word 'moon' came into my mouth as though fed to me out of a
silver spoon. Held in my mouth the moon became a word. It had the round-
ness of a Concord grape Grandpa took off his vine and gave me to suck out of
its skin and swallow whole, in Ohio." By responding to the intonation of
speakers, she began to understand the secret sense of the words and to distinguish truth from lie. "I had to grow up and learn to listen for the unspoken as
well as the spoken—and to know a truth, I also had to recognize a lie."

Every event, every detail of life is considered from the point of view of its
influence on the artist's formation. ⟨. . .⟩

As in Welty's fiction, subtle psychology is combined with thoroughly
described details of everyday life to create an adequate image of the American
situation. To a great extent this is also due to the writer's chosen position of a

detached onlooker who estimates herself, other people and events from the distance of time and experience. Welty calls such a point of view a necessary precondition of the creative process.

> Getting my distance, a perspective of my understanding of human events, is the way I begin work. . . . My temperament and my instinct had told me alike that the author, who writes at his own emergency, remains and needs to remain at his private remove. I wished to be, not effaced, but invisible—actually a powerful position. Perspective, the line of vision, the frame of vision—these set a distance.

The formation of Welty's artistic method was greatly influenced by her taking up photography when she worked as a junior publicity agent. It was photography that taught her to fix the visual images and then to hold transient life in words. Writing in *One Writer's Beginnings* about the dependence of the writer's imagination on the impressions got from the external world, Welty confessed the great role in her fate as an artist played by the travels through which she first became aware of the outside world, through which she found her "own introspective way into becoming a part of it."

> The trips were wholes unto themselves. They were stories. Not only in form, but in their taking on direction, movement, development, change. They changed something in my life: each trip made its particular revelation, though I could not have found words for it. But with the passage of time, I could look back on them and see them bringing me news, discoveries, premonitions, promises—I still can; they still do. ⟨. . .⟩

The movement in space is transformed into the inner movement of memory in time and into the creative movement of imagination. And this inward journey acquires a specific form, leading the author's memory "through time—forward or back, seldom in a straight line, most often spiraling" ⟨. . . .⟩

For Welty, writing is first of all the result of a specific correlating of the artist's personality with the outside world and of creating a new artistic world. Her autobiography is not only the consecutive story of the author's life and historical reality, but also the description of a creative process which is as much an inseparable part of the artist's fate as life and history. This is a specific type of autobiography which to some extent combines in itself both lines peculiar to American literature, certainly in their modified forms. The sphere and means of this combination is art itself and this fact is not occasional for the southern writer, because one of the specific traits of the southern character is an artistic approach to life and attention to its aesthetic features. ⟨. . .⟩

⟨. . .⟩ Answering the question, "Does the serious writer have any obligation to his society?" she says, "To have deep feelings about it—to try to understand it—to be able to reflect on things—to know what's happening and to care." But "a book should only reflect and present—not lecture people," and the great problems should not be solved in an obligatory way in philosophical and political terms, which are to her mind alien to fiction. The field of fiction is the human character and eternal categories: "love and hate, justice and injustice . . . truth and lies." Welty sees the artist's task in self-expression, on the completeness of which depends the work's success and its impact on the reader's mind. She considers her fiction to be autobiographical in the sense that she never invents the feelings of her heroes and describes only such emotions as she has experienced or can imagine. "I never have felt a divorce between my life and work, except the act itself, of course, which is something done in solitude and with much thinking."

Welty tries to reflect the great in the little, the eternal problems—the inner world of a person—and she is convinced that all human joys and troubles can be concentrated on one small patch of land. She says, "I shall always keep my belief that good literature is always about one subject—mankind. We in the South may portray the South, northern writers may portray the North; indeed, Chinese writers may portray China. But if their works are good, they are really about mankind, everybody everywhere." Welty thinks that "to write about what might happen along some little road like the Natchez Trace—which reaches so far into the past and has been the trail for so many kinds of people—is enough to keep you busy for a life." This is a typical southern conviction, because the southern consciousness is obsessed with the sense of time and place. The flow of time, the limits of place, the shelter of one's family—all these factors inherent in the story of human life and in autobiography as genre—are also inherent in southern culture and literature. Welty's autobiographical works manifest the evolution of southern literary traditions and their merging with the new trends in modern American literature which place more attention on personality.

—Ekaterina Stetsenko, "Eudora Welty and Autobiography," *Southern Quarterly* 32, no. 1 (Fall 1993): 17–20

B I B L I O G R A P H Y

A Curtain of Green and Other Stories. 1941.

The Robber Bridegroom. 1942.

The Wide Net and Other Stories. 1943.

Delta Wedding. 1946.

The Golden Apples. 1949.

The Ponder Heart. 1954.

Selected Stories. 1954.

The Bride of the Innisfallen. 1955.

Losing Battles. 1970.

One Time, One Place: Mississippi in the Depression: A Snapshot Album. 1971.

The Optimist's Daughter. 1972.

The Collected Stories of Eudora Welty. 1980.

One Writer's Beginnings. 1984.

Eudora Welty, A Writer's Eye: Collected Book Reviews. 1994.

JADE ʃNOW WONG
b. 1919

JADE SNOW WONG was born in 1919 (or 1922, according to some sources) in San Francisco, California, to Hong and Hing Kwai Wong. She grew up in a poor section of the city's renowned Chinatown, bound by the behavior required of women in Chinese culture. Throughout her childhood, she struggled to define herself as an individual against the authority of her parents, her church, and her community. Even though she graduated from high school as class valedictorian, her parents withheld financial support for college because she was female. Nonetheless, a determined Wong attended San Francisco Junior College, supporting herself by working as a cook and housekeeper. She graduated in 1940 with the highest honors.

At 20, Wong enrolled in Mills College on a scholarship and again graduated at the top of her class. From 1943 to 1945, she worked as a secretary with the War Production Board and while there won a National Congressional Award for an essay on the cause of absenteeism. In 1945, she published *Fifth Chinese Daughter*, an autobiographical coming-of-age story recounting her early struggles to reconcile the demands of both Chinese and American cultures. *Fifth Chinese Daughter* became a best-seller and is today considered seminal in the history of Asian-American literature.

An innovative potter and sculptor as well as a writer, Wong has received many awards for her work, and she opened a ceramic gallery in 1946 in San Francisco's Chinatown. Her pieces are included in collections of both the Metropolitan Museum of Art and the Museum of Modern Art in New York. In 1950, she married Woodrow Ong, with whom she has raised four children and started a travel agency. Wong considers the products of her artistic life a vehicle for creating understanding between Chinese and Americans, yet she is deeply committed to her family and community. In an interview for *Contemporary Authors* she has asserted, "I give priority to women's responsibility for a good home life; hence, I put my husband and four children before my writing or ceramics."

No Chinese Stranger, Wong's second book, published in 1975, details the 30 years of her life after the publication of *Fifth Chinese Daughter*. Largely a collection of travel notes and a summary of events, this book does not offer the same insight into the struggles of second-generation Asian Americans as her first. However, as she describes the paradox of feeling acceptance among the people of China yet rejection as a minority in her native United States, Wong makes a significant statement about identity and assimilation.

Acknowledging her literary contribution, Mills College conferred upon Wong an honorary doctorate of humane letters in 1976. A documentary film was made about her at the same time. Although she has not published other books, Wong is an occasional contributor to such publications as *Holiday* and *Horn Book Magazine* and writes a column in the *San Francisco Examiner*.

CRITICAL EXTRACTS

LOWELL CHUN-HOON

Probably the best-known and most lucidly written autobiography for the study of Chinese-American identity is Jade Snow Wong's classic account of a Chinese girlhood, *Fifth Chinese Daughter*. Published in 1950, it has enjoyed success as a best seller in America as well as being translated into Chinese, Japanese, Thai, German, Austrian, Urdu, Burmese and Indonesian under the auspices of the United States State Department.

Fifth Chinese Daughter is enlightening for a variety of reasons. It is an accurate and vivid account of growing-up in San Francisco Chinatown during the 1920's, 1930's, and 1940's, an entertaining autobiography of a young woman, and the success story of an immigrant member of a minority race in America. Most significant in the present day context, however, is the fact that *Fifth Chinese Daughter* is the story of an education in Chinese values, and the struggle of a Chinese-American to reconcile the conflicts between the values of a minority culture in the larger majority society. Rightly perceived, this unique book is a window not only into the past, but into the present and future as well. To understand it thoroughly is to begin to understand the forces at work shaping the fate of Chinese-American identity.

One of the principal unifying themes of *Fifth Chinese Daughter* is the concept of Chinese cultural authority and the series of confrontations between Jade Snow and her parents over the question of parental authority and filial piety. In American society we have come to accept such confrontations as natural and indeed a necessary part of the maturation process. Children are expected and encouraged to become as independent as possible and are ultimately allowed, at least in theory, to choose their own role in life. In traditional Chinese society this was of course not the case at all, and in Jade Snow Wong's early childhood the traditional Chinese ways are dominant. ⟨. . .⟩

Jade Snow Wong represents the transition in Chinese-American identity from a purely Chinese emphasis upon rigid obedience to the proscribed Confucian dictates of the situation to a Chinese-American reconcilation which legitimates individual and personal initiative when it is successful in bringing honor to the larger Chinese-American community or a given Chinese-American family. Those values rewarded and deemed successful in American society may replace the pure hierarchies of filial piety and obedience in Confucian thought as the primary criterion for behavior. One might say this is a form of adopting American values of success, in the name of upholding the success of Chinese values.

In evaluating the transitional lifestyle evolved by Jade Snow Wong, we come to what appear to be fundamental contradictions. If the primary means for enhancing, honoring, and promoting Chinese cultural identity remains individual success in a culture which requires individual creativity and initiative then the very values necessary for success and the temporary furtherance of Chinese-American identity simultaneously undermines the traditional Chinese identity rooted in obedience to Confucian authority. To state the problem in its most pessimistic perspective: Chinese identity, when transplanted from China, contains within itself the seeds of its own doom. For instead of succeeding through obeying the dictates of Chinese cultural authority, and restraining his individuality, the Chinese-American succeeds through his own individual initiative.

However, once the notion of individual initiative takes hold, it triggers a potentially irreversible and anarchistic process. If Chinese American identity depends on the reverence of tradition and obedience to the persons and ways of previous Chinese generations, this reverence will inhibit success in America to the extent that it will inhibit creativity and self-assertion. There are people like Jade Snow Wong who can utilize their creativity and independence for the Chinese community and can remain both culturally Chinese and individually successful by American standards.

—Lowell Chun-Hoon, "Jade Snow Wong and the Fate of Chinese-American Identity," *Amerasia Journal* 1, no. 1 (March 1971): 52–53, 61–62

ELAINE H. KIM

Jade Snow Wong is ⟨a⟩ proponent of the notion that Asian Americans are a unique blend of "Asian" and "American" cultures. For Park No-Yong the conciliation was perfectly embodied in the doctrine of the mean, a notion that could be found in both Western (ancient Greek) and Chinese philosophy. For Wong it lies in "personal balance": "Each Chinese American like me has the opportunity to assess his talents, define his individual stature, and choose his

personal balance of old and new, Chinese and Western ways, hopefully including the best of both." Paradoxically, a combination of the fundamental aspects
of the "best" of both means Western civilization—thought, social relations,
creative thinking, mental work, way of life—combined with far less critical and
pivotal aspects of Chinese civilization, such as food and holiday celebrations.

Ultimately, through the blending of the "Chinese" and "American" qualities, Wong becomes a mere curiosity to both cultures. She admits that after
attending college she feels more like a spectator than a participant in her own
community. When she invites her economics class to her father's sewing factory, she feels "suddenly estranged" from "observing the scene with two pair of
eyes." When she establishes her pottery business in Chinatown, her wares are
purchased and appreciated only by whites; the Chinese buy not one single
piece. Both whites and Chinese talk about her while she works as if she were
a blind deaf mute, as though she were not even present. In a taped interview
twenty-five years after the publication of *Fifth Chinese Daughter*, she admitted
that she still felt "unaccepted in Chinatown" because of "lack of understanding" on the part of the Chinese there.

In the end, Wong's response to her particular dilemma as an American-
born Chinese was to work harder, to seek comfort in certain aspects of her
Chinese identity, and to refuse to admit the existence of discrimination.
According to Wong, there is no escape from race prejudice; one must simply
decide "how much to accept and utilize." This response marked her as a
Chinese American success story.

Wong was encouraged to write *Fifth Chinese Daughter* by English teachers
and publishing house editors, who were largely responsible for the final version of the book. The editor who asked her to write the book, Elizabeth
Lawrence, cut out two-thirds of the manuscript, and the teacher, Alice
Cooper, helped "bind it together again." When asked in an interview whether
or not she was satisfied with the final results, Wong replied that she was willing to accept the better judgment of her editors: "Some of the things are missing that I would have wanted in. Then, you know, it's like selling to Gump's or
sending to a museum. Everybody has a purpose in mind in what they're carrying out. So, you know, you kind of have to work with them." When asked what
had been left out, Wong replied that aspects that were "too personal" had been
eliminated by the editors, adding, "I was what, twenty-six then? And you
know, it takes maturity to be objective about one's self."

Whether because of the editors or not, the emotional life that Jade Snow
Wong might have expressed in her autobiography never fully emerges. We
know that she was driven by a "desire for recognition as an individual," a desire
she felt was thwarted by her family. We also know that she was almost venge-
fully anxious to "show everyone" that she could succeed in becoming a model

of social propriety. She felt lost in a "sea of neglect and prejudice" at home. But in the end these sporadic glimpses into her emotional life are subordinated to descriptions of Moon Festivals and egg foo yung recipes. The submergence of the self so contradictory to her insistence on individuality is epitomized by her reference to herself in the third person singular throughout the book.

—Elaine H. Kim, *Asian American Literature: An Introduction to the Writings and Their Social Context* (Philadelphia: Temple University Press, 1982), 70–72

KATHLEEN LOH SWEE YIN AND KRISTOFFER F. PAULSON

⟨A⟩ close analysis of *Fifth Chinese Daughter* shows that Wong faces a world as frustrating, fragmented, and confusing as that of ⟨Maxine Hong⟩ Kingston. Furthermore, Wong reveals her successful integration of identities in a masterful blending of the autobiographical and of her natural modesty which is derived from the Chinese culture which demands the literal submergence of the individual. "Even written in English an 'I' book by a Chinese would seem outrageously immodest to anyone raised in the spirit of Chinese propriety" ⟨vii–viii⟩. The result is a rarely used and unusual form—the third person autobiography. So rare is this form that Henry Adams' *The Education of Henry Adams* is the only example that comes readily to mind and appears available for comparison. And like Adams, Wong too treats herself "as the object of a process of education." ⟨. . .⟩

⟨. . .⟩ Throughout *Fifth Chinese Daughter's* third person narrative one is always aware of Wong as simultaneously the protagonist and the author: "But Jade Snow still had to make her own decision" ⟨150⟩. If the sentence were read as it must in an autobiography, "But I still had to make my own decision," the tension of the continuous recognition that both the character and the author are thinking and acting as separate entities and yet are one and the same person completely disappears.

Jade Snow Wong writes the narrative biography of Jade Snow. The singular "I" dissolves and re-emerges transformed and re-created in the objective third-person "she." Jade Snow is once removed from the author, as an objective and fictive character within a novel is once removed from the author, and yet she can not be removed, because the character Jade Snow and the author Jade Snow Wong are one and the same person. Yet the separation has been accomplished. The genius of Wong's form lies in the tension of its inherent paradox. ⟨. . .⟩

⟨. . . Her⟩ bi-cultural narrative will not fit into and cannot be contained within the "strictly autobiographical" form. Her narrative voice breaks the form apart. The division, contradiction, tension, paradox and "bursting" are right there in the form itself. The reader is constantly aware of the divided consciousness of the narrator in the divided voice of author and character. The constant tensions reinforce the dual nature of the narrative voice and constantly make the reader aware of the fragile balance between author and character within one dual but identifiable human being. Jade Snow Wong's choice of form cannot be easily designated because we have no name, no term, to identify the contradictory third person autobiography. And Jade Snow Wong's choice of this very unusual form and divided narrative "voice" arises directly out of her bi-cultural identity. For her to use the "I" form would be to deny the Chinese part of her bi-cultural identity ⟨vii–viii⟩.

What the form compels Wong, or any author, to do is to examine her individual character and her society from without, from an objective and aesthetic distance, as well as from an inner and individual point-of-view. That is, her self-examined individual being is also her objective imagined fiction. *The Education of Henry Adams* provides comparison. In their third person autobiographies both Adams and Wong treat themselves as fictional characters, submerging the individual ego, the "I," within the influences of the forces which surround them. For Wong the chief forces are the many opposing demands of her Chinese-American heritage.

Fifth Chinese Daughter ⟨. . .⟩ like Adams' *Education*, is a work of the imagination—more a work of creative fiction than a simple transcript of events and facts. Jade Snow is a fully rendered, fictional character whom Wong develops within a structured thematic purpose to depict Jade Snow's successful search for balance within the forces of the fragmented world of Chinese-American women.

Wong chose, as Kingston would thirty years later, an extraordinary literary form, one which effectively renders the divided consciousness of dual-heritage. Wong's achievement, however unheralded and unrecognized, is a foundation stone for ethnic literature, for feminist literature and for American literature.

—Kathleen Loh Swee Yin and Kristoffer F. Paulson, "The Divided Voice of Chinese-American Narration: Jade Snow Wong's *Fifth Chinese Daughter*," MELUS 9, no. 1 (Spring 1982): 53–54, 57–59

AMY LING

Even if one's life is not complicated by parents of different races or by geographic relocations, one cannot escape the between-world condition as a non-white in the United States. Both Jade Snow Wong and Maxine Hong Kingston, a generation later, were born to two Chinese parents in the United States and reared in California Chinatowns, San Francisco and Stockton. And the between-world consciousness is central to their autobiographical texts,

Fifth Chinese Daughter (1945) and *The Woman Warrior* (1976). Though Jade Snow Wong's autobiography has been disparaged by a number of Asian American commentators, Kingston herself considers Jade Snow Wong a literary mentor, describing her as "the Mother of Chinese American literature" and the only Chinese American author she read before writing her own book. "I found Jade Snow Wong's book myself in the library, and was flabbergasted, helped, inspired, affirmed, made possible as a writer—for the first time I saw a person who looked like me as a heroine of a book, as a maker of a book."

The two books are greatly divergent in style and temperament, each text largely affected by the personalities of the two women and by the period in which each was produced. *Fifth Chinese Daughter* ⟨. . .⟩ was written for a white audience during World War II, and its popularity, to a large extent, was due to white readers' need to distinguish between friend and foe; thus, of necessity, it contains many explanations of Chinese culture and customs. Another reason for its popularity may be that it was, as critic Patricia Lin Blinde put it, "a Horatio Alger account in Chinese guise," demonstrating the greatness of America in that even a minority woman much repressed by her family could attain the American Dream. *The Woman Warrior*, an outgrowth of the Civil Rights and Women's Liberation movements of the 1960s and 1970s, is a much more personal text, written not as an exemplum for others but as a means of exorcising the personal ghosts that haunt the author. It is written for the author herself, as well as for other women, and for Chinese Americans, whom at one point she directly addresses (5–6).

Fifth Chinese Daughter is subdued in tone, polite, restrained, well-brought up ⟨. . .⟩ a sober, straightforward narrative delivered in chronological order, as though to tell this much were effort enough.

—Amy Ling, *Between Worlds: Women Writers of Chinese Ancestry* (Elmsford, NY: Pergamon Press, 1990), 119–20

SHIRLEY GEOK-LIN LIM

As artifacts of the imagination, there is little to differentiate between *Fifth Chinese Daughter*, the autobiography of Wong, who was born in the United States, and *Chinatown Family*, the novel by Lin Yutang, born in China. Both books, published around the same period, treat the myth of the cultural drive to success in immigrant Asian society, derived from the dogma of the patriarchal network in which the individual finds value through contributive work. In fact, Lin Yutang's novel remains throughout at the level of social stereotyping. ⟨. . .⟩

Wong's book, written in the third person, makes for more powerful literature. While, like Lin Yutang, she has deliberately manipulated the structure of the book so as to create opportunities to trot out all the phenomenology that forms the common opinion of Asian experience (Chinese cooking, foods, celebrations, familial duties, and so on), *Fifth Chinese Daughter* has an element of the unpredictable that challenges these stereotypes and promises every now and again to expose these racial myths. The father, a domineering patriarch, is also an ambiguous figure infected by his new country's vision of equality. The underlying drama of the daughter's challenge to her father contradicts and exceeds the given ideas of Chinese familial relationships. In confronting the limitations of popular perceptions of Chinese traits, Wong appears in some danger of offering only a reversal of attitudes. The pieties associated with Asian Americans (based on the primacy of the patriarchal family units, on obedience, and on formality of behavior) observed in conflict with white American countervalues (the importance of individuality, freedom of speech and action, and spontaneity) are unsympathetically portrayed through the point of view of the author's persona, the socially and professionally ambitious daughter.

This book, however, is more than a neat, hostile overturning of Asian pieties. Its power rests on the unconscious paradox that holds together in a larger frame the simpler narration of conflict as the daughter becomes assimilated into white American culture and therefore apparently less filial. While Chinese attitudes frustrate and demean the protagonist in her daily life, her purpose as she develops is to prove worthy of approval from her father who symbolizes Chinese patriarchal society. Unlike conventional fictions of conflict and identity, *Fifth Chinese Daughter*, although it presents the ambivalence of living in two cultures seemingly inimical to each other, does not clearly set up opposing points of view. The narrative does not contain a rejection of or an attempt to integrate the Asian paradigm to a white American model.

Finally, the author subverts her own endeavor and reveals her hidden agenda: not to rebel against her family but to compel her family to recognize and accept her. Actions lead to a reintegration of the individual *into* the Asian paradigm; the latter part of the book is a series of individual accomplishments seen as significant only insofar as they impress the patriarchal structure. The narrator-persona felt triumph at winning an essay competition run by the War Department, for example, because "this was the first occasion when the entire Wong family was assembled in pride of their fifth daughter" (198).

In the book's conclusion, the father tells his daughter of a letter he had written to a cousin long ago: "I am hoping that someday I may be able to claim that by my stand I have washed away the former disgraces suffered by the women of our family." As readers we are shocked by his self-ignorant and arrogant assertion—that he was the agent in the daughter's push for her rights—when his past actions had shown him to be reactionary. But it is even more distressing to discover that the author-narrator is herself taken in by his hypocrisy. "For the first time in her life," Wong tells us at this supreme point of paternal approval, "she felt contentment" (246). The absence of irony where it seems to be most pertinent makes *Fifth Chinese Daughter* a peculiarly Asian document. Despite the detailed expressions of conflict between the protagonist and her Chinese milieu, in her incapacity for irony Wong demonstrates the single vision in her autobiography—a vision that is unswervingly Chinese and only incidentally occidental.

—Shirley Geok-lin Lim, "Twelve Asian American Writers: In Search of Self-Definition," *Redefining American Literary History*, ed. A. LaVonne Brown Ruoff and Jerry W. Ward, Jr. (New York: The Modern Language Association of America, 1990), 238–39

SHIRLEY GEOK-LIN LIM

In the tradition of Chinese American lifestories, *Fifth Chinese Daughter* would be considered the mother text to *Woman Warrior*. ⟨. . .⟩ Yet, on first appearance, *Fifth Chinese Daughter* seems to be the antithesis of ⟨Maxine Hong⟩ Kingston's book. Wong explains in an author's note that her use of the third person is a racial and ideological choice ⟨. . . .⟩ Significantly, Wong's second book, *No Chinese Stranger*, is written in two parts; in part 1, "To the Great Person of Father," the author again addresses herself in the third person. Part 1 ends with the literal and figurative death of the patriarch: "At thirty-six, she could no longer turn to him as head of their clan, a source of wise counsel, philosophical strength, a handy Chinese reference" (149). Part 2, consequently, is titled "First Person Singular," when, after the father's death, the narrator/author is able finally to take on her full subjectivity, and speak (write) in (as) the first person. In *The Woman Warrior* the narrator first-person is foregrounded, and the voices of female rebellion, impatience, anger, and assertiveness produce the figures of female outlaws, warriors, shamans, and storytellers. The ideological choice of speaking as a Chinese or as an American is also reflected in the authors' choices of pen names. Jade Snow Wong chose an Anglicized translation of her Chinese name, while Maxine Hong, married to an Anglo-American, adopted her Anglo husband's name. *Fifth Chinese Daughter* would appear therefore to be a Chinese text, where Kingston's flamboyant use of the first person would make *The Woman Warrior* an American text.

Both books, however, treat the knotted theme of race, made even more difficult by the threat of male, legalistic power and shame over female sexuality. ⟨. . .⟩

Between *Fifth Chinese Daughter* and *The Woman Warrior* is a breathtaking leap in female consciousness. The fifth Chinese daughter, struggling in her schooling in the father's strict patriarchy, escapes and does not escape his narrow definitions. The third-person separation of autobiographical subject from narrative point of view subtly reinforces this "distancing" or "muting" of female subjectivity. The narrative never escapes the logocentricism of chronological documentation. It is a life presented as always controlled by the demands of narrative "history" with its emphasis on apparent "objectivity," "facticity," "chronological ordering," "the third-person point of view." *The Woman Warrior*, however, is an "over-writing" of given Chinese-Americans stories. In this attempt to "over-write," all stories are equal, whether from history, myth, legend, family lore, or individual invention. The first person dominates, and in overflowing female terms. Thus the book is replete with nouns and pronouns referring strictly to female gender: mother, aunt, she, girl babies, etc. More significantly, the presence of mother, aunts, and daughter places it in a woman-gendered tradition, whereas the constructing/constraining pole of the normative and Confucianist patriarchy locates *Fifth Chinese Daughter* in a male-constituted society. The daughter in Wong's autobiography defines herself against and through negotiations with the other gender; she is above all the patriarch's daughter. On the other hand, the presence of the daughter's discourse in *The Woman Warrior* is a "talking-back-to" the mother culture, which is also the racial culture. The appropriation of the mother's talk-stories, the conversion of oral to writerly tradition, is both the American daughter's reclamation of her Chinese mother's story (history) and her vanquishing of it, swallowing of it into her American presence (present). Logocentricism is repeatedly shattered; in its place are what appear to be fragments, of stories, ideas, thoughts, images, asides, which circle around and accumulate to form the expression of the idea of Chinese American female subjectivity.

The Woman Warrior, therefore, unlike *Fifth Chinese Daughter*, has not an autobiographical story to tell but a racial and gendered consciousness to intimate and create. It shares with another contemporary Asian American woman's text, ⟨Joy Kogawa's⟩ *Obasan*, in interrogating identities and reconstituting in their place an emergent daughterly subject, just as *Fifth Chinese Daughter* shares with Sone's *Nisei Daughter* an earlier generation's submergent subjectivities and eventual submission to patriarchal discourse. The differences between the two books are arguably differences of generational thematics; read together, *Fifth Chinese Daughter* and *The Woman Warrior* deepen each other's cultural constructions of Chinese American daughters, moving from any kind of single or singly divided consciousness to an expression of multiple subjectivities, the consequence of American daughters resignifying their Asian origins.

—Shirley Geok-lin Lim, "The Tradition of Chinese American Women's Life Stories: Thematics of Race and Gender in Jade Snow Wong's *Fifth Chinese Daughter* and Maxine Hong Kingston's *The Woman Warrior*," *American Women's Autobiography: Fea(s)ts of Memory*, ed. Margo Culley (Madison, WI: University of Wisconsin Press, 1992), 256–57, 263–64

B I B L I O G R A P H Y

Fifth Chinese Daughter. 1945.
No Chinese Stranger. 1975.

VIRGINIA WOOLF
1882–1941

ADELINE VIRGINIA STEPHEN was born in 1882 into a family known for its beautiful women and intelligent men. Julia Jackson Duckworth Stephen, her mother, was a beautiful and accomplished hostess, who entertained the intellectual guests of her husband, Sir Leslie Stephen, the editor of the *Dictionary of National Biography*. The young Virginia, designated early as her father's literary successor, had the difficult task of bridging this gender gap. The gap was quite clearly represented by the fact that while her brothers were educated at Cambridge, Virginia was educated at home. Indeed, she had no formal education—a lack she resented all her life.

Woolf's two autobiographical sketches and her autobiographical fiction are, in part, attempts to understand her childhood, her parents' relationship, and her relation to them within the confines of Victorian home life. The central moment of these autobiographical texts is the death of her mother when Woolf was 13 years old and the transformation of her father into a morbid and demanding parent. The first piece, "Reminiscences," charts the passing of the position of "Angel in the House" from Woolf's mother, briefly to her half-sister Stella Duckworth Hills before her untimely death, and then to the young Vanessa. Woolf is notably absent from this rite of passage. Woolf later said she had to kill the Angel in the House in order to write. She also said that if her father had not died in 1904, she would not have become a writer. With his death, Virginia, her sister Vanessa, and their two brothers moved to Gordon Square. Their brothers' friends from Cambridge, including Roger Fry, John Maynard Keynes, and Lytton Strachey, were soon congregating there, forming the intellectual Bohemian community known as the Bloomsbury Group.

Vanessa's marriage to Clive Bell in 1907 began prompting everyone to say "Virginia must marry." But Virginia was not interested in marrying yet, and many of the men of Bloomsbury were homosexual. Two years later Lytton Strachey, believing that marriage was a convenient step for homosexuals to take, proposed to Virginia. Their engagement lasted less than twenty-four hours. Not until Leonard Woolf, one of the original Cambridge friends, returned from Ceylon did Virginia settle on the right man. They were married in 1912.

Virginia had been writing reviews for the *Times Literary Supplement* since 1905 and had written her autobiographical sketch before her first novel, *The Voyage Out*, was published in 1915. In 1917 she and

Leonard founded the Hogarth Press, which published her second novel, *Night and Day*, in 1919 as well as the rest of her novels. In 1915 Woolf began the diaries she would keep almost daily for the rest of her life, which when published in 1977 totaled five volumes. Woolf alternately saw her diary as a less formal place for working out her ideas about writing, a record of her observations of life, and a source for her memoirs.

In the 1920s Woolf entered into a passionate relationship with Vita Sackville-West, and she established herself as one of the leading exponents of modernism with her critical essay "Mr. Bennett and Mrs. Brown" in 1923. Her later novels, including *Orlando* (1928), a fictional biography of Vita Sackville-West and her home Knole, reinforced her standing. *A Room of One's Own* (1929), based on two lectures on women in fiction, is considered a feminist classic. Along with her other works, it suggests the possibility of satisfying lesbian relationships for women, as in the well-known "Cloe liked Olivia" passage: "Do not start. Do not blush. Let us admit in the privacy of our own society that these things sometimes happen. Sometimes women do like women."

A short time before committing suicide in March 1941, prompted by a return of mental illness and the threats of Nazi Germany, Woolf returned to writing about the childhood scenes of 22 Hyde Park Gate. Many critics argue that with *To the Lighthouse* (1927), Woolf was able to overcome the obsessive hold on her imagination of her parents' memory and deaths. But not until she wrote "A Sketch of the Past" did she exorcise another hidden trauma of her childhood—sexual molestation by her two older half-brothers. In this piece of writing the ghosts of the past and Victorian reticence are both put to rest by Woolf's philosophical technique of exploring moments of being. By standing firm in the present and looking back to the past, Woolf delineates her "I now, I then," showing those moments in which reality breaks through the "cotton wool" of daily life. In this, one of Woolf's last pieces of writing, she brings her modernist perspective and technique developed over several decades of writing to the subject matter of her "Reminiscences." In "A Sketch of the Past," Woolf explores her crucial moments of breaking through the confines of Victorian sensibility.

C R I T I C A L   E X T R A C T S

CHRISTOPHER C. DAHL

Woolf's autobiographical works need to be seen not only as indicators of her development as a novelist, but also as products of a long tradition of autobiographical writing in the Stephen family. From this perspective, Woolf's growth as an autobiographer is a journey in which she begins in the late Victorian world of "22 Hyde Park Gate," proceeds through "Old Bloomsbury"—to use the titles of two of her memoirs—and ends up in thoroughly modern territory. To observe this journey is to see how Woolf takes materials and techniques inherited from her father and previous writers of autobiography in the family, revising them and using them for her own purposes, until she is finally able to transcend the limitations of Victorian autobiography in her last and finest work, "A Sketch of the Past." To observe this journey is also to see how an important English writer makes the transition from Victorian to modern literature.

⟨. . .⟩ The works collected in *Moments of Being* are in fact the most recent offshoots in a long time of autobiographical writing which begins in the early nineteenth century with the remarkable *Memoirs* of Woolf's great-grandfather, James Stephen, Master in Chancery, and includes no fewer than nine full-scale works by members of four successive generations of the Stephen family. Virginia Woolf is thus an inheritor of, as well as contributor to, an on-going process of meditation and imaginative commentary on the individual in relation to other members of the Stephen family, and her writings take their place in an almost organic tradition spanning more than a century of British intellectual and literary history. ⟨. . .⟩

⟨. . .⟩ In Woolf's low opinion of both her fiction and her autobiographical writing at this point, one can see the presiding figure of her father.

That presiding figure is very much evident throughout the "Reminiscences." As ⟨Jeanne⟩ Schulkind observes ⟨in her introduction to *Moments of Being*⟩, Virginia Woolf follows Stephen family tradition in addressing her memoir to the next generation and in writing autobiography under the guise of depicting the life of another member of the family, in this case her sister Vanessa. But, even beyond these resemblances, the mode and style of "Reminiscences" are shaped in many other places by the precedent of the *Mausoleum Book*. The similarities between the two works are striking. Both, for example, are a series of portraits held together by the first-person voice of their author, whose relation to the various figures portrayed is the real focus of each work. In their depiction of Julia Stephen (and to a lesser extent in their portraits of Stella Duckworth), the two works obviously overlap ⟨Love, *Virginia*

Woolf: Sources of Madness and Art, 287⟩. Indeed, it is not unreasonable to see her "Reminiscences," with their preoccupation with death and bereavement and their attempt to memorialize two beloved figures who have been lost, as Virginia Woolf's own version of her father's *Mausoleum Book.* ⟨. . .⟩

Though all the Memoir Club ⟨the informal group of Bloomsbury friends⟩ contributions criticize the Victorian past in one way or another, they, like "Reminiscences," point directly back to various aspects of Stephen family tradition in the nineteenth century. "A Sketch of the Past," Woolf's last and finest autobiographical work, is, on the other hand, far less reminiscent of previous autobiographical writing in the Stephen family. To be sure, it grows out of Woolf's earlier writing and therefore out of family tradition, but Woolf's methods as an autobiographer are ones she has developed on her own. In "A Sketch of the Past," written in 1939 and 1940 ⟨. . .⟩ Woolf achieves the potential for the "proper writing of lives" which one would expect from her fiction and from her lifelong interest in memoirs and biographies. ⟨. . .⟩

"A Sketch of the Past" is not only Woolf's most accomplished piece of autobiographical writing. It also fulfills the promise of the "very subtle work on the proper writing of lives" alluded to in her letter to Clive Bell at the time she was working on "Reminiscences." In a certain sense, "A Sketch of the Past" is the chronicle of Woolf's successful quest for an appropriate form for her own autobiography. ⟨. . .⟩

⟨. . .⟩ What emerges in "A Sketch of the Past" is an autobiography in which sharply perceived "moments of being," enduring as part of the continuing present which makes up Woolf's inner self, are blended with careful descriptions of more ordinary events, accounts of Woolf's relationships with other members of her family, and precise evocations of the social milieu which impinges upon the individual at every point and shapes her outer self. Woolf's narrative proceeds by a sort of free association, working its way from her earliest recollections to later events, pausing to fill in details of historical background, and easily shifting between past events and present awareness. The freedom and seeming informality of Woolf's writing suggest the confidence of an author firmly in control of her art, very much in contrast to the difficulties revealed by the formal tone and complex syntax of "Reminiscences." Though Woolf would probably have further revised "A Sketch of the Past" if she had lived longer, the condition of the typescript version of the first two-thirds of the work makes it safe to conclude that the version printed in *Moments of Being* is fairly close to the author's final intentions. The informality and freedom are products of careful art, not inattention.

As this brief account of her techniques implies, in "A Sketch of the Past" Woolf has entirely abandoned the Victorian "factual" mode of autobiographical writing employed by her father. She is no longer dependent upon the crude techniques of analogy and comparison she used in "Reminiscences."

Indeed, at one point in "A Sketch" she explicitly maintains that she cannot compare Stella Duckworth or her mother to anyone else, "either in character or fact." What replaces the Victorian mode of description by analogy and comparison is a mode which might be described as "scenic," based upon sensory images and recollection of physical sensation rather than reconstruction of factual data. ⟨. . .⟩

⟨. . .⟩ Woolf's tentativeness in criticizing the Victorian manner ⟨. . .⟩ perhaps suggests that she has achieved a balanced view even of the literary tradition she has rejected, but the remarks on her early articles remind us again of the path of her development as an autobiographer. She has indeed progressed from the world of Victorian convention exemplified by life downstairs at 22 Hyde Park Gate, to the witty debunking of that world in Bloomsbury, to a broader and more balanced perspective—both personal and literary—in "A Sketch of the Past" which somehow contains and evaluates both worlds. The autobiographical writings, then, reflect Woolf's own journey from Victorian to modern and, strangely enough, from self-doubt and insecurity in "Reminiscences" to a kind of acceptance of her own identity in "A Sketch of the Past," even though the latter work was written against the backdrop of World War II and within four months of her own death.

—Christopher C. Dahl, "Virginia Woolf's *Moments of Being* and Autobiographical Tradition in the Stephen Family," *Journal of Modern Literature* 10, no. 2 (1983): 175–77, 180–81, 189–91, 193–94

Daniel Albright

As a young woman ⟨Virginia Woolf⟩ tried on several occasions to keep a diary, but this resolution did not stick until 1915 when she began the enormous set of daybooks which she kept up more or less continually until her death in 1941. In the opinion of many, this project is one of the masterworks of modern letters. In many places in her diary she announces that her purpose is to provide material for her memoirs, to be written by an elderly Virginia Woolf, an alter ego often addressed in the diary as a presiding dowager queen. Of course when she did come to write her memoirs, in 1939, she abandoned herself at about the age of 21, as if the adult Virginia Woolf were in no need of literary recall. However, the diary itself constitutes a kind of autobiography, though an autobiography of an oddly loquacious, yet oddly reticent sort. Therefore we have two elaborately shaped narratives of childhood, both of them concocted with every literary resource, neither of which extends so far as her father's death in 1904; an astonishingly replete record of the years of her full maturity, 1915–1941 (except for 1916, a year of illness); and, to cover the gaps, three papers which she wrote for the Memoir Club of Bloomsbury, the first two of which describe the quality of her life from late adolescence until

1912. But of her marriage to Leonard Woolf, in 1912, she has scarcely a word to say anywhere. Indeed the period from 1907, when she began her first novel, *The Voyage Out*, until the beginning of the first World War, seems to have required almost no self-explanation. All the autobiographical writings I have mentioned, except the diary, are collected in a handy volume called *Moments of Being*; these writings, with the diary and the novel, *To the Lighthouse*, constitute Virginia Woolf's attempt to elucidate her being.

Yet in this great autobiographical project one often feels that something is missing, and that the missing thing is Virginia Woolf. It is as if this vast self-attentiveness existed as much for camouflage and deception as for revelation. In the autobiographical writings, as in the novels, the reader is drenched in impalpable subjectivity, in which the subject is not a definite body or face but a watery medium. It is a kind of autobiography which seems, in mysterious ways, to exclude the author. In her diary she even announces this: she lampoons the great hostess and lionizer Ottoline Morrell for writing a diary devoted to her "inner life" by reflecting "that I haven't an inner life" (22 November 1917); in later years she reminds herself repeatedly that she had banished her soul as a topic for her diary (19 February 1923), though at times she wonders whether she should not cancel this vow (21 June 1924) and describe the more interesting of her violent moods. Her diary, then, aspires to be a record of external things, of the weather—indeed, whole pages are devoted to flowers, fields, rain, and mushrooms—of a gallery of portraits of acquaintances, of the burdens of running a printing press and haggling with stingy editors. But just as Bernard in *The Waves*, strolling through London in a trance of self-forgetfulness, notes, "One cannot extinguish that persistent smell. It steals in through some crack in the structure—one's identity"—so the soul of Virginia Woolf cannot be exiled far from the matter of her day-to-day life; it seeps in everywhere, but in ghostly fashion, not as explicit self-revelation. Virginia Woolf in her diary is largely a creature of cadences and tonalities, not of character traits. She will explain that she is elderly, dowdy, fussy, vain (28 September 1926), and the phrase "I'm a failure" chimes mournfully on many a page, but these are not sober assessments of character, only symptoms of melancholia. She will occasionally acknowledge that she was especially brilliant or fizzy at a certain dinner party, but for the most part she regards her public self with anxiety and fears that she has got a reputation (for example) of being querulous about bad reviews. The public self is largely embarrassing or irrelevant; the soul resists definition, is incapable of record, an "odd immeasurable soul" (28 September 1926), painful but interesting, which one generally tries to suppress. Sometimes it even seems that the diary is a kind of therapy, designed to engage its author with the external world so that the urgencies and irrationalities of the inner self may be ignored or anesthetized. If this is not too farfetched, then self-exclusion is one of the real purposes behind the whole project, and the diary is composed in order to omit Virginia Woolf.

⟨. . . The diary approaches⟩ the state of engorged subjectivity characteristic of Virginia Woolf's fiction. In 1924 it struck her that "in this book I *practise* writing; do my scales; yes & work at certain effects. I daresay I practised Jacob here,—& Mrs. D. & shall invent my next book here" (17 October 1924). As these études become more and more prominent, the diary loses something of its diary-like character and assumes a quality of metaphysical ego-apprehension.

In a normal autobiography, the author and his or her acquaintances stand on the same footing as independent, rational, equable beings—a society of *selves*—but in Virginia Woolf's autobiographical writings all distinctness, all character and idiosyncrasy tend to disappear into uncanny intimacies and terrors, as if all love were informed by self-love, all loathing by self-loathing. Just as Virginia Woolf in the fields, in the passage quoted above, becomes what she beholds—a diffuse, cloudy intelligence—so she tends in the company of other people to resemble those around her; compulsive merging is always the fate of the ego in its quickest, most inflamed states. Of course her sketches of her friends are often polished and satirical, the proper stuff of autobiographies; sometimes, though, these character studies take on a strange quality, as if she were rehearsing possibilities for her own identity in her descriptions of others, as if the cast of characters summoned up in her diary were a repertory company of potential Virginia Woolfs. It is not odd that one would feel a condition of almost antenatal intimacy with one's sister—she speaks of running to her sister Vanessa "as the wallaby runs to the old kangaroo" (20 June 1928)—but it is perhaps unusual that one would feel continually shaped, molded, even remade by people toward whom one feels indifference or contempt. During a harried time in 1922, Virginia Woolf felt herself in danger of being ruined by society, either "rasped all over," as she put it, by the company of her enemies, or likely to "soften & rot in the too mild atmosphere of my own familiars" (22 August 1922). In either case the acuity, the expansiveness of the private self is threatened. To confront society one must become social, that is, fragmentary, incoherent, edgy, and superficial, and the least intruder is sufficient to evoke this unpleasant public identity ⟨. . . .⟩

⟨. . .⟩ ⟨H⟩er diary provided her with an instrument useful for studying aspects of her ideas, herself, as embodied among her acquaintances, as if her social community existed for the sake of evoking in her a variety of Virginia Woolf's, alternately gregarious and elevated, sympathetic and snide. She told Lytton Strachey, concerning her character as a novelist, "Yes. I'm 20 people."

—Daniel Albright, "Virginia Woolf as Autobiographer," *The Kenyon Review* VI, no. 4 (Fall 1984): 1–2, 5–6

JEANNE SCHULKIND

This collection of autobiographical writings, although diverse, nevertheless reveals the remarkable unity of Virginia Woolf's art, thought and sensibility. The beliefs and values that underlie her work are shown in these pages to be an outgrowth of the sensibility which marked her responses to the world, from the very beginning, with a distinctive quality. The need to express this vision was perhaps the chief impetus behind the experiments with structures, techniques and style which place Virginia Woolf's novels among the most highly innovative and personal contributions in the history of the genre. These memoirs also reveal the unusual degree to which Virginia Woolf wove the facts of her life—the people, the incidents, the emotions—into the fabric of her fiction, thus testifying to the firm artistic control she exercised over that material in creating works having the coherence and inner necessity which distinguish the highest artistic achievement. ⟨. . .⟩

The diversity of purpose which characterizes these memoirs—written for different audiences and occasions and spanning a career that lasted almost four decades—might well have resulted in an absence of coherence, a random heaping together of fragments of a life. Yet the fragments do arrange themselves into a meaningful order; a pattern emerges which expresses Virginia Woolf's view of the self generally, and herself in particular, in ways that a conventional autobiography could not have done.

That self was an elusive will o' the wisp, always just ahead on the horizon, flickering and insubstantial, yet enduring. She believed the individual identity to be always in flux, every moment changing its shape in response to the forces surrounding it: forces which were invisible emerge, others sink silently below the surface, and the past, on which the identity of the present moment rests, is never static, never fixed like a fly in amber, but as subject to alteration as the consciousness that recalls it. As she writes in "A Sketch of the Past", when she thinks she may have discovered a possible form for the memoirs: "That is, to make them include the present—at least enough of the present to serve as platform to stand upon. It would be interesting to make the two people, I now, I then, come out in contrast. And further, this past is much affected by the present moment. What I write today I should not write in a year's time." ⟨. . .⟩

⟨. . .⟩ In the first memoir, "Reminiscences", there is a self-conscious adoption of a literary 'manner', not unexpected in a writer just learning to gauge the spread of her wings but nonetheless distracting, particularly at those moments when the forced flights of the poetic imagination leave feeling far behind on the ground or the tentative starts into areas of originality are cut short by hasty retreats into the safety of conventional formulas. The self-consciousness, with its hint of vulnerability, no doubt reflects a slight unease regarding her audience. Virginia Woolf had intended the 'life' of Vanessa to be read by her new brother-in-law with whom she was not yet on a completely free and easy footing and by her sister with whom she was conscious of reestablishing relations on a new basis. Indeed, so omnipresent was Clive Bell at this period that she felt she might never see Vanessa alone again. This situation may partially account for the occasional disconcerting shifts of tone, from an affectionate intimacy to a stilted, formal manner like that which Virginia Woolf later associated with the 'Victorian tea table manner'.

"A Sketch of the Past" provides a sharp contrast with its easy, unaffected manner revealing an ego so unaware of itself that it appears almost impersonal. So confident is she now, so much a master of her material, that she need not even be bothered to decide on a form before beginning: "So without stopping to choose my way, in the sure and certain knowledge that it will find itself— or if not it will not matter—I begin: the first memory." The memoir is characterized by a flowing, ruminative expansiveness; it presents a consciousness which follows its own peculiar byways rather than a pre-ordained route as it ponders the meaning of reality and the mystery of identity. ⟨. . .⟩

The greatest insights afforded by these memoirs into Virginia Woolf's life, her thought and sensibility and the development of her art, are not, however, those brought about thus fortuitously but those which emerge when she consciously sets out to explore the origins of the beliefs and intuitions which shaped and ordered her vision of life and which, as she began to write fiction, gradually came to shape and order that as well.

One such belief is that the individual in his daily life is cut off from 'reality' but at rare moments receives a shock. These shocks or 'moments of being' are not, as she had imagined as a child, simply random manifestations of some malevolent force but 'a token of some real thing behind appearances'. The idea of a privileged moment when a spiritually transcendent truth of either personal or cosmic dimensions is perceived in a flash of intuition is, of course, a commonplace of religious experience and in particular of mystical traditions of thought, as well as a recurrent feature of idealist philosophies from Plato onwards. But in these memoirs Virginia Woolf sets this belief in a uniquely personal context and shows it emerging, almost inevitably, from her own intense and highly individual susceptibility.

—Jeanne Schulkind, "Introduction," *Virginia Woolf: Moments of Being* (New York: Harcourt Brace & Co., 1985), 11–12, 15–17

SHARI BENSTOCK

⟨It⟩ is the question of place—of space—that absorbs the autobiographical writer's attention as much as the proverbial issue of time. The mother, who occupied "the very centre of that great Cathedral space which was childhood," becomes an "invisible presence" in Woolf's later life. Indeed, it is her removal from temporal and spatial existence that provides the central trauma of Woolf's narrative, an absence over which scar tissue knots this narrative and refuses to let the story unwind itself over the years. Like Gertrude Stein's obsession with the year 1907 (the year Alice B. Toklas entered her life, changing its contours and directions), Virginia Woolf's continual return to the morning of her mother's death, the morning she awoke to news of this loss and was led to her mother's bedroom to kiss her goodbye, constitutes a symptom of the writing, or a scab that is picked until it bleeds and forms again. Significantly, this scene is repeated twice in the memoir fragments, is reconstructed in *The Years*, and marks the moment of temporal absence ("Time Passes") in *To the Lighthouse*. For Virginia, Julia Stephen was "the creator of that crowded merry world which spun so gaily in the centre of my childhood. . . . She was the centre; it was herself. This was proved on May 5, 1895. For after that day there was nothing left of it." ⟨. . .⟩

⟨. . . T⟩he workings of memory, crucial to the recollection implicit in life writing, are found to be suspect. They slip beyond the borders of the conscious world; they are traversed and transgressed by the unconscious. Every exercise in memory recall that Woolf tries in these autobiographical efforts demonstrates the futility and failure of life writing. What is directly gazed upon in the memory remains absent; what is "revealed" comes by side glances and hints, in the effects of sound, light, smell, touch. Returning to the peculiar power of the "two strong memories" that initiate "A Sketch of the Past," Woolf comments, "I am hardly aware of myself, but only of the sensation. I am only the container of the feeling of ecstasy, of the feeling of rapture." She wonders whether "things we have felt with great intensity have an existence independent of our minds" and whether "some device will be invented by which we can tap them." She believes that "strong emotion must leave its trace." Finding a way to tap these resources, to rediscover these traces, becomes both the overriding desire in her memoir writing and the cause of its failure. She is forced to discount memories: "As an account of my life they are misleading, because the things one does not remember are as important; perhaps they are more important." Woolf attempts to explain away the intellectual difficulties posed by the problem of remembering and not remembering by dividing life into "moments of being" and "moments of non-being." She constructs a tapestry in which there is "hidden a pattern" that connects both the being and nonbeing of everyday life. She tries to find a means by which to include in the "life" that which is excluded in life writing: everything that forms the background of perception and action. ⟨. . .⟩

⟨. . .⟩ On 25 October 1920 she had admitted to her diary the happiness that writing gave her: "and with it all how happy I am—if it weren't for my feeling that it's a strip of pavement over an abyss." Her fictional narratives (all of which could be termed "autobiographical" to some degree) were the strip of pavement over the abyss of self. While these fictions were in some sense a pretense against the primordial split subject (and were created "out of" that split), the memoir posed the question of selfhood directly; it forced Virginia Woolf to look into the abyss—something she could not do. Using a metaphor that explores surface and depth, the "experience" of present and past, along narrative movement, Woolf writes: "The past only comes back when the present runs so smoothly that it is like the sliding surface of a deep river. Then one sees through the surface to the depth." This "sliding surface" is not available to conscious thought and practice; indeed, it demands an *unconsciousness* of the present. The present cannot call attention to itself (the "pavement" or "platform" of the present must be invisible). That is, "to feel the present sliding over the depths of the past, peace is necessary. The present must be smooth, habitual." Later in the same paragraph, Woolf reverses this process in an effort to restore a "sense of the present": "I write this partly in order to recover my sense of the present by getting the past to shadow this broken surface" (98).

Woolf concludes her contemplation of the autobiographical act and its relation to writing, memory, and self-consciousness by returning to its initial impetus—what she calls "scene-making":

> But, whatever the reason may be, I find that scene-making is my
> natural way of marking the past. Always a sense of scene has arranged
> itself: representative; enduring. This confirms me in my instinctive
> notion: (it will not bear arguing about; it is irrational) the sensation
> that we are sealed vessels afloat on what it is convenient to call
> reality; and at some moments, the sealing matter cracks; in floods
> reality; that is, these scenes—for why do they survive undamaged
> year after year unless they are made of something comparatively
> permanent?

It is the very admission of "irrationality" that interests here. Woolf views the past not as a "subject matter"—a content as such—but rather as a method, a scene making. Such scenes arrange themselves (much as the matter in the "hold all" composed itself) in moments when the "sealing matter" of identity and selfhood cracks. Unable to argue logically the ontology of autobiography by means of self-consciousness, Woolf moves toward an "instinctive notion"

that the "sealed vessel" of selfhood is an artificial construct, that it "cracks" and
floods, allowing access to that which in conscious moments is considered
wholly separate and different from self—"what it is convenient to call reality."

> —Shari Benstock, "Authorizing the Autobiographical," *The Private Self: Theory and Practice of
> Women's Autobiographical Writings*, ed. Shari Benstock (Chapel Hill: The University of North
> Carolina Press 1988), 26–29

NANCY WALKER

In the autobiographical writings of Emily Dickinson, Alice James, and Virginia
Woolf, both the search for—rather than the certainty of—the "self" and the
sense of "shared identity with other women" are strikingly evident. Each seeks
in different ways to assert an individuality by rejecting the "normal" role of
women (a rejection that results in mental and/or physical anguish); each
addresses the page/reader from behind a series of identities or "masks"; and
each makes clear that her "private" writing is addressed to some "public" with
which she has an uneasy relationship. ⟨. . .⟩

⟨. . .⟩ ⟨I⟩t is the immediacy of the letter or journal entry that engages us;
we feel closer to the humanity of the writer as she or he records the minutiae
of life, and are better able to surmise the influences on more formal and public utterances. It is the sense of immediacy that Virginia Woolf, in the midst of
writing a biography of Roger Fry, almost despairs of capturing as she speaks of
the "invisible presences" that affect each individual life: "Consider what
immense forces society brings to play upon each of us, how that society
changes from decade to decade; and also from class to class; well, if we cannot analyze these invisible presences, we know very little of the subject of the
memoir" (*Moments of Being* 80). The letter or the diary can bring us closer to
these "invisible presences" than can the autobiography or the memoir. ⟨. . .⟩

Virginia Woolf's consciousness of a specific "you" or public for whom she
wrote is far greater than that of James or Dickinson; she was a prolific and
widely published author. Yet she used the strategies of retreat and role-
playing, as did they, as a means of claiming space for herself. As the author of
A Room of One's Own, in which she argues clearly that women who wish to be
professionals must have space and time belonging only to themselves, she
struggled continually with this need. The Woolfs' constant movement back
and forth from London to the appropriately named Monk's House in Sussex,
as well as her recurring bouts of madness, are motifs of engagement and
removal in her life, and her diaries and letters frequently reflect these motifs.
London social life was a magnet she could not resist, yet comments such as "I
feel more and more inhibited and irritated by London life: I feel its meshes
closing in—" reveal her need for the peace of Monk's House, where "one can
sit on the fender and read." Similarly, she vacillated between intense mental

activity and periods during which, like Alice James, she had to "abandon" her brain because of severe headaches or depression. But whereas James saw her mind as dominant over her body, Woolf gradually came to see her periods of illness as times of incubation for ideas. In a 1930 diary entry, Woolf comes to the conclusion that her "mind works in idleness. To do nothing is often my most profitable way." She uses the analogy of a chrysalis to describe this productive dormant state:

> I believe these illnesses are in my case—how shall I express it?—partly mystical. Something happens in my mind. It refuses to go on registering impressions. It shuts itself up. It becomes chrysalis. I lie quite torpid, often with acute physical pain. . . . Then suddenly something springs.

Woolf sees herself as apart from her mind, and watches as it gathers strength to "spring" into activity again. Illness was, for Woolf, a form of enforced solitude, but solitude could also be sought consciously, and she frequently equates isolation and thought with a sense of confronting the most important things in life. In a diary passage that approaches stream-of-consciousness in style, Woolf connects "interruption" with "children," and says that she has stopped wanting children since "my ideas so possess me." A life of solitude, without interruptions, allows her to "get my utmost fill of the marrow, the essence." ⟨. . .⟩

That Woolf was conscious of human role-playing—of the deliberate selection of a self to present to others—is clear from numerous comments in her letters and diaries. In her worst moments, she felt that all life was a facade. She records in her diary in 1929: "I shall make myself face the fact that there is nothing—nothing for any of us. Work, reading, writing are all disguises; & relationships with people. Yes, even having children would be useless." In more positive moods, she played with the idea of identity, especially as identity is assumed to be conferred by names. In correspondence with several people she uses nicknames for them and/or for herself; most are names of animals. ⟨. . .⟩

—Nancy Walker, "'Wider Than the Sky': Public Presence and Private Self in Dickinson, James, and Woolf," *The Private Self: Theory and Practice of Women's Autobiographical Writings*, ed. Shari Benstock (Chapel Hill: The University of North Carolina Press 1988), 274–75, 292–93

HARRIET BLODGETT

An avid diarist, because the activity gratifies her, though perpetually driven to justify it, Woolf can see various good reasons, philosophical and practical, for her diary habit. On the second anniversary of her diary, she decides that she is continuing it "[partly] I think, from my old sense of the race of time. 'Time's winged chariot hurrying near'—Does it stay it?" the sentiment recurs in 1922 and again in 1939. ⟨. . .⟩ She can moreover rely on her diary for maintaining her equilibrium, both personally and professionally. When "it becomes a necessity to uncramp," "Once more, as so often, I hunt for my dear old red-covered book," for "this does not count as writing. It is to me like scratching; or, if it goes well, like having a bath." ⟨. . .⟩

Yet even though Woolf knows herself attracted to the diary as an emotional resource and restorative, her diary is not confessional. Instead it inclines, with the concrete particularity that is her strength of style, to the reportorial and descriptive, to what she has done, encountered, or, with a piercing eye, observed. Often (and especially so in the thirties), it specializes in the faces and voices of others: brilliant portraits of their natures and dealings with her and detailed transcriptions of their conversations, so that her diary provides a remarkable social document of literary-intellectual England as Woolf saw it for a quarter of a century. Of self-exposure, however, Woolf is chary. ⟨. . .⟩ Indeed, Woolf conducts an ongoing struggle to keep her innermost self out of her pages. She early envisions her diary as uninhibited: "The main requisite . . . is not to play the part of censor, but to write as the mood comes or of anything whatever." And yet, despite her frankness on many subjects, she is aware that she reserves a large part of herself for silence.

When she boasts of her diary-keeping at Garsington in 1917, Woolf discovers that Lady Ottoline Morrell "keeps one . . . devoted however to her 'inner life'; which made me reflect that I haven't an inner life." One can trace a path of her concern not to let the inner life of "soul" into her diary—revelations of her inmost personality and intimate feelings—even though she considers herself a lesser diarist for keeping it out. In 1923, she ponders "How it would interest me if this diary were to become a real diary: something in which I could see changes, trace moods developing; but then I should have to speak of the soul, & did I not banish the soul when I began?" A year later she contemplates cancelling her vow against soul description, but she cannot; instead, in 1926, she rationalizes that "one can't write directly about the soul. Looked at, it vanishes"; it can only slip in indirectly, while one focuses on objective matters. Thus, in 1929, she is still contemplating an "idea"—"to break my rule & write about the soul for once"—and in 1932, still hesitant to do so. In 1937, she admits herself "rather ashamed" to be so evasive. But as she acknowledges ruefully in 1939, "I never reach the depths; I'm too surface blown."

⟨. . .⟩ The leitmotif of Woolf's diary is her well-known struggle to have faith in her talents and to transcend criticism, for she suffers sorely from "the curse of a writer[']s life to want praise so much, & be so cast down by blame, or indifference." Woolf's need for reassurance from Leonard and her agonies over what bad reviews may imply about her talents are demoralizing, and she cautions herself in 1921, "for my own good, . . . I must get out of the way of minding what people say of my writing. I am noted for it," yet she cannot, and the struggle goes on. Early to late she reassures herself that she has transcended criticism; that, as she says in 1915, "My writing now delights me solely because I love writing & don[']t, honestly, care a hang what anyone says." But the truth is, "When I say we must discuss our works, without caring for praise, am I sincere? Could I do it?" Despite certain other evasions, the inner Woolf in all her tortured insecurity is very much present in her pages. ⟨. . .⟩

However, for reasons both aesthetic and personal, the diary is curiously unintended to highlight her either. That is, Woolf endeavours to exclude her soul partly by artistic conviction. The sense of art that makes her reach after impersonality in her fiction persists even in such presumably relaxed circumstances as the diary. "I think writing must be formal," she insists, not speaking of the diary here but expressing a habitual attitude to writing; "The art must be respected . . . for, if one lets the mind run loose, it becomes egotistic: personal, which I detest." Her diary too therefore is largely "formal," controlled; it strives to sustain impersonality, not only through exclusion but also through artistry. Because of her aesthetic (and her psychology), the fully improvisational, ideally unselfconscious, mode of the diary form is antipathetic to her. Instead, she writes with active awareness of herself as a diarist and of the diary as a literary form to be mastered. ⟨. . .⟩

Instead of writing of anything whatever as the mood comes, from the outset Woolf demonstrates the professional's urge to be selective and to shape language and structure. ⟨. . .⟩ In 1919, she rejoices in her rapid diary-writing—again expressing herself eloquently on the subject—

> I have just reread my year[']s diary & am much struck by the rapid
> haphazard gallop at which it wings along, sometimes indeed jerking
> almost intolerably over the cobbles. Still if it were not written rather
> faster than the fastest typewriting, if I stopped & took thought, it
> would never be written at all; & the advantage of the method is that it
> sweeps up accidentally several stray matters which I should exclude if
> I hesitated, but which are the diamonds of the dustheap.

Yet in fact this passage, which Woolf recopied for her diary book from an earlier version composed on loose sheets, has been rewritten, its style and themes heightened. The diamonds of sentence two once lay in a less alliterative "rubbish heap"; "If I took thought" once lacked the buttressing of "stopped" and "if I hesitated." The more Woolf extols diaristic freedom, the less she enacts it.

Nonetheless, a more practised diarist by the second volume, she does become more relaxed about the content and the organization of entries, though still careful about phrasing. More of her inner life is deemed transmissible; entries are less obviously arranged. Although she is rather uneasy about it—"I sometimes think that I have worked through the layer of style which suited it [my diary]—suited the comfortable bright hour after tea; & the thing I've reached now is less pliable"—she has found an approach for her diary that will prevail until the later thirties.

—Harriet Blodgett, "A Woman Writer's Diary," *Prose Studies* 12, no. 1 (1989): 58–61

LuAnn McCracken

Because women's autobiographies frequently represent experiences of the world and the self that are outside canonical definitions of autobiography, they have often been misread or ignored completely. ⟨Smith, *A Poetics of Women's Autobiography*, 1987, 3–19⟩

More recently, however, structuralist and poststructuralist theories have contributed to the revision of essentialist notions about the self by calling attention to the self as a rhetorical construct, and feminist critics in particular have drawn attention to the role of gender in autobiography and in autobiography theory. If men and women have different cultural experiences, their representations of their experiences in the rhetorical self-creation that is autobiography will also differ. By reading autobiographies by both men and women for the multiple identities created and not created by language, we avoid the exclusive binarism—with its implied hierarchies—of stability/instability, public/private, which have been characteristic of much theoretical work in the past, including earlier feminist work like Jelinek's, and we admit all versions of self-creation as valuable representations of particular personal and cultural moments. ⟨. . .⟩

⟨. . .⟩ Woolf clearly rejects the self-focus that is an important part of the autobiographical tradition inscribed by her male relatives and particularly her father: she may adopt Leslie Stephen's methods for lack of one of her own at this early stage in her writing, but she fails to adopt his egotistical sense of identity. If we were to read "Reminiscences" according to autobiography theories that assume a transcendent ego—or according to revisionist theories that simply invert this (male) model and assume a woman's fragmented ego—we would miss what is actually contained in Woolf's first memoir: the literal absence of an individualized identity or an identity of her own.

In "Reminiscences," there is no account of Woolf's early childhood nor, indeed, of the present in which she writes the text; there is no description of her relationships with others. When Woolf ventures an opinion of someone, she frequently qualifies it, as though she fears to assert herself. When, for example, she attempts to describe Julia's first marriage to Herbert Duckworth, Woolf undercuts her authority as narrator. ⟨. . .⟩

⟨. . .⟩ For Woolf, the task of achieving a sense of her own identity was doubly problematic: she needed to achieve separation from the identity of her mother, yet the death of her mother at the crucial beginning of Woolf's adolescence (she was thirteen) meant that Woolf lost the figure from which her identity derived. It is not surprising, then, that "Reminiscences" reflects Woolf's uncertainty about her identity and the process by which she attempts to distinguish it, a process she did not feel she had completed until she was forty-four, when she described her mother in *To the Lighthouse* and so achieved separation from her. Further, it is not surprising that "Reminiscences" is centered on the mother-figure, represented by Julia Stephen, Stella Duckworth, and Vanessa Stephen. In her first attempt at autobiography, Woolf tries simultaneously to merge with and separate from the lost mother, the embodiment of and barrier to Woolf's own identity.

Although Woolf excludes direct expression of feelings from the text of "Reminiscences," she includes them obliquely in her account of the effect of Julia Stephen on both Stella and Vanessa. Stella's relationship with her mother was extraordinarily close:

> Living in close companionship with her mother, [Stella] was always contrasting their differences, and imputing to herself an inferiority which led her from the first to live in her mother's shade. Your grandmother too was, I have said, ruthless in her ways, and quite indifferent, if she saw good, to any amount of personal suffering. It was characteristic of her to feel that her daughter was, as she expressed it, part of herself.

Woolf's comment on this relationship is one of the rare instances in the memoir when she clearly associates herself with an opinion:

> It was beautiful, it was almost excessive; for it had something of the morbid nature of an affection between two people too closely allied for the proper amount of reflection to take place between them; what her mother felt passed almost instantly through Stella's mind; there was no need for the brain to ponder and criticize what the soul knew.

Woolf's position is ambiguous; the relationship is both "beautiful" and "excessive," demonstrating Woolf's own ambivalence to her mother. Yet the decisiveness of the declarative sentences at this point—"it was" and "it had" without a "perhaps" or "seems"—suggests that Woolf's emotional investment in the subject is great enough to overcome her confusion of identity and allow her to assert herself. ⟨. . .⟩

In "Reminiscences," then, Virginia Woolf makes her first attempt to confront the importance of her mother for her own sense of identity. The narrative method she chooses for her presentation, that of observer rather than experiencer, reflects her insecurity in her identity—as well as in her own voice as writer—and suggests her attempt to separate herself from the stifling influences upon her, to prevent her self from merging with the figure of her mother. ⟨. . .⟩

⟨. . .⟩ I suspect that Daniel Albright, who complains that in her autobiographical writings Woolf attempted "to retain the plasticity, the abandon, the evasiveness of the ego," would be among those critics who omit women's autobiography from the canon because of its formlessness: he seems to base his judgment on male experience. ⟨Albright, "Virginia Woolf as Autobiographer," *The Kenyon Review*, 1984, 2⟩ Woolf's willingness to become a part of her past by imagining scenes signals not her submergence of her present self, but her emergence from her earlier self-in-crisis; she asserts a positive identity that allows relationship.

> —LuAnn McCracken, *"'The synthesis of my being':* Autobiography and the Reproduction of Identity in Virginia Woolf," *Tulsa Studies in Women's Literature* 9, no. 1 (1990): 61, 63, 65, 66–67, 73

SIDONIE SMITH

Roaming back and forth through time and memory, Woolf, while acknowledging some need for a "thin pattern"—the memoir in fact carries forward the history of the body noted above—eschews the conscious use of memory to construct a linear narrative of evolutionary selfhood, eschews the narrative tendency to put these people and these memories in their right place. Constructed plots, tracing the development of a strangulated individuality invite authorial control and promote an authoritarian stance on the part of the narrator toward both the subject of the memoir and his or her past. When she registers her response to rereading an early draft of the "Sketch" in the diary, Woolf registers her resistance to plotting with its insistence on distorting crises: "Then I dipped into my memoirs," she writes, "too circuitous & unrelated; too many splutters; as it stands. A real life has no crisis; hence nothing to tighten. It must lack centre. It must amble on. All the same, I can weave a very thin pattern, one of these days, out of that pattern of detail." Far from being prelude to the present and thus a point on a narrative line, time past for Woolf constitutes the presentness of the present. ⟨. . .⟩

Nor is the subject of the "Sketch" in control of the past. Scenes from the past break upon the present moment, deluging the autobiographical subject in memory. Moments of being in the past, these scenes are moments arbitrarily revisited, not scenes entered into purposefully or consciously by the autobiographical subject. Revisited, these moments sometimes become "more real than the present moment." 〈. . .〉 Thus the narrator is subject to memory, not its controller, not its authority. Neither predictable nor easily maneuvered, memories come and go. 〈. . .〉

Moreover, life for Woolf encompasses moments of nonbeing as well as moments of being; but the unsaid, the unconscious, the unknowables exist in an elusive subtext, forever unavailable. The invocation of the remembered implies the silences of the unremembered. Woolf was only too aware that any attempt to capture the history of the subject is doomed. As she concludes after describing her early memories, "the things one does not remember are as important; perhaps they are more important." This acknowledgment of the unremembered in one more way undermines the authority of the memoir's subject to "capture" the past. 〈. . .〉 The narrator also rejects the tendency to pin down and to know other people and their lives as she constantly undercuts her attempts to understand others, for instance, her mother or her father. Others cannot be consolidated in a singular gaze. That is the interpretative action of a strangulated individuality, the violence of the patriarch. Any subject needs to be refracted through multiple gazes, as "Virginia" is refracted through her mother and father, Stella, Vanessa, and Thoby.

Everywhere the narrator of "Sketch" concedes the impossibility and the undesirability of the old autobiographical project. Breaking the power of the central protagonist of autobiography as a figure present unto itself, controlling, unitary, Woolf disperses herself into the past, into the stories of others, into a communalized subjectivity, refusing to name the truth, refusing to contain her narrative in a coherent chronology, resisting the position of authoritative narrator. This anonymous, interdependent subjectivity enables her to escape into a stream of life, into that fluid time and place of history, memory, being, nonbeing, where the subject is constituted provisionally through the contextualities of history, family, and individual experience.

—Sidonie Smith, "The Autobiographical Eye/I in Virginia Woolf's 'Sketch,'" *Subjectivity, Identity, and the Body: Women's Autobiographical Practices in the Twentieth Century* (Bloomington: Indiana University Press 1993), 99–100

B I B L I O G R A P H Y

The Voyage Out. 1915.
Two Stories (with Leonard Woolf). 1917.
Night and Day. 1919.
Kew Gardens. 1919.
Monday or Tuesday. 1921.
Jacob's Room. 1922.
Mr. Bennett and Mrs. Brown. 1924.
Mrs. Dalloway. 1925.
The Common Reader. 1925.
To the Lighthouse. 1927.
Orlando: A Biography. 1928.
A Room of One's Own. 1929.
Street Haunting. 1930.
On Being Ill. 1930.
Beau Brummell. 1930.
The Waves. 1931.
The Common Reader: Second Series. 1932.
A Letter to a Young Poet. 1932.
Flush: A Biography. 1933.
Walter Sickert: A Conversation. 1934.
The Years. 1937.
Three Guineas. 1938.
Reviewing. 1939.
Roger Fry: A Biography. 1940.
Between the Acts. 1941.
The Death of the Moth and Other Essays. 1942.
The Moment and Other Essays. 1942.
A Haunted House and Other Short Stories. 1944.
The Captain's Death Bed and Other Essays. 1950.
A Writer's Diary: Being Extracts from the Diary of Virginia Woolf. Ed. Leonard
     Woolf. 1953.
Virginia Woolf and Lytton Strachey: Letters. Ed. Leonard Woolf and James
     Strachey. 1956.
Hours in a Library. 1958.
Granite and Rainbow: Essays. 1958.
Contemporary Writers. Ed. Jean Guiget. 1965.

Nurse Lugton's Golden Thimble. 1966.

Collected Essays. Ed. Leonard Woolf (4 vols.). 1966.

Stephen versus Gladstone. 1967.

A Cockney's Farming Experiences. Ed. Suzanne Henig. 1972.

Mrs. Dalloway's Party: A Short Story Sequence. Ed. Stella McNichol. 1973.

The London Scene: Five Essays. 1975.

Letters. Ed. Nigel Nicolson and Joanne Trautmann (6 vols.). 1975.

Moments of Being: Unpublished Autobiographical Writings. Ed. Jeanne Schulkind. 1976.

Freshwater: A Comedy. Ed. Lucio P. Ruotolo. 1976.

The Waves: The Two Holograph Drafts. Ed. John W. Graham. 1976.

The Diary. Ed. Anne Olivier Bell and Andrew McNeillie (5 vols.). 1977.

Books and Portraits: Some Further Selections from the Literary and Biographical Writings. Ed. Mary Lyon. 1977.

The Pargiters: The Novel-Essay Portion of "The Years". Ed. Mitchell Leaska. 1978.

Women and Writing. Ed. Michele Barrett. 1979.

Melymbrosia: An Early Version of The Voyage Out. Ed. Louise A. Delsalvo. 1982.

Virginia Woolf's Reading Notebooks. Ed. Brenda R. Silver. 1982.

Pointz Hall: The Earlier and Later Typescripts of Between the Acts. Ed. Mitchell A. Leaska. 1983.